A HISTORY OF FEELINGS

A HISTORY OF
FEELINGS

ROB BODDICE

REAKTION BOOKS

For Liz, David, Gerry and Inge,
with feeling

Published by
REAKTION BOOKS LTD
Unit 32, Waterside
44–48 Wharf Road
London N1 7UX, UK

www.reaktionbooks.co.uk

First published 2019
Copyright © Rob Boddice 2019

Printed and bound in Great Britain by Bell & Bain, Glasgow

A catalogue record for this book is available from the British Library

ISBN 978 1 78914 067 5

CONTENTS

INTRODUCTION:
FEELING FOR HISTORY

I remember a particular high-school history project, from around 1993. I was about fifteen years old. In a former mining village a couple of miles outside Burton-on-Trent, my peers and I were charged with exploring the historical experiences of local people during the First World War. Burton had been among the first places in Britain to undergo aerial bombardment, so naturally the Zeppelin raids were an integral part of our local focus. The task: write an 'empathetic account' of what it was like to experience a Zeppelin bombing raid in Burton in January 1916. We were given resources: local newspaper cuttings, secondary sources describing the events and their consequences, technical details about Zeppelins and how to defend against them, as well as local historical context about Burton, its industrial and economic importance and so on. Armed with this information, we were told to engage our historical imaginations and empathize with an imagined character from the past, hiding under a kitchen table, or dealing with the loss of friends and neighbours to this distinctly modern killing technology. No small task.

I think, from memory, that this task was to encompass all of 1,000 words. It would be fitting and highly complimentary to the framers of GCSE History examinations if I could locate this as the moment that I started out on the path to becoming a historian of emotions and experience. It was not (*pace* David Frater, my erstwhile history teacher). In fact, I begin with this anecdote in order to make two serious points. The first is that empathy is something that people might take for granted as an exercise in exploring the emotions of others that is easily and readily applied to the past. This hinges on the assumption that what I can imagine about my feelings if I were

7

in this situation will work as an approximation of what it actually felt like to be in this situation. Our qualification for making this leap is that we share a common humanity and a common set of basic emotions and building blocks of experiential life. A bombing raid is frightening. This is what I feel like when I am afraid. I would have hidden under a table. That must be how it was. Yet empathy does not work like this. It cannot be reduced to some biological uniformity. Empathy involves experience, shared context, shared knowledge, shared emotional prescriptions, shared gestural cues and so on. We empathize, primarily, with what we ourselves know how to feel.[1] Faced with an unfamiliar circumstance, we may still try to empathize, but we may fall well short of approximating what it feels like to *be the other*. The further from our experience a situation is, the less likely we shall be able successfully to empathize with it. Some situations that are particularly alien may not even trigger an attempt to empathize at all. I ask now whether I had sufficient information to hand in order to empathize with a resident of Burton in 1916, about their work, lives, speech, identity, struggles, gestures, about the layers upon layers of emotional regimes – family, class, community, nation, allies – and about the processes of othering that made for enmity and hatred in a time of war. I conclude that I did not.

The second serious point, then, is that while empathy seems to mark out one of the limits of history (or historiography, properly speaking), there are yet reasons to be sanguine about transcending those limits by other means. There was something of a backlash against historical empathy as I was being trained as a history undergraduate in the late 1990s. As the discipline of history reeled from the onslaught of postmodernity, which threatened to reduce historical writing to a highly selective and emplotted process, arising from the imagination of novelist-like historians, the primacy of evidence, empirical research, contextualization and the inherent limitedness of historical narratives was reasserted.[2] To empathize was to wax imaginatively, to pluck thick description out of thin air, as one critic once railed, to ascribe affective values to historical events where no such thing was indicated in the archives.[3] 'The past is a foreign country' remains a rallying cry. And, just as with encounters with people of actual foreign countries, sometimes empathy is not readily to hand. Yet the drive to try to get at what it felt like to be in a certain historical moment remains a signal fantasy of those who think about the past. Understanding takes time, work and effort, but these things do not put understanding out of reach. While we cannot any longer simply begin an empathetic account of the past, we can attempt to understand what it felt like to be *there*, *then*, according to the terms of historical actors themselves, and through a thorough reconstruction of the affective worlds in which people *moved*.[4] We can get at a history of feelings, but only if we first relinquish the primacy of our own as a guide. This is not historical practice as a practice of empathy, but the surrender of empathy in order to try to find how the dead once felt.

THE HISTORY OF emotions, now a major focus in the discipline of history, has taken off in the last decade. Still, one could be forgiven for wondering where the history of emotions is. Despite the great explosion of work being produced by historians on feelings, passions, emotions and sentiments, few have attempted general coverage, and none have attempted a narrative from antiquity to the present, to unfold a story of the history of emotions across historical time.[5] This book brings together for the first time a messy history of feelings over the extremely *longue durée*. In many respects, this book is a companion volume to *The History of Emotions*, a book focused entirely on the theory, methods, practices and challenges in the history of emotions as a field of historical enquiry.[6] I wrote that book because of the difficulty I perceived for anybody wishing to begin work in the history of emotions. The array of methodological and theoretical texts was diffuse and difficult to connect. A starting point seemed to be at once everywhere and nowhere. While those pages were about the historian's craft, I did note in them that we still want for an example of a history-of-emotions narrative that transcended traditional historical periodization and limitations of expertise. In these pages, therefore, I seek to exemplify how to *do* a history of emotions in the broadest possible strokes. It is not a close academic study of a small moment or a single place, but an attempt at a narrative of affective life in the epic mode. There are a thousand ways such a story could be told and I make no pretence that this is the definitive narrative. But it is one narrative, a story to begin with, for others to challenge, embellish, colour and augment.

This book rejects a universal theory of the emotions and adopts a biocultural approach to argue that how we feel is the dynamic product of the existence of our minds and bodies in moments of time and space.[7] Emotional encounters and individual experiences alike are explained in historical and cultural context to rehabilitate the unsaid – the gestural, affective and experiential – of traditional historical narratives. We are accustomed to the historical focus on reason, in which the loud, if not screaming, claims of strong feelings are dismissed as *irrational*. I assume that division, between reason and the irrational, to be false, but we must still ask how historical actors from different periods theorized and experienced the irrational. In many cases we find that feelings were not rationality's 'other' after all, but part of a relatively stable understanding of sympathy between body and mind, *ratio* and *passio*.

Insofar as the book is limited to *historical* time, it eschews the kind of neurobiological narrative that seeks to find in human bodies the 'deep' evolutionary structures that are pre-cultural. I have said elsewhere that while it is all very well to speculate on what is 'automatic' in human behaviour – naturally occurring processes, as it were – it is impossible to conceive of a human being outside of culture.[8] Should someone object that, somewhere in the deep recesses of time, human beings were pre-cultural, I would counter that those beings were pre-human. All of the stuff of historical work – the traces left – involves culture, be it language, meaningful gesture, art, social organization or whatever. Meaning is made exclusively in cultural formations, interactions and dynamics, and if there is no meaning there is nothing to talk about from a historical point of view. It is essential that the histories of the emotions, the senses and of experience liberate themselves from the temptations of a sort of transcendental biology.[9] The risks of not doing so are, according to some, portentous of a new 'dark ages', in which the humanities have surrendered all their power to research what it means to be human, since all meaning is supplied by evolutionary science.[10] It reminds me of the objection of Sartre to the psychologists, when talking about the phenomenology of emotion. Emotion '*does not exist*, considered as a physical phenomenon', he wrote, 'for a body cannot be emotional, not being able to attribute a meaning to its own manifestations'.[11] Search all you like for the biological roots of mind, you will not find *meaning*, or *signification*, in lumps of human stuff. Meaning always has to be made, and it is always made in context, in culture, and in society. The brain and body are themselves *in the world*. They are themselves historical things. The very plasticity of the brain-body, its adaptability to and within cultural formations, is an essential foundation for the history of emotions, for without this we are left only with the veneer of experiential change sitting atop an otherwise stable biology. The history of emotions is more profound than this. Work in neuroplasticity,[12] microevolution[13] and epigenetics[14] in particular is providing historians with an empirical justification for their search for experiential change over time, and an antidote to the universalizing tendencies of a more rigid evolutionary biology or a universalist train of thought among affect theorists.[15] It is not the case that historians have to put their accounts of change in the terms of these sciences – there is no need for us to defer on these matters – but there is no harm in acknowledging an empirical foundation for our arguments about the substance of historical change, which these sciences supply. When I talk about feelings in the past being *different* from the present, intelligible only through layers of historical-cultural scripts, it is important that this is understood as a historicization of the human itself. Feelings are formed and experienced in a dynamic relation of brain-body and world. Neither factor logically precedes the other: while the brain-body functionally delimits the range of feelings that can be experienced, the colour of experience is culturally prescribed. Individuals and groups have both to work out what they feel in a given circumstance and strive to *emote*, to express that feeling, in a way that makes sense in the context. Neurological and physiological activity in the brain-body are implicated in this *effort* (however unconscious the effort may be), such that culturally bound expression feeds back on, and changes, the feeling itself. This, in short, describes what William Reddy called an 'emotive', a shorthand way of describing the dynamic process of feeling–expressing in cultural context.[16] It handily combines both an understanding of the socio-cultural construction of emotion and the inherent embodiment of feelings. Since he coined the term, significant social-neuroscientific strides have been taken that essentially confirm its existence.[17] To put it succinctly, how we *do* emotions – an essentially culturally bound set of activities or practices – is bound up with how we experience them.[18] Since it is absolutely beyond doubt that the way emotions have been *done* has changed over time – the doing includes the words we use for affective experiences, the gestures (facial and bodily) that we use to express them, and the cultural scripts that determine the when and the how of expression – so too must experience itself have changed. What a dreadful waste of time it would be to argue that only the faces of emotions have changed, while the emotions themselves are timeless. Rather, each is implicated in, and formative of, the other. This is not circular, but dynamic, contextual and mutable. When we see these dynamics practised in the past, we are given cause to reflect: who or what shapes the parameters of my own experience? How do I feel – really *how*? Such reflections, I will argue, are empowering precisely because emotional prescriptions or emotional regimes only really work because those who build them also strive either to make them seem 'natural' or else invisible. By exposing the constructedness of so-called 'natural' orders, and by shining a penetrating light on what would be hidden, emoting in context becomes conscious and people become the agents of affect change. The human brain-body–culture system has therefore become a new frontier in historical research.

The coverage I offer here is geographically diverse, though it centres largely on the European experience of emotional encounters with each other and with more distant Others. From the deceptively simple wrath of Achilles among the Trojan ranks to the complex phenomenon of happiness in the late twentieth century, *A History of Feelings* explores the politics and possibilities of affective engagement with the foreign, the friend and the foe, as well as the emotional management of the self. It documents the ever-changing diction, definition and experience of feelings themselves. Of course, in a single volume one cannot hope to capture every facet of affective life from around the world and across all of time. I have tried to make selections that characterize important epochs and historical moments. To some extent, even though each chapter shows change over brief periods of time, the book is broken up into snapshots of affective style and substance that define moments in time and place. Yet in juxtaposition, these snapshots show an enormous overall change in both the language and experience of affective life, as well as marking its shifting centres of influence, from Greece to Rome, to Renaissance Florence and the salons of Paris, and to industrial and scientific London. Doubtless some will find this to be a rather European limitation – a criticism that I am prepared to own – but I challenge others to do what I have done, in broad strokes, for other centres of civilization.[19]

Two important points should be raised at the outset. First, I do not label this book as a whole a history of *emotions* because the very word 'emotions' already implies a conceptual and experiential category that has no real meaning in the vast majority of the historical record. Not only does it preference a particularly Anglophone context for what affective experience is, it also skews analysis to what psychologists and physiologists in particular have tended to think of since the middle of the nineteenth century when they think of emotions. Some might say that there is nothing wrong with such a backward projection of contemporary science, but that is both to misunderstand history and the contemporary science of emotions itself. From a historical point of view, it should be clearly understood that what matters is the experience of historical actors as they understood it themselves. This makes for some strange and, in some cases, distinctly odd encounters with affective experiences that we probably do not recognize. We cannot assume that we can readily enter into the experiential worlds of historical actors, any more than we can enter into their social, domestic or political worlds. Understanding takes work, contextual reading, analysis. Sometimes presenting the past as a place impossible to empathize with is a mark of a successful history.

From a scientific point of view, there have been a number of recent and significant developments that demonstrate the extent to which the mental and physiological processes involved in emotional experience are 'in the world', which is to say, they are both formative of and formed by the realities in which they are situated. It makes a difference whether we conceive of ourselves as having emotions, understood as internal neurological processes, or if we consider ourselves as suffering passions, understood as external influences on the state of our souls. These are not merely semantic distinctions, and it will not do to aver that one conception is true while the other is patently false. On the contrary, what we think is happening to us really does affect us; it influences not only how we feel but how we act and how others act in relation to us. As I pointed out, research in the social neurosciences is happily confirming this notion, which makes emotion research itself so deliciously uncertain. For whenever anybody tries to nail down precisely what an emotion is they are, quite literally, changing it. Social neuroscientific research leaves room for the possibility that the different cultural framing of affective experience *makes* the brain in different ways, and, conversely, those brains *construct* the world in different ways. There is, in short, a dynamic relationship between culture and the brain-body, with affective experience being both an ingredient and a product of the interface. Emotion change over time and place is a central part of human change over time. It is part of human biocultural history, which tends to witness much more rapid change than if we were to take a more strictly evolutionary view of species variation. Indeed, the narrative of biological evolution is increasingly having to adapt to research that shows the remarkable impact of microevolutionary change among humans because of human embeddedness in cultural contexts.[20] It should not come as a surprise. Charles Darwin (1809– 1882) himself showed that evolutionary forces could be rapidly sped up under domesticated processes of selection and control. It might help to understand the rapidity and extreme diversity of change in human affective experience if we think of humanity as just such a domesticated species.[21]

Given these new perspectives from the world of the biological sciences, it would not do to impose the word 'emotion' on the affective worlds of past actors. To be sure, imposing any category would similarly skew the analysis. By referring in the title to 'feelings' I am not suggesting an alternative label that covers all eventualities, but simply preferring a less loaded term that will allow me, in the course of the book, to discuss the semantic, conceptual and experiential worlds of affective life in different times and places. Often this means leaving historical 'feeling' terms in their original languages, preferring difficult explanations over easy but obfuscating translations.[22] Indeed, revising the easy translations of the language of affective experience in the past into the readily understood emotion categories of the present will be a major and recurring goal of this book. Reader, there will be Greek; there will be Latin. They are not to be feared.

The second important point that I want to raise here is that my narrative does not follow, or at least not always, the 'accepted' line of argument about emotional change over time with its typical characterization of different times and places according to dominant emotional standards. In many cases, I seek to upend such narratives, pointing out a particular focus on the elite, and choosing instead to focus on the obverse affective experiences to those that tend to receive historical emphasis. I do this not so much as a contrarian. Rather,

I am motivated by a suspicion that much of the extant literature that features the emotions has tended to emphasize that which connects 'us' to the past: narratives of change over time that nevertheless point to threads of continuity and that are borne along on the logic of teleology. How we got here from there is a perfectly reasonable incentive for research, but it overlooks all that was lost, and it is in what was lost, especially lost feelings, that history to me comes alive. For in examining what is lost we are forced to reckon with the forces that steer human history into its course.

If by this it is understood that I see emotions to be a causal factor in history, then so much the better. In general, the historiographical record – that is, the narrative of history according to what historians have *made* of it – tends to mark emotions as effects of events. They are the joy and shock that come in consequence of the substantial moving forces in time. Here I take the view that the affective life of humans is as much a moving force as anything else, and in fact is not distinguishable from political, economic or rational dynamics. Affective life is inextricably bundled with human activities of all kinds, such that no practice, no experience, no decision is ever without its attendant feelings, even when the feelings in question are framed as the denial of emotion. Claims to a conspicuous rationality, or to a distanced objectivity, are nevertheless defined by an affective posture, a feeling of coolness or righteousness. Even that which is completely unfeeling – the callous, the *brutal* – is only identifiable because of its exceptionality, in a context where everything is awash with feelings.

To try to make sense of such a long historical timeline, I take an episodic approach to feelings in context. The academic literature on emotions in any one of the periods covered here is already large and complex. I do not want to survey that literature, but rather pass by each period and examine important and influential episodes that, in some way or another, characterize the affective context of the time. As such, this is not a straightforward chronological narrative of change over time. I do not survey schools of philosophical thought about the emotions, or attempt a connected intellectual history of the emotions. The episodes I have selected do not necessarily flow one from the other, and may even seem discordant or disjointed. Each chapter is loosely thematic, but where there seems to be flow, apparent similarities often give way to profound differences. To some extent this is the effect that I want to establish, to demonstrate not just the difference of the affective past to our present, but to show great differences over time and from place to place throughout history. By showing feelings, passions and emotions in context, I highlight how the affective experience of our forebears was rich, distinctive and, in the grand scheme of things, fleeting and unstable. Each of the episodes that I focus upon is treated forensically, attempting to discover the minute particularities of affective language and experience that tend otherwise to be consumed by sweeping categories, such as Platonic or Stoic or Thomist or Cartesian or Scientific.

In part such a focus centres on linguistic differences, but I would not want my argument to be reduced to semantics. As I have said, language does not merely label experience; it influences it.[23] Often the rich texture of feeling words from the past is lost in the attractive temptations of translation. Conceptual elisions are frequently made in the name of making dead concepts intelligible to modern readers. Until the history of emotions developed a theory and methodology, few historians would have looked twice at the sacrifices that are made in turning *menis* into 'wrath', or *misericordia* into 'compassion'. This would have been left to philology, the importance of which cannot be overstated. As will become abundantly clear, I think the losses in such cases outweigh the convenience of translation, and I would rather spend time explicating the context that gave contemporary meaning to a word than to drag it, kicking and screaming, into present-day diction. Often this means leaving the feeling words of the past in the language of the time. To make sense of those words, other sources are used to contextualize or situate an episode. In some chapters, visual and material sources are particularly emphasized, be they paintings, photographs, popular prints, pottery or mosaics. The point is often to use an image to help say what is going on with a feeling, but equally to argue that we cannot really know what is going on unless we understand the context in which the image is produced. At other points, I use aspects of the biographies of individuals, through an examination of private correspondence and public contexts in dynamic relationship, to find the affective style of an individual peculiar to his or her time. Otherwise, publications in the worlds of philosophy, science, medicine and literature supply the component parts that allow for the reconstruction of contexts of feeling. The whole point of the history of emotions is, after all, lost, if we seek to make everything fit into emotion categories that we think we already understand. It is my hope that, by defamiliarizing the feelings of the past, we come to a point where we also jettison the conceit that we already understand our own emotion terms. Without significant reflection on the power and politics of emotional language and emotional prescription, we risk being able to know how we feel only dimly, through the refracted light of others.

Doubtless a question will be raised about the justification for the selection of these particular episodes. I cannot give a general answer to this, save to say that the focus points here seem either particularly influential – they have had an enduring impact on society, politics, culture, education and so on over many generations – or else particularly illuminative of the distance between past feelings and present. They are, in many cases, the episodes that I have continued to return to over the last decade or more, as things that are at once compelling but beguiling, resistant to being easily placed into emotional boxes and defined by our own emotional terminology. They are some of the things I habitually hold up to those who hold to a position of universal human emotions and ask: explain this! There is not, therefore, a seamlessness in the narrative here presented, though I do aim to show that an apparently continuous interest in and engagement with particular emotions – happiness, for example – is a deceptive effect of translation. The politics of feelings also dominates the discussion. Experiences are overwhelmingly affected by the prescriptions and delimitations of those in power. Humans emote according to the range of expressions deemed acceptable in a given context, and those parameters are never set by the poor, the weak, the othered (by gender, race, age, ability) or the disenfranchised.

By embracing such a large task in such a small space, I have had to push the limits of my own expertise, but I have done so to exemplify a point made in *The History of Emotions*. The methodology for emotions history applies to anywhere and any time, principally because it begins by throwing out all assumptions about categories of experience in the past. Affective lives, styles and systems have to be reconstructed in context. In the process, traditional periodization comes into question, for affective threads do not always run or end when our common markers of continuity and change would like them to. That said, I have preserved a chronology that may look familiar enough, but within each chapter I attempt to disrupt common assumptions about the emotional styles of this period and implicitly question what kind of work has to take place in order for such assumptions to be made. Hence the *Iliad* turns out not to be about rage after all; Platonic disgust resolves into desire; early modern rationalism is recast as conscious *movement*; the 'age of sensibility' is marked by its preoccupation with *brutality*, or lack of feeling; and our own highly emotional age is shown to be prescriptively servile. Moreover, the chapters sometimes overlap each other in terms of periodic coverage. By shaking up the narrative of affective experience over time, my hope is that future historians will go further and adopt a radical new periodization based on novel understandings of the emotional life of the past.

IN THE SUMMER of 2017 Thomas Dixon, the historian of emotions, science and religion, asked me over dinner in Helsinki why I thought that the history of emotions had suddenly taken off in the last ten years or so. We ruminated on public displays of grief and on an inevitable scholarly fascination with such outpourings. But neither of us was satisfied with such an explanation, which in any case only reasserted the question as well as inspiring new ones. On reflection, I have come tentatively to the conclusion that the history of emotions is so vibrant now precisely because our own emotional lives, whether construed individually, socially, culturally or as polities of various dimensions, have diminished. Emotion in the neoliberal age seems vague, empty or else crude. This is not to say that there is not, at present, extreme anger and grief, for those emotions seem inescapable. It is rather that a complex refinement of emotions, and a complex language with which we can talk about them, has been replaced (or at least degraded) in popular culture. Magnitude has taken the place of this refinement. There is anger, yes, and extreme anger, and *tremendous* anger. The emotional life of the past began to arouse the interest of historians at the moment that past emotions became visible as something unfamiliar. As with most historical investigations, the need to explore the emotions of the past speaks volumes about our own sense of doubt about the emotions in the present. Perhaps we are looking to recover or to reclaim. Or perhaps we simply want to know about the forces that limit and/or control how we feel. In that sense, the history of emotions is not so different to other historiographical innovations over the last fifty years or so. It seeks to expose the instruments of power in order to disrupt them.

I do not want to overstate the political intentionality of this book, but emotions are political, and historians of emotions have debated the kind of impact their work might have. William Reddy, in particular, has argued for our capacity as historians (and anthropologists) to judge emotional regimes according to the degree of emotional liberty an individual has. In other words, to what extent can a person have 'free' play with exploring what she feels through a rich variety of potential expression scripts? I have argued elsewhere that even a strict emotional regime might afford an individual the impression – and therefore the reality – of emotional liberty, and that taking up a position from which to judge is always fraught.[24] Nevertheless, if one turns this approach on its head, I think there is something to pursue. Historians ought to be able to work out the extent to which past actors were consciously aware of the emotive limitations of their experience. To be aware of constraint – that the natural is cultural and political, and that the invisible can be seen – even when the constraint is not an unhappy one, is to be conscious that one is not free. In this book I will show a number of examples of people and societies who were powerless to bring about change in the affective regime that bound them, but who nonetheless knew they were so bound. Insofar as they suffered, this made the suffering worse. But insofar as they struggled, this gave the struggle focus, direction and, the regime notwithstanding, an extra dynamic affective element. By having us reflect on our own emotional regimes (with which this book concludes), on that which binds and restricts or channels our experience, I do not suppose I am supplying a means to emotional liberty. But understanding the shackles is a necessary precursor to picking the locks.

To what extent do we know if we are 'happy', 'compassionate' or in 'pain'? The scare-quotes around each word denote their respective contingency and mutability. There is, as this book will show, nothing intrinsic, objective or timeless about any of these things. The ways that affective behaviour is evaluated are also shown to depend on historically specific configurations.

ONE

ARCHAIC AND
CLASSICAL PASSIONS

The archaic and classical periods in ancient Greece are among the best-studied for the meaning, value and experience of the passions. Much of the scholarship is based on the literature and philosophy of the age, for the sources are rich and their implications and influence are profound.[1] I cannot, therefore, hope to offer complete coverage, much as I can scarcely hope to cover any period in its entirety. Instead, I offer a series of selections that exemplify the complexity and the unfamiliarity of Greek passions, as they were written, certainly, but also as they were experienced (insofar as anybody can begin to guess at this).[2] I take, therefore, four 'emotions' that, on face value, will sound familiar and uncomplicated: rage, fear, shame and happiness. What I aim to demonstrate, through a reading of the *Iliad* of Homer, of Thucydides' (*c.* 460–400 BCE) *Peloponnesian War* and of Aristotle's (384–322 BCE) *Nicomachean Ethics*, is that these bare labels – rage, fear, shame, happiness – obscure more than they reveal about what is meant to be conveyed in the Greek. Indeed, though I refer at the outset to these familiar emotion nouns, I will show that such terms should be used only with care and with explication, for they do not mean what they appear to mean. For that reason, and I make a humble non-apology here, I have found it necessary to detail the Greek words in question throughout this chapter (with English transliteration, for ease of reading). I do not profess to great expertise with ancient Greek, but I have learnt enough to know that there is a tangible danger in flattening out the meaning of the Greek in the name of a nice translation. I see no risk, on the other hand, of going to some lengths to explain what the Greek terms actually mean. For that reason, it will be just as well if the reader, expecting an account of rage, fear, shame and happiness, leaves instead with an appreciation of μῆνις (*menis*), φόβος (*phobos*), αἶσχος (*aiskhos*) and εὐδαιμονίᾱ (*eudaimonia*).

Godlike Menace

In the beginning there was the word *menis*. The very first word in the Western literary canon is usually translated as wrath, or rage (μῆνιν – *menin*, the singular feminine accusative of μῆνις – *menis*). Homer's epic poem the *Iliad* seems fundamentally to be about the extreme anger of Achilles. The *Iliad* is a logical starting point for me. The influence of the *Iliad*, perhaps composed around 800 BCE or a little later, cannot be overstated.[3] It, along with a small number of other epic poems, dominated the educational life of Greece, such that an Athenian in the time of Plato (*c.* 400 BCE) would have had a deep familiarity with this work and would have drawn fundamental life lessons from it. The *Iliad* continues to be a cornerstone text in liberal education as well as a popular 'classic' in its own right. That it begins with, and is framed by, what we would recognize as an emotion word makes it of no small importance if we are seriously to entertain a history of feelings. It is not so much that the *Iliad* represents a factual account of a war and the actions in it, but that it was used, for centuries upon centuries, as a model of heroism and virtue. Both these things are steered by passions of the soul and by what look like emotions, but which encompass something more grandly cosmological.

If we acknowledge that the *Iliad* is about something like rage, then we must also enquire what it is about rage that we are supposed to learn. In pursuing this question, I have found that the *Iliad* is not really about something like rage after all, and this in turn has led to a host of further questions about why translators have made it so. Numerous scholars have pointed out that *menis* is a special and rare word in the *Iliad*, reserved for Achilles and the gods, and distinct from the more prosaic anger of the other characters, who tend to suffer χόλος (*cholos*), which is rooted in the body, like bile or gall.[4] Achilles' *menis* is, in its connection with the gods, cosmic in its magnitude and its importance. Leonard Muellner has called *menis* 'cosmic sanction' in a teleological reading of the *Iliad* that ascribes to *menis* the power to re-right a world that has been put out of shape by a profound threat to the social order.[5] In most instances, it is unleashed by a god to prevent a human who acts 'like a god' from overreaching the limits of his nature, but it is also used to keep the order of the gods itself in line. Achilles is not a god; he is a demigod, having an immortal mother, but more importantly he is a king of equal status to Agamemnon. At the beginning of the *Iliad* Agamemnon humiliates Achilles by taking his prize slave girl Briseis. In so doing, he threatens the delicate social structure of kings among kings, also upending carefully observed rituals about the share of plunder. Achilles is justly angry, but does this personal humiliation and risk to the stratification of Greek society account for his *menis*?

The second word in the Western literary canon is 'praise', and this gives us a huge clue as to what we should come to understand about Achilles' *menis*. Homer begins the account by asking the Goddess – Homer's muse – to praise it. Most modern translations have Homer invoke the Goddess to 'sing' the rage of Achilles, but this rather neutral choice comes, as far as I can tell, from a sense of incredulity that the *Iliad* can be dedicated to an account of wrath as a virtue, or at the least as a positive emotion. To the same end, most modern translations use the words 'rage', 'wrath' and 'anger' somewhat interchangeably. The crucial distinction between a humanly rooted rage and cosmic *menis* is lost. For example, in Robert Fagles's celebrated translation, rage becomes a leitmotiv of the whole epic, making the text come to life as a densely populated landscape of enraged kings and gods.[6] It works, as far as it makes for a wonderfully lucid and gripping narrative, but it sacrifices a crucial distinction in the bargain. In 2006, when I first taught the *Iliad* to students, I remember one student suggesting 'praise' as a potential translation of ἀείδω (*aeide*), which was met with consternation and surprise by the assembled classicists. With gratitude to that student I suggest that translation now, and await the further consternation of classicists.

It is not, on the face of it, a controversial translation of the word. Most lexicons suggest it. What makes it implausible in the *Iliad* is our contemporary understanding of rage, and Achilles' rage in particular, as negative, out of proportion, obscene, vicious, callous and irrational in the extreme. It is hard for us both to understand why Achilles' wrath boils along so consistently throughout the epic, and why any of Achilles' deeds are worthy of praise. The overall effect in many modern translations is to encompass the actions of Achilles after he rejoins the battle at the end of the *Iliad* into an account of his rage. This effect, given the extreme lengths of Achilles' battle murderousness, makes it hard to countenance the idea that his *menis* is praiseworthy. This leads to difficulties of both understanding and analysis.[7]

The *Iliad* provides an exciting potential starting place for an alternative history of feelings that would be at once strange and yet vital; for the upheaval and reversal of the virtuous and the vicious in the *Iliad* has come about through a radical change in the evaluation of certain passions. This change is reflective of a history of emotions itself. To read Homer through the eyes of his critics is to begin to flesh out the narrative of that history. Over the course of time, as understanding about the *menis* of Achilles ebbed, so the human qualities and emotional complexities of Hector came to the fore. Hector, according to modern readings, is the hero of the *Iliad*, a gallant and valiant underdog whose fate is sealed by a brute whose passions cannot and will not be checked. If there is *pathos* in the epic, it is to be found embodied in Hector's plight.[8] In the scheme of the *Iliad* itself, it is precisely such humanness that disqualifies Hector from top billing in the pantheon of epic heroes. Understanding why Hector has received the plaudits over the centuries depends on the shifting interpretation of the value of the respective heroes' emotions. To be clear, Hector becoming the hero and Achilles the villain of the piece is not reducible to a shifting moral interpretation of the text, nor to a simple change in the evaluation of certain emotions (like anger, or fear), but suggests an experiential distance from the context of the poem. Achilles becomes the villain because it is no longer possible to account for his experience of *menis*, or the profundity of his grief and the actions it brings about. The most important critical reading of Homer is perhaps the first and most famous, which resides in large parts of the Platonic dialogue that makes up the *Republic*. It is here that we first find a clear critical discussion of the difficulties of accepting Homer's Achilles as a virtuous, and therefore exemplary, hero. The implication, in classical Athens, is that Homer might be banned for his corrupting influence. In contradistinction, from the medieval to the Victorian period, Hector was refashioned to become the chivalrous heroic loser of the *Illiad*, held up as an exemplar of courtly manliness. In order to do so, however, Hector and Achilles had to be recast so as to accord with later sensibilities about the meaning and value of anger and valour. Achilles was to become the arch-villain, while the vanquished Hector would be the model of a pyrrhic victor. Anger, especially unrestrained anger, could not be countenanced as a positive trait. The cosmic significance of *menis* was lost, coming as it did from a ritual-dominated polytheistic society, wholly unintelligible to a monotheistic culture profoundly influenced by stoicism.

Hector is reputed to have become 'a recognizable romance hero' by about 1400 in the anonymously written *Laud Troy Book*, and his fame as such can be read as far as Elizabeth Barrett Browning's poem 'Hector in the Garden' (1846).[9] In 1869 Gladstone expressed his dismay that the

> character of Homeric Hector has been so exaggerated, and so defaced, by the later tradition, that it has lost every distinctive feature of the original, and has come to stand as a symbol of the highest bravery and chivalry. But neither bravery nor chivalry are, in a proper sense, distinctive features of the Homeric Hector.

Gladstone struggled to make sense of Hector's 'inconsistent' character traits, between extreme bravery and 'palpable signs of cowardice', which shows how difficult it was to access precisely what it was that made Hector afraid. Perhaps, Gladstone wonders, 'the total absence of vice ... in his character, co-operated with other causes in bringing about his adoption in the Christian literature of the middle ages, as the model, for the olden time, of the heroic man'.[10]

According to Saul Levin:

> From remote times, a picture of certain heroic types was communicated to every generation of Greeks, in the *Iliad*, which they read or listened to from childhood on. Whatever the contemporary environment might make of a Greek, he was, through the poem, insensibly molded by his distant ancestors, or rather what his ancestors admired. Yet the Greeks of the Golden Age were less touched by some parts of the *Iliad* than by others. They could and did slight one of the two leading personages – Hector – who moves most modern readers and even scholars far more than Achilles.

We would rather be like Hector; but are we as close to the feelings of the poet and his Achaean audience as their descendants were, who saw in Achilles alone the great hero of the *Iliad*?[11]

My notion is that we are many times removed from the feelings of the poet and his Achaean audience, and that to understand why Achilles is the hero of the *Iliad* one has to work hard to understand the stakes of his *menis*. I want therefore to entertain the idea that Homer's poem does in fact open as it appears to open, with an exhortation to the Goddess to praise *menis*, and that the *Iliad* as a whole is just such a praiseworthy account of *menis*. If Achilles is the hero and Hector the despised villain, how can we make sense of all of Achilles' dreadful deeds as positive, proportional, seemly, virtuous, feeling, rational and just? I posit that such a reading is possible, and that this is the way the Greeks understood Homer's hero. In fact, Achilles derives his honour from Zeus for his *abstaining* from battle. His rejoining of the fray signals the *end* of his *menis*. Therefore, I humbly submit a novel suggestion for a new translation of the first two words in Western literature: 'praise godlike menace'. *Menis* is not a mere passion and cannot be equated readily with what we call an emotion. It does not arise from within, but has both social and cosmic stimuli. In my reading, it makes more sense to translate *menis* as *menace* (there is some cause to connect the two words, not least because they sound almost exactly the same), which carries with it an implicit affective disposition of extreme anger, as well as an implication of violent threat that defines the actions of its subject and disrupts the experience of all in that world who encounter it. *Menis*, after all, does not merely describe the feeling of Achilles; it underscores and justifies all of his (in)actions and the course of the war until he finally relinquishes it and rejoins the fray. Menace, as a noun, is understood today as 'a person or thing that is likely to cause harm; a threat or danger', when applied in the singular, as well as a 'threatening quality or atmosphere'. In the context of the *Iliad*, precisely such a threat is warranted because of the social and ritual rupture caused by Agamemnon's treatment of Achilles.

Achilles' *menis* causes blood to flow in rivers among the Argives. What is its cause? On a simple reading, where we assume *menis* to mean 'rage', it is almost impossible to avoid the conclusion that

Achilles acts out of all proportion to the wrong done to him. In book 1, Agamemnon strips Achilles of his prize, the slave girl Briseis, as compensation for having to give up his own prize woman, Chryseis. He is compelled to give up Chryseis to her father, who is a priest of Apollo. Initially, and against cosmic and ritual notions of justice and order, Agamemnon had refused to ransom Chryseis, whereupon Apollo had visited a great plague upon all the amassed Greeks. This is the *menis* of Apollo, and the collective suffering it causes compels Agamemnon to change his mind in order to restore order and end Apollo's menace. But as compensation for having to give up his own prize, and in order to not lose face, he takes the prize of Achilles. In turn, Achilles cuts all ties with all the Greeks who implicitly condone Agamemnon's action by allowing it to happen. If we understand Achilles simply to be very angry, for having lost face or for having been dishonoured by Agamemnon, or because he lost his Briseis, then we shall not fail to consider him truculent and petulant in the extreme. Can his dishonour really justify all the grievous harm that his *menis* brings about? But Agamemnon's unjust seizing of Briseis does not simply anger or enrage Achilles on a personal level. It signals in much broader terms a disruption of the order of worldly things, a disruption that follows quickly on the heels of the disruption of cosmic things. Agamemnon has twice risked *menis*, first of Apollo, second of Achilles, by acting out of all regard to deeply embedded and encoded ritual practices concerning status, exchange and honour. Achilles' menace is praiseworthy because it will ultimately restore things to the way they are supposed to be.

The teleological purpose of Achilles' *menis*, for the majority of the action in the *Iliad*, is not for him to unleash violence but for him to withdraw from violence. Achilles is all restraint in his *menis*. He is marked by *inaction*. He is restrained (by himself or by Athena or by Thetis). See, for example, the first-century CE fresco from Pompeii in which Achilles' *menis* is first transformed by Athena into control and withdrawal. It is worth noting, *en passant*, that most ancient depictions of Achilles do not portray any visible or obvious facial expression. If one is looking for an archetypical sign of anger in facial affect, one will not find it in Achilles, the supposed archetype of rage. In another depiction, on a cup dating to 480 BCE, which captures the moment of Briseis being removed to Agamemnon's custody, Achilles sits motionless, wrapped in a mourning shroud, the only

Fresco of Achilles and Agamemnon, Casa di Apollo, Pompeii, 1st century CE.

Athenian red-figure cup depicting Briseis being taken from Achilles, c. 480 BCE.

visible expression being the placement of his hand on his forehead. While it might serve to see this as a physical gesture of his personal grief, in the context it makes sense to interpret it as a visible sign of his *menis*. He is inert, grieving not merely the state of his personal fortune, but the state of the *world*.

Thereafter, Achilles simmers by the ships, his *menis* continuing to be the cause of the Argives' struggles. The *Iliad* is always already a retelling of a story with a known outcome, hence Achilles' *menis* portends the violent conclusion that inevitably arises, but it also permits the violence visited upon the Greeks by other hands. It is a withdrawal designed to unleash hell upon the Achaeans by allowing Hector and the Trojans the advantage in battle. With the chief source of military resistance out of the picture, the Trojans slaughter the Argives. This is the will of Zeus, but Zeus' *menis* is actually in this case the active adoption of the *menis* of Achilles. Zeus becomes, in Muellner's terms, 'the active agent' of Achilles' *menis*.[12] Zeus accedes to the request of Achilles, via his mother Thetis, that the Achaeans should all suffer for the transgressions of Agamemnon, transferring the unusual human *menis* of demigod Achilles to the 'cosmic sanction' of an actual God, who justly punishes the whole social group associated with he who put the world out of sorts.[13]

The impact of Achilles' *menis* only gives way when he unleashes Patroclus onto the Trojans. The rout of the Argives by this point is sufficient punishment for the injustices done to Achilles' honour, and in sending Patroclus into battle *as if* he were Achilles himself, Achilles takes the first step to rebuilding those bonds that were shattered by Agamemnon at the outset of the poem. Patroclus' death – experienced not simply as the death of a loved one, but as if this were his own death, such was the identity between them – ignites in Achilles a profound grief that finally launches him into battle. Modern translations almost inevitably confuse this return to activity as a continuation of Achilles' rage, in an admixture of other powerful emotions: love and grief. It is only reasonable, by our own standards of what constitutes rage or wrath, that the extraordinary violence that issues forth from the hands of Achilles must be borne by nothing other than this. But insofar as Achilles' actions are undertaken out of grief, and for the benefit of all of his comrades, we have to see his relentless murderousness as the sign that his *menis* – the theme of the *Iliad* – has dissipated.

Whereas in his *menis* he was completely inert, in his killing rampage he is described as being 'like' the *menis* of the gods. Achilles comes only figuratively to embody the kind of menace unleashed from on high, and only once his own *menis* has been given up in the name of rejoining the human and ritually bound fold.[14] When Homer styles Achilles, immediately prior to his mortal wounding of Hector, with 'violent [or wild] soul full of might' (μένεος δ' ἐμπλήσατο θυμὸνα ἀγρίου – *meneos d' emplesato thumona agrion*) his passion is explicitly re-grounded in the stuff of earth, in the natural rather than the cosmological realm.[15] Achilles is 'fury incarnate', as Stephen Scully has it, but this is finally a mortal body, a human body and a human, grief-driven rage.[16] Here, and again just prior to Hector's death, modern translations usually render μένος (*menos*) as 'rage' or 'wrath', conflating this word for might, power, force, strength or violence with the categorically distinct *menis*.[17] Importantly, and this is often overlooked, as Achilles refuses to hand over Hector's body and insists he will become food for dogs and birds, he wishes he had μένος καὶ θυμὸς (*menos kai thumos*) to eat Hector's flesh raw.[18] Fagles translates this as 'my rage, my fury'; A. T. Murray styled it 'wrath and fury'.[19] Both are in keeping with the theme of an enraged Achilles, where 'wrath' here is indistinguishable from the *menis* that opened the whole poem. But the implication of the passage is clear. Achilles does *not* have the necessary passion to eat Hector raw and nor does he ever attempt it. The passage might just as well read: 'would that I had the vital strength (*menos*) or heart (*thumos*) to eat you raw'. It would be more in keeping with the narrative arc of Achilles' character, who has, by this point, fully relinquished his more cosmic *menis*.

Fear and Cosmic Things

At the crucial moment of encounter in book 22 of the *Iliad*, Hector, having talked himself into a one-on-one showdown with Achilles, nevertheless loses his nerve and bolts in fear. Achilles pursues him relentlessly around the walls of Troy, and it is only the deception of Athena, appearing to Hector as an ally to help him fight Achilles, that makes him stop running away. Why, having resolved to fight, does Hector run? It is, for those who promote Hector to primacy among the epic heroes, the most difficult moment to interpret. Given his exploits throughout the *Iliad*, is it not completely out of character for Hector to 'tremble' (τρόμος – *tromos*) and to 'flee in fear' (φοβηθείς – *phobetheis*)?

A basic tenet of the history of emotions is that it is not sufficient to mark changes in the *object* of emotions, for such changes also alter the experience of emotion itself. As David Konstan, the most prominent historian of emotions in antiquity, has said, 'emotions are not instinctive and universal responses, but are conditioned by values specific to a given society ... they are cognitively based and socially constructed'. They 'depend essentially on judgments', but such judgements are made, in Sara Ahmed's formulation, *as if* naturally.[20] They happen so fast that there is not a conscious feeling of the working out of the appropriate demeanour. Emotions are not performed, they happen. But they happen, nonetheless, in context, and they involve an implicit understanding of that context. To understand why Hector ran, it will not suffice to say 'because he was afraid', nor will it do to qualify 'because he was afraid of Achilles'. Both of these constructions only lead to a further question. How does such a fearless warrior suddenly come to tremble?

To understand it, we have to understand the relatively shallow depths of human heroism in the overall cosmic scheme that Homer constructs. To help imagine Homer's narrative as a kind of surface interpretation of the heroic, let us turn to Homer's own description of another surface: Achilles' shield. It is given to him before he finally rejoins the battle, his *menis* abandoned, forged by the god Hephaestus.

Oliver Taplin's scheme of how the shield might have been configured is a useful guide. The shield is, in his view, a microcosm of the universe.[21] It contains, crudely, the elements of life (and they are mainly good). In five concentric circular bands, the cosmos – earth, sky, sea, sun, moon and stars – is at the middle of the shield. Outside it, two cities, one at peace, one at war, depicting two kinds of justice ('straight justice' and the justice of bronze and blood). Beyond this scene is a band of rural life, depicting the seasons and their activities. The next band depicts a dance, and the final, widest band, is the ocean. War is put, for the only time in the *Iliad*, in the perspective of a much greater whole, depicting the good life, or at least an holistic life.

But why give this shield, with this design, to Achilles? Of all the people in the *Iliad* Achilles consciously chooses war, a glorious death, over a long and peaceful life. Achilles' power is based on his virtuosity as a fighter. His *raison d'être* is contained in only one half of one of the circles, and not at the centre. It is not the kind of shield we see elsewhere, depicting the head of the Gorgon, or thunderbolts and lightning. On the contrary, Achilles' shield is a reminder of the day-to-day: farming, 'peaceful' quarrelling, dealing with the vagaries of nature, frolicking. Life is limited by the heavens and the oceans, and the breadth of experience is, most of the time, quite narrow. Its themes connect to Hesiod's *Works and Days* (*c.* 700 BCE). The description in *Works and Days* is of the everyday. Things to do and not do. The seasons and the land. About futile quarrels. Its limits, from Hesiod's point of view, are the ocean, which is best avoided, and the gods, who are immanent. And in the sense that Hesiod describes the repeating seasons, and the repeating calendar, it is essentially circular in structure. Structurally, the shield and *Works and Days* therefore have something in common, but the similarity goes, I think, beyond this superficial likeness.

The point is about not trusting in the appearance of superficiality. Hesiod's message seems to be that even though the everyday, on the surface, is mundane, it is nevertheless important because it is the will of the gods; life, in all its circularity and with all its repetitions, is in its essence divine. Likewise Achilles' shield fashions, in a plane surface, the mundanity of life. The Trojan War slots into a far grander scheme in which it becomes a mere detail, dwarfed by the grander forces at work. All the actions of the heroes on the battlefield become obscured in the army as a whole, and subsequently in the wider scheme of life in all its forms. We are given the surface of life as it was known, and the actions of our heroes become unimportant. It is not a universally happy depiction of the world, but in its entirety it shares with *Works and Days* its mundane attitude. The conclusion is the same, however, as for *Works and Days*. After all, this is a shield forged by the divine, and represents the presence of the divine in all things, beneath the surface. The value of the hero, his status as warrior, is undercut and the hero emasculated by the broad view. Whatever the exploits of battle, and however famous (or infamous) the hero, his reputation is dwarfed by the influence of the divine, and the power of the sea and stars. It is therefore crucial that this mundane, yet divine, image is forged at the pivotal moment in the whole of the *Iliad*, as Achilles finally relinquishes his *menis* and joins the battle in grief and rage. It is as if we are given a forethought that what we are about to hear or read has its place. The poem as a whole is put into perspective. Achilles bears before him the grandeur of the universe.

While we may again be consumed by the heroic exploits that follow, the motifs of peace and a world other than, and larger than, that of the battlefield (and the human) recur. As Achilles dresses for battle in book 19 we are told that his shield 'spilled light around it as if it were the moon. / Or a fire that has flared up in a lonely settlement / High in the hills of an island, reflecting light / On the faces of men who have put out to sea / And must watch helplessly as rising winds / Bear them away from their dear ones.'[22] Heavens, Earth, Sea. At a stroke the structure of the shield is recapitulated. It is recapitulated again as Achilles dons his helmet, shining 'like a star', the horsehair placing us on the earth, but 'rippling in waves' to remind us of the sea. And finally, as Achilles mounts his chariot, he is 'shining in his war gear / Like an amber Sun'.[23] In the context of the cosmos, what will happen in the concluding books of the *Iliad* are small deeds indeed.

Stephen Scully has argued that this stark reminder of the insignificance of human deeds explains the inability of Achilles' Myrmidon army to look at the armour. Achilles can observe it with pleasure because he has already accepted his impending death, and the emptiness of human action. Achilles is, it must be remembered, a demigod. For the same reasons, Hector only runs away when he sees the shield, having not yet reconciled himself with his mortality, and with his place in the grand scheme. At the precise moment of Hector's death we are again reminded of the cosmic scheme: Achilles is rage itself, but notably 'behind the curve of his shield'. The description again mirrors the shield's universal structure: the rippling of his helmet's crest, like the sea, the thick golden horsehair as an emblem of the land, and his spearpoint glistening 'like the Evening Star'. 'Such framing of the human within the broader settings of Earth, Heaven, Sun, Moon, stars, and River Ocean', Scully tells us, 'is Olympian, and a distancing vision of the mortal that only Achilles in his transcendent fury can long sustain'. I would suggest that it is Achilles in the fury of grief, accepting his fate to die in battle, that can sustain this vision, since his 'transcendent fury' – his godlike menace – has, by this point, passed. To see these separate rings of the universe as a 'unified whole' is terrifying to those only concerned with their own mortality: 'That synoptic and inhuman perspective breaks the sense of the special status of the human by placing it within the context of a larger cosmos and Zeus' will.' This particularly affects Hector at the moment of his confrontation with Achilles. Scully refers to 'a sense of godhead made present', a vision of the cosmos bearing down on him brandished by Achilles. To behold such a scene is to be reduced to the infinitesimal. But the shield was more than 'Gorgon-like in its effect upon humankind'.[24] It inspired *awe*, that particular fear of the divine that is intermixed with a sense of overwhelming grandeur.

The narrative of the *Iliad* demonstrates to us that actions speak louder than words; indeed, that words are impotent without actions. A good speaker who cannot also brandish a sword or hurl a spear *ought* not to be heard. Nevertheless, this observation is contained in a poem, the medium of words (and presumably *not* sword-brandishing) par excellence. Homer's description of the shield, the reminder of the superficiality and partiality of all that happens in the *Iliad*, is a pointer to the fact that the poet sees divinity in universals, not particulars, *and is able to describe them*. Heroes come and go, as does glory, fear and rage. Actions last for the moment in which they are acted. They make but a fraction of the whole scheme, and yet it is through the whole that God works. Likewise, words transcend time and space and encompass the whole. The poet's vision is truly heroic since it puts things in context and has its domain in the universal, much like the divine. It accesses the divinity below the surface of the whole. Achilles says of the shield that 'no / Mortal could have made' it, yet the shield *is made* by the poet.[25] The convincing nature of the description affiliates poetry with the divine. The instructional value in the *Iliad*, the rendering of heroic examples to which to aspire, is always, therefore, accompanied by the following caveat: if it were not for the poet, we would not have access to these heroes, or to the exemplar of Achilles' godlike menace, at all. The immortality, in the popular mind, of Achilles or Hector, is always secondary to the immortality of the poet who told their story. It is *words* that prove to be the hero of the *Iliad*, for their power in revealing the heroic and its limits. For while the hero either breaks under the power of awe, or else is only able to inspire awe in knowledge of death, the poet is the only one who gets inside *menis* and awe, to outlive the hero and look the divine in the face.

Shame and Human Things

In stark contrast to the consideration of the human as belittled by cosmic grandeur, the absence of cosmic considerations in Thucydides' account of the Peloponnesian War squarely centres the action on human things, on a grand but nonetheless human scale. To understand human things, including the history of the affective lives of human beings, we need to know what a human is. This has been the allure of emotion studies in disciplines that attach it to the word 'science', for emotions seem to offer an unimpeachable insight into human nature, which in turn could explain the experience of being human everywhere, and for all time. The circularity of such research is apparent. To explore the vagaries of human experience we need to investigate what a human is, which we can find out by investigating the vagaries of human experience. Studies of emotion often do not know what their object is, but they tend to make one giant assumption or another: either they claim to know, for all time, what a human is, or else they claim already to know, for all time, what an emotion is. Reading critically across works in psychology, philosophy, evolutionary biology and so on, one concludes that these assumptions are usually wrong.

Not that we should be at all surprised that such assumptions are made. In many ways the quest to define ourselves is itself definitive. The problem with grand declarations about what we are is that, with the passage of time, we see only too clearly that, no, that is not what we are. The logical conclusion, however, is not that the real and final definition eludes us, lying at the end of some as yet unexplored research agenda; on the contrary, the logical conclusion is that we definitively resist definition. If categorical assertions about the quality and meaning of being human do not seem to hold up over time, maybe it is because that quality and that meaning have themselves changed. Central to the argument of this book is that the human being is not fixable, just as Linnaeus classified our species, *homo nosce te ipsum*: human know thyself. The slipperiness of subjectivity is built right in. It was precisely the distinction between Hector and Achilles that marked them out, ultimately, as vanquished and hero: Hector had not recognized what it meant, in that context, to be human (mortal); Achilles had. One might summarize the shifting fortunes of these two characters as the rise in importance of worldliness and the falling away of godliness. In any case, they offer a curious and compelling study of the mutability of conclusions about what a human is and does.

Historians have not been immune to the temptation to define or seek to define human nature, however. One of the most conspicuous means by which they have done so is through the art of translation, whereby ancient historical writing has been made to serve presentist preoccupations with human meaning. The *Iliad* is a case in point, as we have seen. To further this insight I will dwell here in particular on the use historians have made of Thucydides' *History of the Peloponnesian War*, for it is by repute a narrative about the timelessness of human nature, especially as concerns its emotional or irrational qualities, but it is firmly grounded, unlike the *Iliad*, in a war that historians can reliably date, locate and contextualize. What will become clear is that this reputation of Thucydides' work for its communication of the timelessness of human nature has been implanted by historians into a text that actually allowed for the mutability of human things. By taking a historiographical journey through the stakes of translation in Thucydides, we shall ultimately arrive at an appreciation of the importance of particularity, not universality, in his original account of the war. And this particularity, this context-bound understanding of human dynamics, necessarily includes experience at the affective level.

Thucydides (*c.* 460–400 BCE) was an Athenian general serving in the war between Athens and Sparta that began in 411 BCE. He is known as the father of history, reputed for his evidence-based and 'objective' storytelling. His account of the war, which he styled the greatest war of all time, is noted for the absence of gods and supernatural forces, and for its focus on human zeal and human fear as major factors in the movement of polities towards and within conflict. Elsewhere I have styled Thucydides' work as the first history of emotions, for events are emplotted in such a way as to show the tendency of humans to succumb to passions that they are reputed to be able to resist.[26] Insofar as it contains many exemplars of Athenian political reasoning and rhetoric, its action is moved along by consequences of fear and ambition, by prescriptive passions and by the transgression of those prescriptions.

The feeling that things that go around will come around has been central to modern understandings of what Thucydides claimed to be the lasting importance of his work – that he was describing a war that others would subsequently identify with their own, later, wars. But in large part that sense of identity with Thucydides' account has been manipulated by the numerous readers and translators of Thucydides over the centuries, who have sought to make the Thucydidean narrative fit with their own sense of history, of the progression of time, and of the meaning of that central character in the history of history, the human.

The illustrious Mary Beard, doyenne of TV historians, remarked in 2010 that Thucydides' Greek is 'made almost incomprehensible by neologism, awkward abstractions, and linguistic idiosyncrasies of all kinds' that led a later Greek historian, Dionysius of Halicarnassus, to denounce Thucydides' 'forced expressions' and 'riddling obscurities', noting that 'if people actually spoke like this, not even their mothers or their fathers would be able to tolerate the unpleasantness of it'. They would need 'translators'. Beard concludes that those translations that are 'fluent and easy to read . . . give a very bad idea of the original Greek. The "better" they are, the less likely they are to reflect the flavour of what Thucydides wrote.' Her cautionary note is that Thucydides 'simply did not write many of the bon mots attributed to him'.[27] There is an overwhelming sense in Thucydides of a human experiential universal. On a simple reading, we might see this as the permanent presence of, or at least potential for, zeal and enthusiasm, in particular in relation to power; and where that zeal for power exists, somebody somewhere else feels fear to the same degree. These human factors of lust for power and fear of power afflict each individual according to his proximity to the instruments of power or the location of fear. In Thucydides' opening account of the whole war he announces that these kinds of things will happen again, and he bears this out himself episodically in his narrative of the war, where lust for power and fear of power seem to take Athenians and Peloponnesians alike into remarkably similar scenarios of troubled waters and defeat. We might identify it as an emotional frailty, a collapse of caution and reason in both the quest for power and the rise of fear, that defines Thucydides' account, and the essential humanness of this frailty works as a universal cause for why this kind of war will happen again, or at least, why wars will appear to be fundamentally in common.

In line with Beard's scepticism, we must ask how we reach this impression of the red thread in Thucydides' narrative. Certainly, it stands in stark contrast to Aristotle's assessment of what historians do, and the charge is so candid that presumably he did not read in the Greek of Thucydides any such claims of being able to forecast the future according to the character of human nature:

> The historian and the poet are not distinguished by their use of verse or prose; it would be possible to turn the works of Herodotus into verse, and it would be a history in verse just as much as in prose. The distinction is this: the one says what has happened, the other the kind of thing that would happen. For this reason poetry is more philosophical and more serious than history. Poetry tends to express universals, and history particulars . . . Even if in fact [a poet] writes about what has happened, he is none the less a poet; there is nothing to prevent some of the things which have happened from being the kind of thing which probably would happen, and it is in that respect that he is concerned with them as a poet.[28]

Despite this, Thucydides' reputation stands almost impenetrably to the contrary. The reason, I suggest, is in the conceit of Thucydides' translators, who staked out a claim for history that Aristotle reserved for poetry.[29] The historiographical importance of the work is usually located in book 1, part 22. The key phrase in Thucydides' Greek looks like this: κατὰ τὸ ἀνθρώπινον (*kata to anthropinon*). To give a characteristic translation with context, Steven Lattimore puts it thus, with the key phrase in italics: 'Yet if they [my words] are judged useful by any who wish to look at the plain truth about both past events and those that at some future time, *in accordance with human nature*, will recur in similar or comparable ways, that will suffice.'[30] That line, 'in accordance with human nature', gets a variety of treatment in translation, but the tendency to invoke something timeless and 'natural' is characteristic of translations appearing after the Second World War. Rex Warner, for example, translated it as 'human nature being what it is', and Robert Lisle plumped for 'so long as men are men'.[31] Even the most recent translation in English, by Martin Hammond, tends towards the same emphasis: 'I shall be content if it is judged useful by those who will want to have a clear understanding of what happened – and, *such is the human condition*, will happen again at some time in the same or a similar pattern' [emphasis added].[32] This rings true of translators into other languages: Vretska and Rinner's German translation reads '*gemäß der menschlichen Natur*', which literally reads as 'according to human nature' in English.[33] In sum, Thucydides is presented as a man whose satisfaction with his work rested on its usefulness as a timeless exemplar of what human nature is and what it does. It is a blueprint for understanding why humans act the way they do in situations that arise according to that nature.

Earlier translators left more ambiguity in this line. Thomas Hobbes, Thucydides' first English translator, settled for 'according to the condition of humanity', whereas Benjamin Jowett, the arch-Victorian classicist, rendered it 'in the order of human things'.[34] Both these translations are ambiguous, for the first suggests that the condition of humanity is contingent, and the second references a category – 'human things' – that is not readily intelligible. In the early 1980s Marc Cogan wrote a whole book on 'the human thing', which he argues is the literal translation of *anthropinon* that so many others render as 'human nature'.[35] It is such a rare usage in Greek, appearing only once in Thucydides, that narrowing down its meaning is impossible unless we read it in the context of Thucydides' work as a whole. What should be clear right away, however, is that Thucydides' pronouncement of the universality of human nature that makes history repeat itself is precisely one of those bon mots that Thucydides did not write. We can be sure that it definitely does not refer to 'human nature' because Thucydides does in fact refer to this (ἀνθρωπείαν φύσιν – *anthropeian phusin*), literally, elsewhere in his account of the war.

If the importance of Thucydides' work lies in its interpretation not of human nature, but of the 'human thing', then it is obviously essential that we try to discern what this is. It is my contention that, far from being a fixed category of nature that makes history a kind of predictive science, Thucydides' principal point was that humans are characterized by their contingency, their fickleness and by their tendency to be overwhelmed by passions when faced with adversity. The only predictive quality this allows for is a sense that humans will behave unpredictably when under pressure. The essential ingredient of this temperamental instability was an affective debility that belied all attempts rhetorically to fix human action within the sphere of rationality.

This is perfectly illustrated by Thucydides' accounts of Pericles' funeral oration, praising the virtues of Athenian character, and of the plague, which follows immediately afterwards. Pericles praises the courage and sense of duty of Athenians and draws attention to the affective disposition of the Athenian populace as a guarantor of these virtues. Athenians are neighbourly and avoid those injurious expressions that cause offence. They are respectful of laws, the breaking of which is a source of shame, dishonour or disgrace (αἰσχύνην – *aiskhune*). They recreated the mind and banished distressing cares (λυπηρὸν – *luperon*) through games and festivals. They loved beauty and knowledge in such a way as to prevent them becoming effeminate (literally, 'softness', μαλακίας – *malakias*), and placed shame not in poverty itself but in failing to struggle to get out of it. Pride, therefore, defined civic life. Not reflecting on the odds of success, but leaving the outcome to hope (ἐλπίδι – *elpidi*), they culminated their lives in glory, not fear (δέους – *deous*).[36] Athens itself, the city, underwrote and formed these qualities, and was itself built upon the qualities of its ancestral citizens. For as Athenians looked upon the city they were to become its lover (ἐραστὰς – *erastas*) and reflect that the power of the city had been acquired by courageous men filled with a duty to avoid disgrace. This dynamic relationship signalled both the dependency of their affective states on the nature of the city and the courageous duty that being part of the city implied. For an overall feeling of contentment and satisfaction with life (εὔδαιμον – *eudaimon*)[37] depended on freedom (ἐλεύθερον – *eleutheron*), and freedom depended on courage, or literally, a goodness of soul (εὔψυχον – *eupsykhon*). War, therefore, in which the city was geared to engage, becomes the natural vehicle of contentment, justified by the logic of collective involvement in the institutions of politics. War, citizenship, courage (the defeat of fear), honour, love and contentment are all mutually implicated in a dynamic relationship of individual and city.[38] No part can be removed.

This panegyric about the affective qualities and heroic virtues of Athenians becomes a dead letter as soon as the plague begins to ravage the population.[39] The shifting context of civic life unravels that tight relationship of virtuous citizenry and glorious city, so much so that every aspect of Pericles' speech is reversed. The population, overcome by fear, abandons its adherence to law and seeks happiness in hedonism rather than through courage. Since death stalks the streets indiscriminately, and since no heroic action can mitigate it, desire has to be immediately gratified. Laws and the system of justice become empty categories in the face of an unchecked pestilence, to the point that the institutions that bind the populace together into a body that is at one with the city crumble, re-individuating the population, who act without restraint on their passions. Neither fear of God nor fear of punishment check their indulgence, which is driven instead by fear of death. Thucydides provides us with both a clear understanding of the passions as a cause of events, and of the dangers of allowing passions to run without the control provided by community harnessing. In the breach, it reinforces the larger point that Athens depended on affective control, on the tethering of human things to the polis.

The mutability of human things was combined with the inertia of human political institutions, wrapping up individuals in the dynamics of the polis. Human things are collective things. Repeatedly, Thucydides' account of the war shows what happens when individuals overcome with passions enact those passions through political institutions, and it is in this dynamic of individuals and institutions that we locate the vagaries of human things. Thucydides' humans are always in a relationship with power and with the institutions of power, which can either be balanced or unequally distributed. In the latter case, in Thucydides' scheme, the powerful succumb to zeal, the powerless to fear. But insofar as either circumstance draws the worst out of men as individuals, it is their institutions that drag them into war. Peloponnesian fear and the Athenian lust for power are nothing without the political structure, the location of men within the polis, that seals their fate. Thucydides, though clearly stating a preference for democracy over oligarchy, nevertheless expects that power dynamics will cause war regardless of the particularities of a regime, and that all regimes are subject to a lust for power or, conversely, to fear in the face of regimes who seek to enhance their power. What humans actually do, how they feel, how they act, is passionately chaotic, but if there is stability in human things it is found not in their biological nature but in the clash of regimes that both bind and alienate people.

Much of the action in Thucydides' text is staged around dialogues and speeches, but the key dialogues characteristically take place not between individual interlocutors, but between cities, each given an individual voice. The most famous example of this is the so-called Melian dialogue, in which Athens demands that the island of Melos become subject to Athens or else be destroyed.[40] In each case, it is the city that speaks, not the individual. I dwell on it here because it exemplifies the Thucydidean account of 'human things' insofar as it bundles a rational rhetorical approach with a thesis about the power of certain passions and the ineffectiveness of others, and hitches all this to an inertia given momentum by the weight of armies and of political institutional logic. It warns that hope leads to the destruction of the weak, and that hatred of the strong is a sign of their strength.

The dialogue begins with a crucial reference to human arguments (ἀνθρωπείῳ λόγῳ – *anthropeio logo*), in which Athens argues that justice is only possible in human arguments when there is an equality of power on each side, whereas in imbalanced situations, the strong take what they can and the weak submit to the extent that they must. Yet strength and weakness here are not qualities of any particular human, or any individual's reasoning. Rather, they pertain to the collective strength of respective polities. The human arguments – in some translations these are 'human considerations' or 'human affairs' – are indistinguishable from civic affairs. The Athenians, as the stronger party in the dispute, therefore demand complete submission of the Melians, or else face total annihilation. Their implicit point, made explicit in due course, is that strength in human affairs demands a certain attitude. They refuse the Melians' neutrality or friendship because, given the power dynamic, such mercy would be a sign of Athenian weakness, and by this point Athens is indeed afraid that it has become weak. The hatred (μῖσος – *misos*) of the Melians, on the other hand, is a sign of and reassurance about Athenian power. Athens's rhetorical position is one in which a collective affective disposition of an enemy is confirmation of their political will to subjugate or destroy.

The Melians, for their part, make a rhetorical appeal to Fortune and to hope: that their fortune in war might be as great as the Athenians', and that by not surrendering they keep their hopes alive. This is dismissed out of hand by the Athenians, who call hope, according to most translators, 'danger's comforter'. It is an indulgence justifiable only when tangible means of success attach to it. The Athenians point out that there are still human means of saving themselves – surrender – and that it would be foolish to mix their hopes with intangible means, such as prophecy and oracles, which combine with hope to bring about ruin. The Athenians articulate hope as a kind of blindfold that prevents men from seeing their fate, which will surely come about if practical steps are not taken to avoid it. The mistaken adherence to blind hope is coupled and bundled with a concern about shame or disgrace that prevents people from doing what is necessary to save themselves, leading to an even greater disgrace in the end, as events overtake the vestiges of a people's pride. The Athenians are convinced of the delusional quality of the Melians' hopes and warn them of utter destruction.

As the Thucydidean narrative tends to do, the conclusion to this dialogue is followed by a matter-of-fact description of the events of that summer, followed by a brief account of further action in Melos the following winter. The explicitly human focus of the dialogue, connecting cities with both reasoning and affective qualities, is immediately lost in the bathetic reporting of events, but the baldness of Thucydides' account, in light of what has come before in the tone of the Athenian view of the order of things, is truly terrifying. For the Athenians had warned the Melians that it was necessary according to nature (φύσεως ἀναγκαίας – *phuseos anagkaias*) for the strong to rule over the weak. The whole of Thucydides' account of the war exemplifies his argument that all human dynamics are reducible to the zeal for power and the fear of power, to strength and weakness in imbalanced proportions. In the end, the Melians' fate is sealed by this axiom of nature, in which human things are bound. After a brief uprising, Athens sends another force to Melos to reinforce the siege. Overwhelmed, the Melians surrender. All the men of military age are put to death. All the women and children are sold as slaves. Melos becomes a colony for Athenian settlers.

The narrative contains many silences where the feelings of the actors would be located. In the months between the Melian dialogue and the destruction of the Melian way of life, we can presume that much of what the Athenians forecast came to pass. The Melians clung to hope and pride, and these were the agents of their ignominious demise. The object of hope, in this scheme, is fantasy, and its consequence is ruin. In this emplotment the Athenians' zeal for power overcomes the Melians' scant resistance, but their destruction comes about through a corruption of fear. Had they feared according to the Athenians' expectations, namely, of their power, then they would have surrendered and accepted their enslavement, but they would presumably have survived. Instead, the Melians' fear focused on the disgrace that would have accompanied surrender. Pride in this instance becomes a colour of fear. The cocktail of hope and pride, a negative mixed with a negative, not only sealed their fate but, in the event, and to the expectations of Athens, made it worse.

Practices of 'Happiness'

If finding the history of feelings in Thucydides involves reading against the grain of modern historiography, finding it in Aristotle involves reading against the grain of modern philosophy. In both cases, modern translation tends to emphasize those categories that make the most sense to contemporary readers, even if something significant is lost along the way. We are, when it comes to our own emotional radar, wedded to a need for familiarity, continuity and human certainty. When these things are upended, and when Thucydides and Aristotle are notable for their unfamiliarity, we feel a sense of disorientation and loss. Yet to truly interrogate who we are and why we feel the way we do involves embracing the unfamiliar. Only in this way can we reveal the politics of experience in our own lives, shedding light on the contingency of our own feelings. To find the strange in the past and to come to understand it is to shine a light on the importance of context in the shaping of experiential categories. There is nothing more tempting, for example, than the category 'emotion' for making sense of how we feel and, in turn, understanding who we are as individual humans and as humans per se.

Resisting the temptation of the universal category of 'emotion' is essential if we are to gain any appreciation of Aristotle's understanding of the connection between passions, virtues and well-being. Here I will focus principally on Aristotle's *Ethics*, as the most clear expression of the dynamic relationship among doing, being and feeling good. Normally Aristotle's scheme is rendered something like this: the ultimate end of life is to be good. The highest good is happiness. Happiness is reached through virtuous activity. The most virtuous activity is politics. Therefore the way to be happiest is to be a virtuous politician. We would have, on the face of it, a recipe for happiness as an activity of the rational soul. There are, however, well-known problems with this apparently simple scheme.

The first and most obvious problem is the word 'happiness'. This is the most common translation of the Greek word εὐδαιμονία – *eudaimonia* – which literally translates to being in the state of good spirit. 'Daimon' refers to an external divinity, a personal guardian spirit, but *eudaimonia* refers, somewhat confusingly, to the disposition of an individual. This disposition is objectively measurable, based on the virtuous training and life experience of a person.[41]

A more acute problem is that Aristotle is most specific that the life of virtue and the experience of *eudaimonia* is an activity of the *rational* soul, which relegates that part usually associated with something like emotions to the background. Something sensational, or experiential, is dependent on careful thought and thoughtful activity. This feeling of the good, of *eudaimonia*, is therefore not well understood as an emotion, or a passion, but rather as a disposition, a concrete quality and not necessarily related to how a person feels at any given moment. It becomes most problematic to call a person 'happy' in these terms if, at a certain point, they might also be described as pained, angry, bereft and so on.

Though it is far from unusual to debate the true meaning and appropriate translation of *eudaimonia*, a favourite topic among philologists, the sharper focus accorded to such phenomena by research in the history of emotions brings a fresh importance to such a debate.[42] For to deny, emphatically, that *eudaimonia* is happiness wrong-foots the history of philosophy and philosophy itself. Even if the 'happiness' translation is deployed with due caution and subtextual notes to that effect, there is still a concern that in reading 'happiness' the Aristotelian concept is read through a contemporary one. All analysis proceeding from this point has, at the very least, the flavour of anachronism.

What to do? My preference would be to leave *eudaimonia* in the Greek. Certainly, it requires explication, but still it is the best option. The whole point of the history of emotions is to emphasize that emotions not only change over time, but they get lost. The past is replete with affective concepts, behaviour and practices that have no name and no equivalent in modern English. Why then would we strive to shoehorn archaic concepts into contemporary ones? If the ultimate aim of classical Greeks was to be good, and the highest expression of that good was *eudaimonia*, then it behoves us to try to understand what they understood by this term, in its own right. Saying what it was like, or what it was akin to or analogous to, is only to miss the very object in question.

If *eudaimonia* is an affective activity of the rational soul in accordance with virtue (*arete*), an objectively present phenomenon of which an individual may nevertheless have no awareness, what then were the affective activities of the rational soul of which an individual was aware? Here we enter into a discussion of passions and their creation, management and purpose, and their relation to virtues, which is to say, to that which is moral.

Two centrally important components stand out: first, moral virtue is not in humans by nature, but has to be cultivated through habit; second, it is in the response to situations that arouse passions that virtue and vice are cultivated. Put another way, the practices and activities that are habituated in the presence of passions determine the moral status of an individual. This kind of passion management directly affects how passions are experienced and what is done because of them. Importantly, when Aristotle delineates the different fields of passion (*pathos*) to which activity attaches, he often conflates the category with practice (*praxis*). There is no feeling without doing. A feeling always elicits a practical response (which has a value). The experience of passions is therefore highly individuated.

In turn, this kind of scheme has the effect of relativizing feeling itself. A given situation may be fearful, but the quality of the experience of fear is absolutely relative to the behaviour, the practices, associated with that fear. A timid man – a coward – will be frozen to the spot in the face of fear, or else he will flee; a courageous man will stand ready to confront the source of fear, to fight or to protect. The activity, for Aristotle, defines the feeling, not the other way around.[43] There can be no inbuilt mechanism for the reception or processing of fear, anger or any other feeling, because it is only through experience and practice that an individual comes to rationalize and understand what is happening to him:

> It is the way that we ... behave in the face of danger, accustoming ourselves to be timid or confident, that makes us brave or cowardly. Similarly with situations involving desires and angry feelings: some people become temperate and

patient from one kind of conduct in such situations, others licentious and choleric from another. In a word, then, like activities produce like dispositions.[44]

A person's disposition, therefore, is entirely dependent on a person's habits, and the process of habit formation from infancy. This, according to Aristotle, 'makes a vast difference, or rather all the difference in the world'.[45] There is no room here to think of emotions or affects as automatic internal processes that are essentially natural or part and parcel of being human because there is no affective experience outside of situated conduct. To absolutely emphasize this point, Aristotle quotes his own teacher, Plato, about the 'importance . . . of having been trained in some way from infancy to feel joy and grief at the right things: true education is precisely this'.[46] An education in affective orientation and practice is the ultimate end of education, because such an education enables virtue. To be clear, Aristotle understands that the soul has the capacity to feel. It is open to 'desire, anger, fear, daring, envy, joy, friendliness, hatred, longing, jealousy, pity', but there can be no evaluation of these things, either by the self or by anyone else, without an appraisal of the conduct associated with them.[47] And it is impossible to imagine a passion without an associated practice. Even complete inactivity is a form of practice that says something about the disposition of the person.

The capacity of the soul to feel certain things does not mean, for Aristotle, that it should feel those things. Indeed, certain passions are said to be decidedly immoral, suggesting that a virtuous person would simply never experience them. Feelings have to be felt 'at the right time on the right grounds towards the right people for the right motive and in the right way', and sometimes not at all.[48] Envy, shamelessness and malice are cases in point. Anyone who experiences such feelings is, in the Aristotelian scheme, simply wrong. At first blush this seems to present a problem, for how could the soul of a virtuous person have the capacity to feel that which is vicious? Aristotle solves this problem by making these vicious passions extreme epiphenomena of other passions. For example, shamelessness (*anaischuntia*) is a deficiency of shame, of which the virtuous passion is modesty or humility (*aidōs*); envy or jealousy (*phthonos*) is an excess of indignation, of which the virtuous passion is righteous indignation (*nemesis*), associated with practices of just retribution. In other words, the soul's capacity to experience feelings that are vicious is equal to the soul's capacity to experience feelings that are virtuous. The feelings aroused in a person at a given time depend entirely on what the person is habituated to *do*. Aristotle provides, for example, a rubric for anger management that might surprise those who suffer with the control of their temper today. An excess of anger leads to irascibility (*orgilotēs*), whereas someone who is not angry enough is said to lack spirit (*aorgēsia*). But the virtuous experience of anger is borne through meekness (*prāotēs*). It is hard to imagine meekness as a species of anger, but it is perhaps more plausible if we think of meekness as a practice of anger management.

While Aristotle is leading us to an understanding of virtue, of the good and of *eudaimonia*, it is worth pausing to reflect on how we might apply these observations to our foregoing account of affective experience in the archaic and classical worlds. What should be most clear is that the activities and practices of people in difficult situations cannot be understood as accounts of the relative failure or success of emotional control. Panic, anger, cruelty and so on are not the results of a loss of control so much as of a failure to exercise temperance in practice. In the classical world, one must look at the appropriateness of what *happens* in a given situation in order to understand the quality and value of affective experience.

All of this is at great remove from the kinds of passions that are enacted in the *Iliad*, for Achilles' *menis* is at once viewed as extreme and appropriate. Yet for the better part of Homer's epic there is something of meekness about Achilles, whose fury simmers outside the sphere of battle. His practice of godlike menace is to withhold his military prowess, which is shown to function in supreme fashion in the absence of a direct expression of anger. After the death of Patroclus, Achilles' return to the battlefield, his merciless slaughter of all in his path, and his degradation of Hector's body, all indicate not disproportionality so much as an outburst of grief in keeping with the magnitude of his love for and devotion to Patroclus. Nevertheless, even the Greeks of the classical period had difficulty understanding the scripts of *menis* and grief in the *Iliad*, as the shifting codes of heroism cast a heavy pall over what seemed to be Achilles' barbarity. The matter-of-factness of the brutality of war was, in the classical period, all too evident and present. As evidenced by Thucydides, shame and fear undermined honour in the face of military power. Rage was of no benefit unless one had the power to enact it. Submission and humility marked the Athenian view of what opponents should feel, or emote, in the face of superior might. It is suggestive of both the mutability of, and the locus of power in, virtue, considered through the rubric of Aristotle. After all, were not the affective failures of the citizenry of Athens in the plague, and of the Melians before the might of Athenian power, simply failures to feel 'at the right time on the right grounds towards the right people for the right motive and in the right way', from the point of view of those in power? And, by way of contrast, what grounds did the Melians have, prostrate before a merciless colonial power, to construct and convey their own understanding of rightness of feeling, even though their protestations were evidence of their conviction that they did indeed *feel right*?

TWO

RHETORICAL AND BODILY FEELINGS

I n this chapter we traverse the ancient world, ending up in early Christendom, with episodes from classical Athens, imperial Rome and North Africa. The focus, however, shifts from questions of definition and experiential categories to the power of rhetoric to *make* affective experience. In turn, we will examine how rhetorical knowledge has implications for both bodily and social practices, such that what people thought they knew about human passions directly influenced how those passions were experienced, created and dispelled. In Thucydides in the last chapter we saw the power of rhetoric used as an expression of an understanding of 'human things', to double down on affective beliefs and practices. Here I want to go a stage further and look at the way in which rhetoric did not merely invoke such things, but was the affective practice itself.[1] Put another way, my argument here is that certain feelings are aroused not, as it were, spontaneously, but rather because they are justified, and that the justification is realized rhetorically. This is about the power of words, where an invocation is also an evocation. Emotions – if we call them that – can be purposeful, situational and, in many instances, *reasonable*. For this reason I advise that we do not call them emotions at all. In some cases, as with Plutarch and Plato here, rhetorical practice is actually designed to evoke feeling at a distance, as it were, to look at and enter into an experience through its absence, in the rhetorical imagination. Again, I want to avoid giving the reader the impression that this chapter is about things called 'anger' or 'disgust', because this privileges a contemporary understanding that actually gets in the way of understanding the rhetorical passions that are here invoked.

Summoning Anger

Robert A. Kaster has shown the lengths one has to go to in avoiding casual translations of ancient 'emotions' into recognizably English ones. By reducing emotional experience to its lexical form and then translating it, we lose the whole drama of what it is/was to emote in context. An emotional process is 'registered' by a lexical reference – an emotion word – but also involves evaluation and response: the

> emotion properly understood . . . is the whole process and all of its constituent elements, the little narrative or dramatic script that is acted out from the evaluative perception at its beginning to the various possible responses at the end. Subtract any element of the script, and the experience is fundamentally altered: without a response (even one instantly rejected or suppressed), there is only dispassionate evaluation of phenomena; without an evaluation (even one that does not register consciously), there is mere seizure of mind and body that is *about* nothing at all.[2]

It is precisely for the reason that much of this process tends to happen unconsciously or with instantaneous, or *as if* natural, responses, that I reject his allusions to acting or performing, though I fully endorse the tenor of his argument and completely agree with the notion of a cultural 'script'. The thing is, cultural scripts are not like screenplays: people learn cultural scripts without necessarily knowing that they are part of what looks, only from the outside, like a drama; an actor learns a script fully intending to 'read' it *as if* naturally, but the process and the drama are always already telegraphed. Hence an emotional drama is more of an improvisation: the reading of scripts that everyone knows but which are invisible; the practice of culture as if it is nature; a dynamic set of interacting cognitive processes that *seem* unconscious.[3]

This insight has the potential to unlock one of the oldest mysteries of the classical period, concerning the way in which Thucydides deploys speeches. In his explanation in book 1 of the *Peloponnesian War*, Thucydides notes that it 'has been difficult to recall with strict accuracy the words actually spoken, both for me as regards that which I myself heard, and for those who from various other sources have brought me reports'. This has been lauded as a kind of scientific honesty: a confession that nevertheless demonstrates his intent to maintain accuracy and objectivity. But Thucydides provides a solution to the vagaries of memory by reference to cultural and rhetorical scripts. 'Therefore the speeches are given in the language in which, as it seemed to me, the several speakers *would express*, on the subjects under consideration, the sentiments *most befitting the occasion* [emphasis added].'[4] The Greek is more compelling even than the emphases I have added, suggesting that the speeches record what was *needed* (δέοντα – *deonta*) to have been said. The circumstances of encounter, which involved dynamics of power and culturally embedded demands for anger, fear, compliance and domination, meant that, rhetorically, procedurally and experientially, situations had to unfold in a certain way, according to an unwritten script that all parties nonetheless knew how to read, however unconsciously. The affective content of speeches was intertwined with, formative of, and at the same time representative of, what was being felt. Insofar as they utter 'emotion' words, they include also the emotive evaluation thereof, and encapsulate the responses thereto. In the Thucydidean exchange of rival speeches, we also see how such scripting is modulated and modified by debate.[5]

The particular speeches to which I want to draw attention here (3.37–49) are exemplary of things that *needed* to have been said. They concern the Athenian response to the revolt of the Mytileneans in 428 BCE.[6] The city of Mytilene on Lesbos had been an ally of Athens, but which then sought to unite all of Lesbos in a revolt against Athenian power. The Athenian response to this challenge was to dispense with the Mytileneans according to the just anger of the betrayed, killing all of the male citizens and selling all of the women and children into slavery. Curiously, we learn of this decision, the result of speeches in the Assembly, without any speeches being recorded by Thucydides. All we know of the exchange is that there was a debate, 'and in anger' a determination to kill and enslave the Mytileneans. This 'anger' – ὀργή (*orge*) – had been encouraged both by the fact of the Mytileneans revolting even though they were not under the Athenian yoke, as other 'allies' were, and the fact that the revolt seemed to have been well planned, with the Peloponnesian fleet offering support. The revolt was a calculated affair, making the betrayal all the more complete.[7]

The passage, and the speeches that follow, have been well studied. It is worth pausing to reflect, however, on how an assembly can act 'in anger'. It is perhaps conceivable that a debate can whip up anger in each individual, such that a decision is reflective of an anger held in common. Yet here the context seems to suggest that the anger was *necessary* given the provocation: not the provocation of one individual against another, but the actions of a city against another, more powerful one. It was the city – Athens – whose anger was justified, as represented by its citizens in the Assembly. Yet the next day, Thucydides tells us that the Athenians had a change of mind (μετάνοιά – *metanoia*), determining that their resolution had been ὠμός (*omos*).[8] Figuratively, the word is usually translated as 'cruel', but it might just as easily be rendered 'uncivilized', for the recanting seems to have to do with the spirit of democracy, of the projection of Athenian values. It is just this that is attacked by Cleon, who demands that Athens return to its original decision.

Cleon reminds the Assembly that while Athens is a democracy, its empire depends on Athenian might, subjection, despotism. It has to be ruled with the fist, not with the niceties of democracy. Thus, according to Cleon, it can only hurt Athens if it waits until its anger is blunted before proceeding against an enemy.[9] Anger is not a passionate accompaniment to debate that, in the cold light of the next day, can be recanted. Anger is the whole essence of the decision to punish, and punishments meted out in the heat of anger are justified by that anger. To revisit such punishments and decide, on reflection, that if it were not for the anger then the punishment might not have been so severe, is to miss the whole point of being wronged. Justice, according to Cleon, demands anger as integral to its administration. He calls on the Athenians to remember how they felt at having suffered (πάσχειν – *paskhein*) at the hands of the Mytileneans and to channel the resulting anger into the delivery of justice. He bids them not to soften or flinch (μαλακισθέντες – *malakisthentes*) at the distress of their enemy, nor show them pity.[10]

For all that Thucydides records what Cleon *would* have said, he nevertheless demonstrates, in the adjoining speech of Diodotus, that he *should not* have said it. A number of scholars have pointed out that Cleon speaks as if in court, persuading a trial judge to dispense justice, and mobilizing anger as the vehicle of that justice.[11] As Harris has documented, the summoning of anger in legal proceedings was an accepted and expected rhetorical device that rationalizes punishment. Cleon's speech is the kind of speech that *would* be made in court. Injustice makes anger (remade in court by the reconstruction of the injustice before a judge), and justice is therefore appropriately measured by and through that anger.[12] Yet Cleon is not in court, but in the Assembly, and as such his attempt to summon anger to the Athenians' cause is out of place. For this reason, Cleon earns the ridicule of his culture by being caricatured in the plays of Aristophanes (*c.* 446–*c.* 386 BCE), specifically both *Knights* and *Wasps*, where the arousal of anger is his métier.[13] We have to assume, given that Cleon claims to be recapitulating his own arguments from the original speeches that Thucydides does not record, that Cleon had initially succeeded in summoning the anger of the city by treating the Mytileneans' rebellion as if they were being *tried*. The change of mind, therefore, comes not from pity, as Cleon charges, but on the basis of a point of order. It is, after all, explicitly a change of *mind* not a change of *heart*. Cleon's words and actions are not the kinds of things that can be said and done in the Assembly. Anger is an anomaly in a place of reason. The anger was *wrong*.

Diodotus' speech in response, therefore, is the kind of thing that *would* be said to someone who had abused the institution of democracy.[14] Its purpose is not to argue against anger or in favour of pity, but to reject entirely the premise that such a forum was a place in which such passions could be evoked. He identified two things detrimental to decision making in the Assembly, namely haste and ὀργή (*orge*).[15] In Diodotus' speech, this word, which was 'anger' in Cleon's speech, becomes 'passion' in most translations of Thucydides, and is coupled by Diodotus with 'an undisciplined and shallow mind'. Here 'mind' is γνώμη (*gnome*) and could equally mean 'opinion' or 'decision', which in fact makes more sense in the context.[16] Diodotus is directly condemning the opinion of Cleon because it is limited or narrowed by anger. This critique is then broadened as a warning to the Athenians: Cleon's speech may appeal because of a shared anger at the Mytileneans.[17] Again, in many translations the word for 'anger' (ὀργή – *orge*) is here translated as 'temper' or even embitterment. It seems to me a fundamental misdirection of the debate to change the terms of it in this way. Cleon summons anger; Diodotus waves it away. This is not a legal case, where anger would be relevant. In the Assembly the question of right and wrong, of justice, is immaterial and out of place. The only question is what is to be done that is most advantageous to the city, and in such work anger has no place. The attempt to create it, through rhetoric, corrupts the city's decision-making abilities.

While Thucydides marks that the vote was close, it was Diodotus who prevailed. With this victory, a mitigated punishment was handed out (only a few more than 1,000 Mytileneans were killed).[18] But we must also infer an affective outcome of the procedure of debating and showing hands. Since Diodotus rejected both anger and pity, and instead proposed only wise counsel in the city's best interests, we must assume that the triumph of his rhetoric also diminished or even eliminated the anger of the Athenians. Remember Kaster's dictum about emotion scripts: 'Subtract any element of the script, and the experience is fundamentally altered.' Diodotus fundamentally alters the experience of Athenian deliberation in two ways: first, he considers the 'emotion' words in the abstract, discussing the merits of their involvement in the debate; second, he denies the Assembly any chance to respond to the invocation of anger in angry terms. Without response, as Kaster remarks, there is merely dispassionate evaluation, which indeed is the whole point of Diodotus' speech. It is a flip side to the Mytilenean debate that is seldom considered: if the power to summon anger through rhetorical means is granted, then presumably rhetoric also has the power to banish anger, or any other passion. How the city *felt*, with the city understood to be an aggregate feeling entity in its own right, depended on how the city deliberated. Passion control was a rational instrument of civic institutions.

In a Bloody Temper

The Mytilenean debate is remarkable for the way in which it disembodies passions, tying them up with procedure and rhetoric. Yet central to any history of feelings, sensations or emotions are epistemologies about the body's role in affective behaviour. The experience of emotional life has always prompted philosophers and medical professionals (most often men) to theorize about what emotions or passions are, how they work, what they do to the body and how to control or treat them physiologically. Passions in particular were linked to pathology for centuries, with the dividing line between disease and distress being a modern contrivance. I include various strains of such theories in this book, sometimes implicitly, but my intention is not simply to provide an intellectual background. On the contrary, the intellectual history of what emotions, passions or affections *are* is an essential ingredient in discerning how those phenomena were experienced. For what we know about a thing influences what we do about and because of that thing. It influences how we reflect on that thing when it is happening to us. And it influences how others reflect on us, and how we reflect on others, when that thing is perceived to be happening to us or them. Institutions, policies and practices all emerge and are reinforced by what we *know*, and this puts a huge emphasis on systems of knowledge.

Of paramount importance, therefore, is to enter into the history of knowledge according to the terms of the contemporary knower.[19] Those intellectual strands of the history of medicine and the history of science that construct teleological narratives showing how we got here from there, looking for the development of successful ideas that turned out to be *correct*, have to be jettisoned from the beginning. We are not interested, as historicists, in whether historical knowledge was *accurate*. We are only interested in the extent to which that knowledge was *known* to be true and beyond the status of belief. Systems of knowledge become essential ingredients in the building of historical contexts, so that practices relating to feeling can be understood.

There are perhaps few systems of knowledge that have had more traction and more influence than that of humoralism. Humoralism ought not to be understood as a theory of the emotions, for such would be a gross anachronism. Rather, it is a theory that encompasses the whole of the human, at the level of character and disposition, health and disease, feelings and fitness for life. It connected the fluids or moisture of the body with the natural elements of the environment, thereby situating the human in the world and the world in the human. It accounted for every kind of disorder, and the remedies to disorders were also defined by it.

Humoralism is ancient, being given formal medical implications by Hippocrates (460–370 BCE) and later receiving canonical treatment by Galen of Pergamon (130–210 CE).[20] The body's humours (χυμός – *khumos* in Greek; *hūmōrēs* in Latin) comprise blood, phlegm, yellow bile (choler) and black bile (melancholy). The temperament of a person (from the Latin *tempere*, to mix) comes from the particular balance of humours in the body. Blood is moist and warm, like the spring. It relates to the element of air. Its predominance in the body makes for a sanguine temperament. Yellow bile is warm and dry, like the summer. It relates to the element of fire and makes for a choleric temperament. Black bile is dry and cold, like the autumn, and relates to the element of earth. It makes for a melancholic temperament. And phlegm is cold and moist, like the winter, and relates to the element of water. It makes for a phlegmatic temperament. The language of humoralism contains many a lexical false friend. Whatever we may currently mean by humour or temperament, or by those character-ized as melancholic, phlegmatic, sanguine or choleric, will have to be ejected if we are to understand the meaning of disease and cure in ancient Rome. Doubtless, these categories are all familiar to contem-porary speakers of English. We use them to denote what kind of emotional disposition a person has, or how their emotions are likely to manifest in certain situations. 'Humour' itself is perhaps the most commonly invoked: having a good or bad 'sense of humour' comes from this field. Young sportsmen whose 'nerves' get the better of them under pressure, causing them either to fail or to lash out, are said to lack the temperament required to win. We think of temperament as a quality, a thing in itself, which is immaterial. Yet, as with all these qualities, they are rooted in a definite material and substantial pres-ence in the body. For more than 2,000 years humoralism defined both the affective character of individuals and races more broadly, as well as being the major factor in the definition of diseases. When the temperament became imbalanced, or was imbalanced by nature, medical treatment was aimed at restoring it. Essential to under-standing this, however, is the ejection of a contemporary psychological understanding of the word 'temperament'. Disposition, in humoral terms, is entirely physical, though it may manifest in what seem like moods, passions and so on. It is important to remember that, in the time of Hippocrates and, later, of Galen, to be diagnosed as 'melan-cholic' was to say something about the temperature and moistness of the blood (melancholics are cold and dry).[21] What we have inherited, very loosely, as *temperamental*, was initially bodily, elemental, physical. Temperament was in the world.

Hippocrates made the connection of climate and temperament explicit in 'On Airs, Waters, and Places', noting, for example, that the Scythians had humid (ὑγρότητα – *ugroteta*, literally wetness) constitutions, for which reason they cauterized their 'shoulders, arms, wrists, breasts, hip-joints, and loins', in order to dry up their humidity through heat.[22] The aim was to improve their physical prowess for hunting and war. Such a people were constitutionally lax, the men having a 'softness and coldness' of belly, which, combined with spending a life on horseback, dulled their sexual appetite. The women, meanwhile, were humid such that the womb malfunctioned, and their humidity also made them 'indolent and fat'. In comparison, European races were said to vary according to the seasons due to the variable coagulation of the semen. Hence Europeans could be 'wild' and unsociable due to excitement of the mind, as well as passionate. For a 'changeable climate' induced 'laborious exertions both of body and mind', from which 'courage' was derived. Seasonal change made the Europeans more warlike, for physical changes caused by fluctuating temperature made the temper wild (ὀργὴν ἀγριοῦσθαί – *orgen agriousthai*) and senseless (ἀγνώμονος – *agnomonos*).[23]

Since disease hinged on temperament, so its cure often depended on bleeding to restore balance. Consider Galen's advice: 'For those going about their normal activities, who have a sense of heaviness or of tension, either in one of the vital parts or in the whole body, evacuation [of blood] is necessary.'[24] I am particularly interested, in this dictum, in the affective experience of 'a sense of heaviness' or 'tension', for here as in many places the sign of a disease or disorder is indistinguishable from its affective experience. The Latin translator of Galen rendered it as *gravatur tenditurve* (weighed-down tension) and Galen's Greek reads: βαρυνομένοις – *barunomenois* (literally being weighed down or depressed) ἤ τεινομένοις – *e teinomenois* (or stretched).[25] One may have a physical, humoral problem – a plethora of blood – but the sign of this is a sensation, a feeling. When afflicted with 'crude humours', the patient, in addition to 'a leaden tint of the complexion', will have 'a sense of heaviness of the body ... with mental sluggishness and a dulling of consciousness'.[26] Again, these are sensations, affective experiences, feelings, rooted in the body, and in stuff. The bloodletting, insofar as it is a physical cure for a physical problem, also inevitably alters the affective experience: one *feels* better.

What follows from the absolute dominance of such theories according to medical expertise is that the expectation of successful treatment must accord with an appreciation of the understanding of the problem. How one feels relates, on the one hand, to what one *knows*, and, on the other, to what one *does* about it. Bloodletting was not merely a medical cure, but an affective practice: a mode of altering one's senses, one's feelings, one's mental state. For this reason, we ought to take bloodletting seriously as a medical practice that *worked*. Of course, such an assessment goes against the grain of medical history and current medical practice, for bloodletting has no currency in current medical training. Its existence is regarded as a marker of past ignorance, and of medical incompetence. At best, experts may say, it was a placebo.

It is precisely in its efficacy as a placebo that I become interested in it, and claim it as a valid area of inquiry for the history of emotions. In everyday parlance, placebo is understood as an *effect* of something that does not have any intrinsic medicinal qualities. It is used as a control to see whether new medications are effective and can be released to the market. The pharmaceutical industry is in a constant battle to outperform placebo.[27] What do people commonly understand the placebo effect to be? A kind of self-delusion? A sign that there was nothing really wrong in the first place? A mysterious psychological phenomenon that has no explanation? I think some mixture of all three would be commonly enough reported, but this is despite a fascinating new research agenda that both takes placebo seriously and has determined to find out how it works, why it works and what makes the effect variable.

Rather wonderfully, for the purposes of the historian of the emotions, pharmaceutical companies are finding their task increasingly difficult. The placebo effect, especially in the United States, appears to be growing stronger, because of a variety of factors related to the anticipation of success. The atmosphere of the physical spaces in which clinical trials take place, as well as blanket coverage of advertisements promising amazing cures, has boosted expectations such that placebo has become more powerful. Some have even called for a redesign of controlled trials, with the introduction of a no-drug control, since the supposed placebo control has become so unreliable (and so high-performing). In part this is due to an apparent genetic variability in the neurotransmitter pathways that allow placebos to take effect, and to a distortion of the body's endogenous systems caused by placebo–drug interactions.[28] In short, the existence of the body in the world, in culture, has demonstrably changed how the body responds to placebo. While placebo researchers try to tackle the implications of this for the pharmaceutical future, the historian is left to wonder about the endless possibilities for speculating on the kinds of placebo–drug interactions of the past, and of the level of the placebo effect in historical cultures. All kinds of factors emerge as tenable analgesics, from prayer in an age of piety, to strange brews and concoctions.

For people suffering pain, a context of reassurance is known to be something of a relief. 'Rubbing it better', taken literally or figuratively, in many cases, actually works.[29] The electrical and chemical signals that go from a sore spot to the brain, and the cascading chemical and electrical response of the brain, can be modified by other signals – such as rubbing – that communicate control or safety and that lessen anxiety or fear. In any given time or context, a person will expect a certain response to the report of a problem, be it a reassuring phrase, a pill, a tonic or a touch. The power of this aspect of placebo lies in expectations being met. It does not matter what the palliative is, so long as the afflicted party believes it will work. The human body contains a powerful internal painkilling system, and much of the history of medicine has unwittingly involved a search for methods to recruit this system to do its job more efficiently. Whereas doctors for centuries and pharmaceutical companies more recently have tended to look at the intrinsic qualities of a drug or practice – trying to understand what it is about a particular chemical compound or procedure that numbs pain – recent placebo research has shown that often the efficacy of a drug lies in its ability to enhance what the human body does by itself. This is thought to be the power of paracetamol (acetaminophen), for example. It actually inhibits the extent to which the body can process an endogenous cannabinoid – an onboard painkiller – causing the body to produce a whole lot more of it in response. Anything that activates the human central nervous system to kill pain is an effective placebo.

In other words, there is a science of placebo that explains how expectation of success has physiological implications. What we *do*, according to what we *know*, will often work because we know it will. That the pharmaceutical effect is entirely endogenous – that is, it is part of the internal physiological functioning of the human organism – is irrelevant. For those feeling weighed down or tense in an era when bloodletting was best practice, chances are bloodletting would make them feel better. The fact that the placebo effect cannot be tied to an intrinsic quality of the method or medicine in question does not discount it from historical medical analysis. On the contrary, when we are looking at the placebo effect in the past, we are looking at the working of the historical body, at its biochemical intertwining with social and cultural practices. It is a subject of the history of feelings, or of neurohistory, par excellence.

The use of cups or leeches for bleeding is an ancient practice with global reach, and was a central part of Western medicine until well into the nineteenth century. Usually, cupping is thought of as a treatment for pain. The purpose was to draw blood to the surface of the skin by applying a cup and then creating a vacuum using heat in order to draw the skin (and therefore the blood) upwards into the cup. In wet cupping, this process was combined with bleeding, to release the excess blood at the site of the cupping. The cup would be applied to wherever the problem was perceived to lie, be it back or breast or knee. The use of leeches is mentioned by Pliny the Elder (23–79 CE) in his *Natural History* as having a similar effect to the use of cupping glasses, 'their effect being to relieve the body of super-fluous blood'. Used once, he claims, and an individual tends to need to use them again annually. He reports that they also help with pain caused by gout.[30]

Every kind of pain gets a remedy in Pliny, and it should be remembered that in all cases the intended effect was physical. For *phlegmoni* – painful inflammation under the skin caused by blood stagnation – he prescribed pounded radishes.[31] For headaches, the root of wild rue (*Peganum harmala*) should be applied topically with polenta. For a more serious headache it could be mixed with barley-meal and vinegar.[32] If mixed with beaten polium (*Teucrium polium*) in rainwater, it was supposed to be effective against the venom of an asp.[33] Attaching dittander (*Lepidium latifoliuim*) to the arm will draw the pain of toothache to it, though pricking the gum with the root of mallow (*Malva silvestris*, perhaps) was also supposed to help.[34] Meanwhile, halimon (*Atriplex halimus*) was said to work against pain caused by sprains of the feet and affections of the bladder.[35] There are, in sum, dozens of remedies for pain and suffering in Pliny, drawn from medical knowledge and popular folk knowledge. It is not so much the point that, in some cases, there may have been an appropriate medicinal agent in the compounds

Glass bleeding cup, Roman, 251–450 CE.

he prescribed. For even though wild rue, for example, might actually have an intrinsic analgesic effect, my premise is that it would probably have indeed been more potent when applied with the barley-meal, or with the rainwater. The power of placebo in context should not be underrated as an affective modifier. Pain states, which are affective states – *feeling* states – par excellence, depended for their remedy on knowledge of what worked. It was part of what Javier Moscoso calls the 'moral economy of hope', which I would augment by reference to the historicity of the biocultural body-mind system.[36]

Blood and Gore: A Feast for the Eyes

Plutarch (46–120 CE) was a Roman citizen of Greek origin. A Platonist, he was a famous man in the empire, becoming a priest of Apollo in later life at Delphi. He is most famous for his works on the lives of the Roman emperors, on *Parallel Lives* (biographies of eminent Greeks and Romans) and for his *Moralia*. Within the *Moralia* are three essays nominally on animals, but cleverly constructed with human morality as their subject. The one that interests me here, in particular for the way it handles blood and guts, is *On the Consumption of Flesh*, or *De esu carnium*.[37]

Plutarch expresses a kind of dismay about the state of the soul of the man who first slaughtered an animal and put the dead flesh to his lips. He seems implicitly to be describing the historicity of disgust. It is to him a given, a commonplace, that to kill and eat an animal is horrifying, or else would take a great degree of steeling or hardness to pull off. Whereas in the person who did it first, Plutarch can only try to imagine the necessary absence of revulsion, which is indicative of a different kind of soul. The soul's capacity to suffer passions is, by such reasoning, not fixed. Yet for all that the consumption of flesh appals Plutarch, he nevertheless espouses that its consumption is unshakeably customary, and that if animals should be eaten and then killed, then the act of slaughter must be framed as an affective practice, lest killing denote a brutal soul. He therefore recommends that animals are eaten because of hunger, not because of 'wantonness', and that they are killed with 'sorrow and pity', and not by 'abusing and tormenting'. At least, such are the standard translations. But the Greek for 'wantonness' here is τρυφῶντες (*trufontes*), which refers to a somewhat luxurious and effeminate sumptuousness of living: decadence. This equates decadence, which we might normally associate with a certain refinement of feeling, with a wilful heartlessness. Moreover 'sorrow and pity', which are employed because they are idiomatic in English, are here translations of οἰκτείροντες καὶ ἀλγοῦντες (*oikteirontes kai algountes*). The first word here denotes a kind of pity, but as David Konstan has explained, *oiktos* refers more often to the 'expression of audible grief or lamentation rather than pity', suggesting that the killing of animals be done through wails and tears.[38] Indeed, the second word here comes from *algos* – bodily pain – suggesting that the process of killing should cause the killer pain and anguish.

This accords with a general rule I have found for expressions of pain in antiquity, which conflates what we might be tempted to separate out into physical and emotional pain.[39] While contemporary pain science is busy joining the two back together, in the Greek and Roman worlds there is no physical pain that is not also *suffering*, and there is no suffering that is not somehow registered in the body as *pain.* Hence Plutarch, lamenting that animals will still be killed and eaten, recommends that humans share in the pain that is part of the process of consumption.

Yet for all that Plutarch seems to register his disgust (though he does not use any of the words typically associated with the English 'disgust'), he strangely seems to delight in recounting the monstrous or frightening (τερατῶδες – *teratodes*) all the same.[40] For his exhortation to kill and eat only with wails and pain is followed by a series of recipes for making meat taste better, listed in horror, but listed all the same:

> some run red-hot spits through the bodies of swine, that by the tincture of the quenched iron the blood may be to that degree mortified, that it may sweeten and soften the flesh in its circulation; others jump and stamp upon the udders of sows that are ready to pig, that so they may trample into one mass (O Piacular Jupiter!) in the very pangs of delivery, blood, milk, and the corruption of the crushed and mangled young ones, and so eat the most inflamed part of the animal; others sew up the eyes of cranes and swans, and so shut them up in darkness to be fattened, and then souse up their flesh with certain monstrous mixtures and pickles.

This might be taken as an example of one essential dynamic of disgust as we know it, for that which is meant to repel also has an inescapable allure. There is nothing fixed about the objects of disgust, and no predictable responses to the sight of the disgusting. Disgust has to be made somehow, in order to be intelligible as disgusting. Plutarch seems to be constructing that which is disgusting by describing the consumption of meat in terms that make it strangely new. He compels us not to look away, but to look closely at what we consume, not as fine cuts and joints, but as dead flesh and sores, the product of slaughter. Plutarch marvels at the first man who 'touched slaughter' with his mouth, and who 'set before people courses of ghastly corpses and ghosts', wondering how 'his sight could endure the blood of slaughtered, flayed, and mangled bodies; how his smell could bear their scent; and how the very nastiness happened not to offend the taste, while it chewed the sores of others, and participated of the saps and juices of deadly wounds'. This is a radical reimagination of a feast, seeing stinking dead animals instead of food. It foregrounds a scene common to all and demands that it be looked at again in a raking and horrific light. In order to be horrified, and in order to be able to be disgusted and to turn away, one first has to come close, engage all the senses, comprehend the scene of death and defilement, reflect on one's past experience of doing such things without thinking or without conscious contemplation of the frame in which the scene is now presented, and *only then*, turn away in disgust.

Yet I return to the nagging sense of disquiet I have that Plutarch does not refer to disgust (or what we are assuming to be the Greek correlates of disgust), σικχός – *sikkhos*, or ἀηδής – *aedes*. Are we reading Plutarch correctly when we read an account of disgust at the ghastly feast? The answer lies in whether we need the word for the experience or whether, in fact, the word blinds us into looking for an experience with which we are familiar, when the particularities might suggest something else entirely. Richard Firth-Godbehere has noted that contemporary neuroscientists tend to assume that disgust is both universal and automatic, not really an emotion but an affective state (like hunger). He has also noted that the meaning of the word has shades of difference in different languages. It is hard to maintain that x = *universal* when people disagree about the definition of x. Moreover, the very disagreements themselves do something to the experience of x that connects the experience to the specific word choice. When x = *disgust*, Firth-Godbehere points out, then x = a particularly nauseating impulse to turn away. When x = *Ekel*, the standard German correlate of 'disgust', there 'is no gag reflex'. It is more neutrally an aversion. He points out that it 'may be that a sensation of revulsion is an evolved trait that is felt by all, and that all cultures have words that relate to that trait', but 'it is not the case that this can always be understood through the lens of modern English disgust'.[41] Furthermore, even if there is some automatic revulsion state, the objects that elicit that response are by no means fixed. What people find disgusting has been shown to vary enormously from culture to culture and across time. Looking through the lens of the history of emotions and to findings about iterations of other emotions in the past, it makes sense to say that whatever revulsion experience a person has, the experience of it is directly and fundamentally intertwined with the meaning of the specific thing that elicited it, in context. To say that this 'evolved trait' is shared by all is, in fact, to say very little about what it is, or what it is like to experience it.

I have challenged that kind of universalizing tendency in the past, pointing out the neurohistorian Daniel Lord Smail's mistake in calling disgust a universal, while at the same time documenting cultural change:

> Starting with a known concept of 'disgust', usually in English, the physiological and gestural signs of this concept are mapped onto people of other cultures who, when representing similar physiological signs and expression, are said to be 'disgusted', even if the local concept in question is worthy of a rich conceptual analysis of its own and does not bear any contextual or experiential resemblance to 'normative' representations of disgust in anglophone contexts. To concede that social emotions 'do different things in different historical cultures' makes it meaningless, even an obfuscation, to say that, 'disgust' is nevertheless 'universal', irrespective of its different contexts, signs and experiences. To quip, 'Same disgust, different object', as Smail does, is to impose a preferred and a priori conceptual definition on a physiological process that does not, in fact, need to be defined by the label of its associated emotional experience in some cultures. Bare physiology does not carry any meaning.[42]

On the contrary, I pointed out, a different object must mean a different disgust, with a different name, a different set of consequences, a different form of interaction with the world and the things in it. The examples of 'disgust' I am particularly fascinated by in the ancient world seem not to be commensurate with 'disgust' in contemporary English terms. In a way, it is just as well that Greek 'disgust' words are missing in Plutarch's account of the consumption of flesh, for if they were there they might make it all the easier to label them 'disgust' and move on.

The challenge, then, is to reconstruct the affective experience in the source without privileging a contemporary one. In the case of Plutarch, the revulsion he feels at the engagement of the senses in the processes of killing and of eating flesh is situated in a Pythagorean cosmology. What makes it monstrous? When I first read Plutarch on the consumption of flesh, I assumed that the appeal was to a general aversion to blood and gore. This turns out to be a superficial reading. The context is of the risk, given a Pythagorean belief in the transmigration of souls, that in killing and eating animals one is consuming that which belonged to a human, perhaps even a friend or a relative. Why, Plutarch asks, would you risk it? Even if you do not believe in the transmigration of souls, if you at least admit of the possibility then surely the gamble is too great. The monstrousness of the feast is in the imaginary that all these dead bodies are human, or at least that the bodies had contained the transmigrated souls of once-were-humans. The scene becomes horrific. Plutarch needs us to look closely at it, to scrutinize it carefully, in order for us perchance to see it the way he does, as a kind of cannibalism at one stage of remove. His whole point is that killing and eating animals, even in the most elaborately excruciating procedures, is *not* at all repulsive to most people. People who eat flesh are inured by custom to anything untoward in any of its processes. It is hard to argue with people's stomachs, Plutarch says, for bellies do not have ears. And in general, he says, consumption of flesh depends upon an emergence of a habituation to killing – a certain blood*thirst* (μιαιφονίας – *miaifonias*). While he is implicitly condemnatory of such things, he is also resigned that the inertia of custom is irresistible. Bellies are blameless. Again, what he is describing is a form of desire, not revulsion. Insofar as he is trying to point to the possibility of revulsion, he has to actually provide a context for a new construction of *horror*. To succeed, we have to desire to see this too.

In English translation it is easy to conflate Plutarch's text with an aversion to *cruelty*, and indeed most translations include the Plutarchian exclamation, 'Oh horrible cruelty!', but the exclamation does not make sense as a concern for either animals themselves or as a concern about human behaviour in the abstract. In my reading, the line ὠμότητος δεινὸν (*omotetos deinon*) does not mean 'horrible cruelty', but rather something like 'fearful rawness', wherein a certain savage disposition is figuratively aligned with uncooked meat. It is a pun. Nineteenth- and twentieth-century translators can hardly be blamed for choosing to overlook the apparent lexical overlap here, since aversion to cruelty to animals has, since the nineteenth century, been a particularly popular public cause. Here, however, Plutarch is recoiling both from dead flesh *and* the rich people whose tables bespeak refinement, but whose souls are *crude*. Some of these people happen to be Stoics, whose dietetics seem to him at odds with their general principles of control. The rest are Epicureans, whom Plutarch is known to reject out of hand. His wonder at the first man to put gore to his lips can be understood in similar terms. Most translations have Plutarch ask something like 'why did the pollution not offend his taste?', but here 'pollution' is μολυσμὸς (*molusmos*) – defilement – which singles out what is happening to the eat*er*, as well as what has happened to the body of the eat*en*. His tirade against the consumption of flesh, which relies so much on rhetorically confronting the senses – confronting them in the imagination of the reader – with blood, shrieking death and stinking gore, is therefore a philosophical and political vehicle, and at the same time an expression of a firm conviction about the immortality of the soul. As such, it is a piece ultimately that beckons rather than repulses, for if it is to persuade it depends upon a close examination of the flesh and the eaters of flesh from his point of view. If, in translation, the mode is disgust, it is because it is difficult to grasp the spiritual affective disposition he takes up. In conclusion, the Greek word for 'disgust' is not present because disgust is not the response Plutarch is going for. When we give in to the temptation to read for disgust, we will surely find it, but we will not understand.

The problem, that when one looks for disgust one inevitably finds it, even if technically it is not *disgust*, leaches into even the best studies of disgust in history. In *The Ancient Emotion of Disgust*, edited by Donald Lateiner and Dimos Spatharas, for example, there is a clear and worthy purpose to try to explicate ancient concepts that pertain to disgust in their particular historical and lexical contexts. Contemporary definitions of disgust are shown to be limited in their usefulness for historical study and also historical products in their own right. Yet, despite all this, such a work sets out to look for *disgust*, to mark out how ancient iterations and experiences of it relate to or differ from contemporary English disgust. All care and attention to historicity notwithstanding, the teleology of such a study is in the end irresistible. Ultimately, the lens used for looking at disgust in the past is a new one. By situating an inquiry within the framework of a contemporary category we are always dancing perilously close to anachronism.[43] Consider, for example, the observation that 'Affect

Francisco de Goya, 'One Can't Look', plate 26 from *The Disasters of War*,
c. 1810–20, etching and drypoint.

responses to loathsome creatures or substances gather in the expressive face. One usually averts the face from a disgust-eliciting source.'[44] Here, and throughout, is an unshakeable assumption that some things are simply and intrinsically 'loathsome', and that the reaction to such things is, at it were, built-in, with the built-in-ness revealing itself on the timeless face. Here the editors append a note: 'Drive-by gawkers at automobile accidents and fatalities deliver a rule-proving exception, but perhaps the facts that passers-by are insulated by their cars and that only a quick glimpse is possible buffers their curiosity. See Socrates' Leontius below.'[45] This is a stunning piece of subtextual sleight of hand, as well as an astonishing intellectual leap between the contemporary ambulance chaser and a character in Plato's *Republic*. In the interest of showing how wrong this is, and in light of what I have said about Plutarch, I will pursue both ends of this linkage at once.

There is no substance to the claim that drivers who slow to look at an accident are an exception to rules about disgust that in fact proves rules about disgust. The throwaway explanation – that they are somehow shielded by their cars – simply will not do. Susan Sontag, in *Regarding the Pain of Others*, took a completely different view on this subject. The mutilated bodies of other people are, in her estimation, *profane*. We look at them precisely because we know we are not supposed to. Taboos conflate powerful forces of attraction and proscription. Those proscriptions define the guilt that comes with giving in to the desire to *see* that which is supposed to disgust. In Sontag's opinion, drivers slow to look at accidents because they genuinely desire 'to see something gruesome'. There is nothing about it that is particular to being inside a car. In my own foot-powered peregrinations around Montreal I have often come across large gatherings of people, craning to see a mangled cyclist or unlucky pedestrian. The phrase 'I cannot look' often accompanies the act of looking, as if body and mind are in opposition. Think of Francisco de Goya's depictions of *The Disasters of War* (1810–20), and in particular plate 26, of an unseen firing squad (unseen save for the ends of gun barrels and fixed bayonets) at the moment the bullets hit the men, women and children. Goya inscribed the image with the words 'No se puede mirar' (one cannot look), yet clearly *he looked*, and remembered, and in putting the work on paper he *made* the image, precisely so that it could be looked at. Not being able to look is a dynamic part of the act of looking. Moreover, there is, however much we might wish to deny this in public, a pleasure in it. As I pointed out in *Pain: A Very Short Introduction*:

> Disgust at the aesthetics of pain, and the fear aroused by putting oneself in the place of the sufferer, ought to drive us from the scene. But disgust and fear, insofar as they are visually inspired, demand to be looked at. How else are we to know what disgusts or frightens us? Thus we are rooted, enquiring, but also enjoying the pain of others.[46]

It is a complex admixture of delight and distress – the sublime, perhaps – that *might* inspire us to helpful action, but it might also simply have us whisper to ourselves that we are glad it is not happening to us. In Sontag's estimation, our indifference to most images that *should* disgust us is guaranteed by the massive amount of exposure we have, through television and other media, to war, to pain, to injury. Our eyes have cataracts when looking at mangled bodies that should inspire revulsion and/or sympathy. The argument – about the rise of indifference – is hardly new. I will say much more about it in Chapter Five. But it does demonstrate that disgust is complex. It cannot be reduced either to the objects that inspire it, or to the facial and bodily signs of it. It will not fit into a timeless schema of revulsion or nausea.

Let us look at the dead bodies in front of Leontius, that car-crash analogy put forward by Lateiner and Spatharas. Let us look with Socrates at this gruesome feast for the eyes and the difficulties of understanding ancient desire. In the translation of Plato's *Republic* that I have read most often – the text with which I have taught – the passage in question (439e–440a) reads as follows:

> Leontius, the son of Aglaeon, was on his way up to town from the Piraeus. As he was walking below the north wall, on the outside, he saw the public executioner with some dead bodies lying beside him. He wanted to look at the bodies, but at the same time he felt disgust and held himself back. For a time he struggled, and covered his eyes. Then desire got the better of him. He rushed over to where the bodies were, and forced his eyes wide open, saying 'There you are, curse you. Have a really good look. Isn't it a lovely sight?'[47]

The passage occurs as part of a discussion of how the soul is divided between the rational, the spirited and the desiring. Socrates uses the example to show how anger (ὀργὴν – *orgen*) allies with reason to wage war on the desires. It occurs 'whenever people are forced into doing things by their desires against the advice of their reason – when they curse themselves, and are furious with the bit of them which forces them to do these things. It's as if there's a civil war going on inside someone like this, with spirit acting as an ally of reason'. The formulation of Leontius can therefore be rendered thus: reason says, do not look at dead bodies, turn away; desire says, look at dead bodies; spirit angrily chastises the whole self for having given in to desire. If this is accurate, and I do not see any great dispute about this, then the reference to disgust seems odd, out of place, and difficult to reconcile with the divisions of the soul as presented. After all, the part of Leontius that has him want to recoil is his *reason*, which is set at odds with his desire to see. In the Greek, he is said to be 'at the same time desirous [ἐπιθυμοῖ – *epithumoi*] to see and unable to endure [δυσχεραίνοι – *duskherainoi*], turning himself away'. The word here that gets translated as disgust is δυσχεραίνοι (*duskherainoi*), which might denote a kind of distress, but which I give here as 'unable to endure'. In the way the argument is set up by Socrates, the part of Leontius that cannot endure and turns away is *reasonable*, not part of his *thumos*, or spirit. Something like 'emotion' only arises when his spirit is activated in anger against his desire to see dead bodies. He is struggling, at war with himself, yes, but the struggle is between reason and desire.

What this tells us is that there is a cultural script running for Leontius that proscribes the desire to gawk at the dead. It is unreasonable to do so. Yet the desire is too strong and wins out. The expression, of himself to himself, of that cultural script manifests in anger. There is, in short, no disgust in this scene at all, let alone a 'paradox of disgust' as Lateiner and Spatharas put it. While there are countless contemporary examples of a paradox of disgust, where in our own terms we feel the tension of an emotional pull towards at the same time as an emotional push away, to reduce what is happening to Leontius to the vagaries of disgust is misleading. Having contextually eliminated disgust from the discussion here, we are left instead with the questions of why it was *unreasonable* to look at dead bodies in the first place, and why anyone might *desire* to see them.[48]

Plenty of ink has been spilt on these questions, and it seems to be something of a philological sport to find interesting pathologies and perversions to apply to Leontius.[49] In this case, this seems to be overstriving. As Carolyn Korsmeyer has pointed out,

> Leontius is not presented as a person of unusual disposition; he is just a man walking home. The discomfort of the divided soul filled with conflicting desires is a phenomenon Plato expects us to recognize readily . . . [W]hat draws him to the corpses is just the grisly sight itself . . . There is no greater purpose that the sight of the bodies serves; Leontius is attracted to something that is just plain nasty.[50]

This seems right to me. We do want to look at dead bodies. It is not more difficult to conceive of than gawking at a car crash, or, as in medieval and early modern Europe, attending a scene of capital punishment. Then, as now, we might fight with ourselves over our wish to see the grisly, but whereas we might think about the complexities of our experience of disgust, Plato wanted us to think about the way the soul is divided, and the way in which reason, spirit and appetite interrelate. The history of emotions is nothing if we arrogate to ignore the experience being described by Plato (through the character of Socrates) and favour instead a contemporary neurobiological reading of disgust. It matters that Leontius' soul is torn. It matters that his affective experience is understood, by himself and by the assembled interlocutors in Plato's dialogue, as *anger* at his own desires, and that the experience is carried out in the mode of self-admonishment. The struggle for mastery of one's desires defines the Platonic corpus, the ethics of Aristotle, and thereafter both Platonic and Stoic schools of philosophy. We have to take Leontius' experience, as it is recounted, at face value.

To round out this discussion, let us return to what is happening at the level of rhetoric here. Leontius only exists for us as a Socratic anecdote, part of a conversation recorded by a fourth party (assuming Socrates to be the third, and Plato the fourth). What is fascinating about such a passage is that it both visualizes a scene for us, into which we can readily enter, and tells us not merely how Leontius felt, but how we also should feel. It tells us how we too are managing our response to the sight of dead bodies. The justification for including a story about dead bodies, as opposed to a more quotidian desire like hunger, is that we cannot seem to avoid *seeing* those bodies too. The mere mention of them, and the description of where they were and who was there (the executioner), means that we have also *seen* them. They are called to mind by the power of rhetoric, but in the context of a discussion about control. Indeed, reason is master in this rhetorical invocation of desire, such that the desire is satisfied without debasing the rational soul. We safely look at the dead bodies without becoming angry. It is a wonderful paradox, not of disgust, but of the power of an image, or sight. In our mind's eye we safely and dispassionately look at Leontius looking at dead bodies and at him becoming angry at himself. And in so doing, we feel *nothing at all*. As such, the dialogue itself becomes the rhetorical vehicle of control – the platform for the master of reason in the soul – that is at the heart of the *Republic*. In diminishing affect to the point of undetectability, it is an affective practice par excellence.

Sense, Sin and the Fear that Endures Forever

Augustine (354–430 CE) knew the heart of one who would look on dead bodies, ripped up ones at that. We can infer from his *Confessions* that he had looked at them, and that he knew it as a pleasure (*voluptatis*). The celebrated Church Father, theologian and philosopher exercised a dominant influence on the nature of Christianity. From his bishopric of Hippo Regius (now Annaba, Algeria), he wrote prolifically. For historians of emotions he has proven enormously influential, for his modifications of Cicero (106–43 BCE) provided a working model for the conceptual range of affective life in the Middle Ages.[51]

For Augustine, pleasure and curiosity were 'functions of physical sensation' (*agatur per sensus*).[52] What appears to be a craving for knowledge or understanding is actually a desire to know the physical world by means of the senses, and through the eyes in particular (and through the metaphor of seeing when talking about the actions of the other senses).[53] Curiosity (*curiositas*) craved (*libidine*) experience and understanding, which explained the 'inherent pleasure in looking at a rent corpse (*laniato cadavere*)', even though it 'makes you shudder (*quod exhorreas*)'. After all, he observed, if there happens to be a mangled body

> lying there, people flock to it to be appalled, to turn pale. Then they are afraid that they will see the corpse in their sleep, as if someone had forced them to look at it when they were awake, or some rumour had convinced them that it was a beautiful sight . . . Monstrous sights are paraded in public shows to pander to this disease of desire (*morbo cupiditatis*).[54]

It seems that Augustine was rather taken by morbid spectacles, with curiosity challenging the singular focus of his heart on a daily basis. In particular, he confesses to being rapt by a hound's pursuit of a hare in the field; he is equally absorbed by the sight of a lizard catching flies, or of a spider consuming its prey in its web. His life, he confessed, was 'full of such moments', and his 'only hope' (*spes*) was the 'overwhelming mercy' (*misericordia*) of God. Such sights were his heart's desire and it was his eyes' propensity to seek for them. Unless intercepted and turned to reflection, they were the cause of vanity.[55]

So what scope was there in Augustine's philosophy and theology for the affective life? Was all feeling a pull towards sin, towards flesh, and away from God?

Augustine's affective language is generally translated into the language of 'emotions', but it loses its clarity in the bargain, as we see in a reappraisal of the ninth part of book fourteen of *The City of God*.[56] Augustine directly impugned Cicero, for the movement (arousal, perhaps) (*motus*) and feeling (*affectus*) he describes are derived from the love of the good (*amore boni*) and from holy charity (*sancta caritate*). To call them vices (*vitia*) is to be categorically confused. To call them diseases (*morbos*) or vicious passions (*vitiosas passiones*), as Cicero did, is to overlook the fact that the feelings followed right reason (*rectam rationem*) when they were appropriately expressed.[57] Indeed, to be without bodily feeling, or without bodily pain, would come at a great cost: monstrousness of soul (*inmanitatis in animo*) and numbness, or unfeelingness, of body (*stuporis in corpore*).[58] The body is an inescapable part of being human, and its feelings are inherent. Here, drawing a parallel with Cicero, who made an obscure translation of *pathos* as disease, Augustine translates the Greek ἀπάθεια (*apatheia*) as *inpassibilitas*, and says that it would be a 'good and extremely desirable state' only as it applies to the soul and not to the body. If it were to mean living 'without those feelings (*affectionibus vivatur*) that are contrary to reason and disturb the mind'[59] then so much the better. This would hardly be an everyday feeling of 'apathy', but rather an existential and essential equanimity. It was clear that, in the present state of humanity – that is, in the world of flesh and sin – such an apathy at the level of the soul was impossible and undesirable.[60]

If (some) human bodily feelings and, importantly, their expression were really virtuous, which ones counted, and in what way were they virtuous? Only those disturbances of the soul (*perturbationibus animi*) and feelings (*affectus*) that are 'right' (*rectos*) are to be found in the lives of the righteous (*vita iustorum*). Those 'citizens of the holy City of God', so long as they 'live in God's fashion', will rightly feel 'fear, desire, pain, joy' (*metuunt cupiuntque, dolent gaudentque*).[61] Augustine is directly quoting Virgil's *Aeneid* (6.733), who in turn is said to have been summarizing the four principal *perturbationes* of Cicero: *voluptas* (pleasure), *cupiditas* (desire), *aegritudo* (sorrow) and *metus* (fear).[62] Yet whereas Augustine otherwise condemns desire and fear, here they are re-treated so as to come together as living in the manner of God.[63]

To be sure, Augustine provides scriptural examples for Christians to experience each of the four categories of feeling, but he reserves distinct meanings for compounds of fear and desire that seem paradoxically to make certain feelings derived from their opposites, a construction that makes sense only in the context of a belief in God and in original sin. Citing the Apostle Paul's fear (*timor*) that the Corinthians might succumb to the Devil, Augustine claims that this fear is 'felt by love and can only be felt by love' (*Hunc enim timorem habet caritas, immo non habet nisi caritas*). This is 'true fear' (*timor vero*) and, he forecasts, it will 'endure forever'. This fear does not lead to flight from possible evil, but keeps a man 'in a good that cannot be lost'. When sin is kept in mind it is feared so that it may be avoided, and this kind of fear, Augustine says, is *securus*: fearless! This kind of fear is an act of will (*voluntas*) – it is, in a sense, *desired*, for to refuse to sin and to guard against sin are the result of desiring those things. They are desired without concern (*sollicitudine*) that we may succumb to sin, but rather with a calmness (*tranquillitate*) that comes from love. Hence the conjunction of fear and desire is clarified and defined as an awareness of the inescapability of sin, the fear of this, the desire to avoid this, in the context that all this derives from the love of God and from God's love. Hence the phrase, 'The holy fear of God that lasts forever' (*Timor Domini castus permanens in saeculum saeculi*). Its reward is endless blessed joy (*perpetuorum feliciumque gaudiorum*) in the hereafter.[64]

From here, a second compound, pain–joy, is explained, for Augustine connects the above dictum with another: 'The patience of the poor shall not perish forever' (*Patientia pauperum non peribit in aeternum*). Patience as a virtue will sound familiar to contemporary ears, but its origins are in the word *patior* – to suffer – which also gives us *passio*. Patience implies the presence of pain, sorrow or grief that is endured (hence, in medical parlance, the 'patient'). The reward of patience in a world of evils is also everlasting joy. Pain itself is therefore virtuous. Since it is God-given, it is a sign of God's love – a theological position that was maintained as far as the twentieth century – and therefore a reason for, in fact a source of, joy.[65]

Ultimately, Augustine's approach to the passions and feelings is to wrest them away from those who would casually intellectualize or disembody them, putting them in purely rhetorical categories that have no bearing on the experience of sinners and believers. By connecting a theory of passions with the lived reality of the passions, Augustine united rhetoric and bodily experience. Humans are crude, physical, fleshly beings. That they feel is inevitable. By rhetorically guiding that feeling in the way of God, Augustine was not merely shaping the words of experience, but the character and the meaning of experience itself.[66]

Here the analysis chimes with the rhetorical evocations we have seen in Thucydides, with the power of naming a medicine or medical practice to improve one's health, and with the rhetorical beckoning of Plutarch to conjure up an image of the mangled flesh. Words, once in the world, are embodied. That body is itself subject to rhetorical and discursive knowledge of what a body is or *was*, and of what it is or was comprised, both in terms of its material stuff and its immaterial essence. In sum, these episodes conjure up a history of feelings that bundles together body, soul, mind, words and world into a single script. If we were to extract any one of these elements and treat them separately we would be led astray.

THREE

MOTIONS AND MACHINATIONS

L ove is . . . Perhaps an ellipsis was never more pregnant with possibilities. It has become idiomatic to say 'it's complicated' in matters of love, but even in the mire of entanglements that define love in the twenty-first century, our own definition of love is rather narrow. It is premised on a particular kind of romantic love that involves (usually) two people who conceive of themselves as individual selves, and between whom there is an 'attraction' and mutual volition. But this love, a shared, sexual, romantic feeling that also involves a conscious practice of loving, is remarkably modern. The liberty to love and to pursue the objects of one's love is not a timeless definition of the practices of love. Even in our own times there are other types of love, such as that of a parent for a child. Yet it is possible to conceive of a time before romantic love, when love took a variety of different forms, whether divine, ennobling or marital.[1] Though this chapter is not exclusively about types of love, it does focus on the physical, spiritual and social factors that allow for different kinds of love across the medieval and early modern periods. It begins with moistness in the soul in twelfth-century Germany, negotiates the politics of love in Renaissance Florence, incorporates Cartesian machinery and terminates in the delicate social conventions of 'inclination' in the salons of seventeenth-century Paris. I cannot hope definitively to say what love is – nobody could ever manage something so reductive; but in a mitigated way, I can begin to say, 'Love was . . .'

A Vision of Divine Love

The work of Augustine, and later that of Thomas Aquinas (1225–1274), are definitive of intellectual thinking on the passions and affects for the medieval period, especially from a theological point of view.[2] Yet the practices of affective life were hardly uniform by the time of Aquinas. Hence my departure from the usual canonical treatment of medieval 'emotions' is designed to exemplify the extraordinary range and sophistication of affective experience, even where affective expression might be thought to have been severely limited by strict policing of heretical practices. I turn to the endlessly fascinating figure of the Cistercian nun Hildegard von Bingen (1098–1179).[3]

Hildegard is famed for her visionary trilogy, her works on medicine and on language, and particularly for her musical compositions.[4] A large repository of her letters also survives, allowing us to piece together her day-to-day world with her record of the meaning of her divine visions.[5] She was famously untaught, or unlearned, meaning that her oeuvre is not built upon classical foundations or on models of composition, but comes directly from the structure and explication of her own visions. As such, she is often described as being unique among medieval prophets. Certainly, as a touring preacher in her sixties and seventies, Hildegard garnered a fame highly unusual for a woman, and through an activity limited customarily to men. She spent her life until the beginning of her lecture tours in cloisters, at the convent in Disibodenberg, about 56 km (35 mi.) southwest of Mainz, and later at her own establishment in Rupertsberg, Bingen, on the Rhine some 29 km (18 mi.) west of Mainz.[6]

The non-canonical nature of Hildegard's compositions makes for a distinctive construction of her affective cosmology, in which the senses, the soul, the Holy Spirit and the body are inextricably bound. I do not want to focus here on the affective qualities of the virtues identified in Hildegard's work so much as on the very essence of *being* as affectively construed. Hildegard's understanding of the world and beyond, though fastened onto reason, is explicitly an inward perception. She sees her visions, and the 'living light' of God, but not with her eyes. She sees them as it were internally, through the receptivity of the moistness and – importantly – *greenness* of her body and soul. What she records, she says, is only that which she has 'seen' in this way. This brief episodic examination of Hildegard therefore focuses on the necessary conditions of body and soul required in order for her to *feel* her way towards God, mirrored in the advice she gives to others about the state of their own souls. In this, much rests on the aforementioned and central concept of 'greenness', and on the affective practices that make such feeling and 'seeing' possible. In turn it depends on the divine nature of the human as begat by divine Love, a personified being in Hildegard's visions that plays an important part in this analysis. Hildegard's corpus is massive, and I can scarcely do her life's work justice here. Instead I focus on three letters that respectively open up the study of Hildegard's affective practices and an essential account of *caritas* that is foundational of her understanding of spiritual/affective life. The letters encompass the whole of Hildegard's public career, from its very beginning in 1146, in a timorous epistle to Bernard of Clairvaux, to an explanatory missive in 1175.

At the heart of Hildegard's affective practice was reading, meditation and writing. Mark Atherton summarizes the life of Cistercian study and prayer as follows:

> According to this approach, meditation was the practice of reading aloud and pondering with the whole person – not only with memory, will and attention, but also with body, mind and spirit – on the meaning of the text. In effect, the meditator had to learn the text by heart and so put its theory into practice. By contrast, reading, so defined, was more careful and guided study of the text, using scholarly aids and commentaries. Meditation could precede reading, but reading aided further, advanced levels of memory and meditation, which allowed the mind to soar, as it were, to heights of devotion and understanding.[7]

That Hildegard engaged in such reading and meditation is highly likely (her claims to being untaught notwithstanding, Hildegard was still widely read, though without scholarly direction). That she extended the practice in which her devotion soared to writing is also beyond doubt.[8] Before beginning to tease apart some of the sensual and affective elements of her visions, it is important to state that on no account should the visions of Hildegard (or anyone else) be gainsaid. What she 'saw' was *real*, in the sense that her particular practices of devotion and her particular context of neurological formation led to these visions. They are outputs of the neuroplastic brain, integral to Hildegard's perception of herself and the world, and cannot be dismissed as metaphors, madness, contrivance or fraud. It is not for me to say that Hildegard did not *really* see the divine. It is only for me, as a historian, to say that Hildegard knew that she really did. It is a statement that goes beyond the confines of belief, which might be said to concern things that are not present and cannot be proven. Since, from Hildegard's perspective, she actually experienced the divine, she had certain knowledge of God.

From the very emergence of Hildegard's voice beyond her own cloisters, the mode in which her visions appeared to her is foregrounded. Her first letter to Bernard of Clairvaux is deferent in tone, begging to be given permission to speak about the visions she sees, and concerned lest her speech be deemed heresy. She is explicit, however, about *how* she sees: 'not with my fleshly eyes but only in my spirit'.[9] The vision 'touches my heart and soul like a burning flame (*que tangit pectus meum et animam sicut flamma comburens*), teaching me profundities of meaning, I have an inward understanding (*interiorem intelligentiam*) of the Psalter, the Gospels, and other volumes'.[10] It is not that Hildegard has not herself read these books, for surely reading and *hearing* them read aloud was a central part of her daily practice. Her point, and the essence of her importance, is that her exegetical insights and her understanding are not built upon formal schooling. It comes entirely from within her soul, through that which she 'sees'. Also important is her claim that her visions are not experienced in a state of trance. She sees the world with her eyes and things beyond the world with her soul, but at the same time.[11]

Towards the end of her life, in 1175, she further explained the experience of her visions to the Monk Guibert. In her visions, she says, her 'spirit rises, as God wills, to the heights of heaven and into the shifting winds, and it ranges among various peoples, even though very far away'. Her perception 'depends on the shifting of the clouds'. She does not hear with 'bodily ears', nor perceive with 'the cogitations of my heart or the evidence of my five senses. I see them only in my spirit'. In many of her visions she sees a bright, burning light, which is sometimes animate. This light, she claims, she has seen in her soul since infancy. 'It is far brighter than a lucent

Frontispiece to a 19th-century copy of a manuscript of *c.* 1175, now lost, of St Hildegard von Bingen's 1150s treatise *Scivias*, showing her receiving a vision.

cloud through which the sun shines.' Its meaning coheres through her religious practice. This 'shadow of the Living Light' reflects the 'writings, words, virtues, and deeds of men' back to Hildegard. She both sees and hears words, not in 'human speech, but . . . like a blazing flame', and her spirit even 'tastes' these words and visions.[12]

Her reading, meditating and writing, in the 'context of possibilities' of the time, transforms inchoate visionary experiences into meaningful knowledge.[13]

Hildegard is an exemplar of biocultural neuroplasticity. Her senses did not sense like my senses do. Her understanding of her soul and body is not one I share, but it absolutely conditioned her experience of the world. She understood that the origins of the world were in the living presence of the world, and therefore what she saw was definitive of what she knew the world and the people in it to be. Humans were the embodiment of Divine Love, their life force grounded in a physical, spiritual and affective quality – *viriditas* – usually translated as 'greenness'.[14] One could easily imagine an entire affective history of *viriditas*, but here I want to focus on the prior quality, namely, love.

The elements of the Grace of God are embodied in the human in wisdom, viridity and moisture, all of which must be looked after lest they degenerate or, literally, dry up. And all, in turn, are the product of divine love, the principal material God used to create. In a letter to Abbot Adam, about 1166, Hildegard describes her vision of Love.[15] She 'saw, as it were' (*vidi quasi*):

> a beautiful girl of such great brightness, with so shining a face, that I could hardly gaze upon her. She had a cloak whiter than snow and brighter than the stars, and she had on shoes of the purest gold. And she held the moon and the sun in her right hand, and she embraced them lovingly. On her breast there was an ivory tablet, and on this tablet there was an image of man colored like sapphire. Every creature called this girl sovereign lady. And to the image on her breast, she said: 'With thee is the beginning in the day of thy strength: in the brightness of the saints: from the womb before the day star I begot thee.'[16]

A voice then tells Hildegard that this is Divine Love (*caritas*). Here I preserve the translation choice of Baird and Ehrman, who point out that Hildegard is juggling different kinds of love in her letter, *caritas* and *amor*, the first of which is this divine personification and source of Creation, the second being a different kind of quality. There are, as Barbara Rosenwein has pointed out, many possible ways to translate *caritas*, and everything hinges on context and intention. Here *caritas* is most specific in its cosmic essence. The explanation that follows is complex. God, wishing to create the world, bent down in 'sweetest love' (*suauissimo amor*) and made provision for everything in 'great ardour' (*magno ardore*). Here ardour might also be a kind of love, though there is a sense here also of heat and light – the two qualities Hildegard most often associates with God – in God's activity. The curious part is that God bends down and acts with *amor*, not *caritas*, betraying a distinction that Hildegard surely meant to be significant. *Amor* defines the quality of God's action, but *caritas* defines its substance, for it follows that '*caritas* was the elemental material (*principio materia*) from which He created all things'.[17] By means of *caritas*, every creature was formed.

The personification of Divine Love then acquired wings of holy humility, necessary to raise up humanity after the Fall: 'divine love created man, but humility redeemed him'. There follows a passage that explains the existence of all the human virtues, according to the qualities of Divine Love with wings of humility. The two master virtues are hope and faith, which 'bring forth all the other virtues'. Each of these master virtues has two qualities of either Divine Love or humility: 'Hope is, as it were, the eye of divine love (*caritas*); celestial love (*amor*), its heart; and abstinence, the link between the two. But faith is, as it were, the eye of humility; obedience, its heart; and contempt for evil, the link between the two.' Hence, it is clarified that *amor* is a quality in the heart of *caritas*, connected by abstinence to hope. All this is relayed to the Abbot as a pretext for telling him to maintain his obligations to his office. Yet the description is absolutely foundational for Hildegard's worldview. Her spiritual sensorium shows her the light of Divine Love, which is the source and maintainer in eternity of the virtues by which the good live. It is at once a cosmogony and a prescription for duty, affective practice and morality. For, so Hildegard assures the errant Abbot, Divine Love and Humility possess 'ornaments of gold and precious stones' in the human soul. They are to be looked after, cherished and served, regardless of burden or fatigue.

Love and Power at Court

The power or capacity to enter into the feelings and affective qualities of other people is proportional only to the power of others to deceive. The power to deceive depends on a readily available and readable script of expressions, practices and performances. It seems reasonable to contend that, in the history of human affairs, important discriminations about feelings, emotions, mode or tone of a situation have been read wrongly as much as they have been read rightly. Perceiving someone's anger, fear or hatred, and acting accordingly, ends badly when it turns out that those perceptions were wrong, just the same as the misperception of love, happiness or friendliness can end in disaster. The archives are littered with such disasters. Much depends on a history of misreading the emotions of others.

While Hildegard drew her power from the capacity to divine truth, the ability to deceive has also long been recognized as useful as part of the management of power dynamics. Niccolò Machiavelli (1469–1527), for example, was explicit that particular affective qualities were not necessary for a ruler to cling on to power, but the power to simulate those qualities was.[18] Indeed, it was just as necessary for a ruler to have the capacity for cruelty as for humanity in the Machiavellian scheme, but as far as keeping the population onside was concerned, it was necessary for a ruler to 'seem' to be completely pious/merciful (*pietà*), completely trustworthy (*fede*), completely honest (*integrità*), completely humane (*umanità*) and completely religious (*religione*).[19] Yet an individual who actually had these qualities would find himself in trouble because of them, whereas one who projected such qualities could reap the benefits of them, but also do their opposite when politically expedient. In short, the ruler was to be a mask to his people, and the more convincing that mask, the more powerful he would be when allowing it to slip for its opposite. Machiavelli is absolutely clear that a ruler has, at times, to be harsh, duplicitous, dishonest, cruel and un-Christian in deeds, and therefore presumably also in heart.

Key to this affective flexibility is an appreciation of the way that circumstances dictate action. Machiavelli is not convinced that all rulers have the capacity to adapt with the times, for the cautious to become impulsive and vice versa, but what is clear is that an effective ruler projects an affective pragmatism, being one thing *and* the other as the situation suggests. In Machiavelli's scheme, virtue (*virtù*) encompasses this capacity to be clement and callous. It is a strength or skill to manipulate and control with effectiveness. It suggests a person whose affective powers are supple: one who knows the available scripts and who can employ them to his own advantage without ever having to feel anything as it were *authentically*. Indeed, authenticity of feeling is absent from the Machiavellian scheme, displaced entirely by the power that inheres in the appearance of authenticity. As a case in point, Machiavelli is at pains to compel a would-be ruler to avoid being hated, either by his army or by his people, for nothing leads to ruin so certainly as being hated. Yet all the methods of avoiding hatred seem to have nothing to do with a ruler's actual personal qualities and everything to do with how he presents himself through his actions. An affective dynamic is implied, whereby a ruler who leaves his subjects' money and their women well alone does so *strategically*, but is viewed as *liberal* or merciful. There is no content on the part of the politician, only cynical form.

In turn, this power depends on the inability of others to question or interrogate appearances, on the one hand, and on the affective authenticity of the masses on the other. For if there is any feeling in *The Prince* that can be trusted, it is that exhibited by the faithful followers of a successful leader. There is no cynical form there, only practical affective content. A leader that could unite Italy against the barbarian invasions would be met, Machiavelli thought, with a thirst for revenge, with obstinate faith, with piety (*pietà*) and with tears. The Italian *pietà* is one of those words that suggest both the need for and the difficulties of producing a history of emotions. It gives us the English words 'piety' and 'pity' as well as the formulaic artistic representation of Mary holding and lamenting the dead body of Christ ('pietà' in English). At first glance it is difficult to reconcile these three categories, which nevertheless coalesce in Italian harmoniously. What we should recognize, first and foremost, is the inseparability of spiritual and what we might call 'emotional' qualities. The scene of Mary cradling Christ emblemizes piety and pity, the sign for both of which is tears. In English, it was once well known that pity was a correlate, though not a direct synonym, of sympathy, of compassion and of humanity (the affective quality, not the species). It was considered not to be an entirely other-orientated phenomenon, where the object of pity is contemptible (this is something like our modern usage), but rather a sort of pleasurable pain that was suffered by he who pitied. By suffering a pleasurable pain, we approach the meaning of *passion* as suffering, which in its neutral sense refers to that which is *undergone*, rather than necessarily referring to something unpleasant or noxious. The proposed relationship here, between ruler and population, with the ruler being met with '*pietà*', does not really map onto a contemporary English emotion word (indeed, David Wootton's translation simply elides the piety with the subsequent tears, so that the former is eliminated and the latter become redundantly expanded into 'tears of emotion').[20] Some have translated this as 'sympathy', but this suggests a kind of equality between ruler and ruled that is not indicated in the original. For the pious have an understanding for the suffering and worthiness of the object of their affections, but, and this seems essential, they cannot see themselves as equal to that object. Here then I leave the translation of *pietà* as piety, connoting the spiritual fidelity – love, if you like – that can attach to the otherwise worldly relation of ruler and ruled. In the previous iteration of this word, I left a double translation – pious/merciful – for the word when applied to the ruler suggests a double connotation unique to his station. Not only is it useful for him to appear to be pious (in a religious sense), but it is useful for him to appear merciful, which is the preference to opt for life when holding the strings of life or death. The word 'pity' would also work here, but as per the foregoing discussion, we do not necessarily recognize any longer the implicit power dynamic in pity, for, unlike piety, one does not pity the strong, only the weak. Pity – akin to mercy or clemency – is an aspect of strength and power. The actions associated with it imply the possibility of their opposites: cruelty, indifference, ruthlessness. A ruler who pities therefore exercises the symbolic violence of obliquely referring to his power to be pitiless. In Machiavelli and elsewhere, it is clear that these are not built-in affective qualities of individual human nature, but matters of circumstance, training and choice.

The loving devotion of a united population, replete with expressions of bleary-eyed loyalty, was a projection to be sure. There are no concrete examples in Machiavelli's extensive range, drawn from all of Italian and Roman history, of such an affectively grateful and committed populace. Yet he gives credence to the possibility: *The Prince* is essentially a manual for bringing about such fidelity, or avoiding its opposite.

If Machiavelli only allowed for the affective dissimulation of a ruler, his near contemporary Baldesar Castiglione (1478–1529) fully explored the affective dynamics of courtly life surrounding such a ruler. Here we find no shortage of prescriptions for display and representation, but there is also a clear connection to the lived experience of affective life in the courtly world. This is immediately clear in the first book of *Il Cortegiano* (1528, commonly translated in English as *The Book of the Courtier*).[21] The atmosphere around the Duchess, Elisabetta Gonzaga (1471–1526), was such that a supreme contentment (*somma contentezza*) prevailed, yet the power dynamic involved in the social situation at court makes for some curious language. The male courtiers around the Duchess were bound in love by a chain (*una catena*), suggesting both a genuine amatory set of relations as well as a restriction of the form of this 'love'. Indeed, Castiglione qualifies this love as 'cordial' (*amore cordiale*), combined with a 'concord of will' (*concordia di volontà*).[22] The qualification of cordiality, though positive, thrusts this love to the surface of sociality, where the good-naturedness of relations was experienced as part of social interaction, performance and script reading. That it was tempered by the 'will' and the checks of decorum owed to such a great lady suggests a tightly controlled atmosphere, of liberal display undergirded by universal restraint.

This is the way that love plays out according to the rhetorical games of the assembled courtiers Castiglione presents. One of them talks of love as a passion that follows from an 'ability to induce' women to love *him*, the pursuit of which requires 'persistent effort'. He resists this effort because of the countenance of love he sees in the faces of other men: 'the continual laments of certain lovers who, pale, sad, and taciturn, seem always to wear their unhappiness depicted in their eyes; and whenever they speak, they accompany every word with tripled sighs and talk of nothing but tears, torments, despairs, and longings for death'. Under such circumstances, where love is not in itself a discrete emotion so much as it is the harbinger of a torrent of negative passionate sufferings, this courtier 'makes every effort to extinguish it' for his 'own good'.[23]

On the other hand, this same courtier is aware of other lovers who seem 'overly happy' (*troppo più che felici*) when in love, to the point that even a lady's arguments (*guerre*), rage (*ire*) and disdain (*sdegni*) are part of the sweetness of passion. Being unable to understand how anger (*sdegno*) can be experienced sweetly, as opposed to fearfully, he asks the assembled company to detail the kind of anger and its causes that induce this happy feeling, so that he might 'venture a little further in love, in the hope that I too may find this sweetness where some find bitterness'. The quest for love becomes an intellectual exercise routed through the causes of anger that is received sweetly. That the courtiers discoursed freely on the causes and manifestations of the 'angers of love' (*sdegni d'amore*) suggests a kind of common-place knowledge about the dynamics of love relations that were particular to courtly affairs.[24]

If love was a fire in the heart, being loved caused inflammation of the soul (as did beauty, manners, knowledge, speech and gestures). This equated to pleasure (*piacere*) and perhaps went some way to explaining how some relational dynamics were a source of pleasure even when marked by scorn.[25] After all, while love did not depend on an appreciation of beauty, a man who could deeply appreciate the bodily qualities of female beauty would be more inflamed than a man who was deficient in this perception, which is an argument in favour of the artist's gaze. Thus the quality of love could be influenced by both the penetration of the male gaze and the degree of beauty of the female body. A perfect match, under such a rubric, would combine the most beautiful outward female form in conjunction with the finest artistic appreciation of that form. Under such conditions, male love could doubtless withstand torrents of womanly wrath.

I *Move* Therefore I Am

Think about the word 'emotion'. What does it literally mean? The Latin prefix *e-* means 'away', or 'outward'. The stem 'motion' is from the Latin *motio* and means 'movement'. 'Emotion', therefore, literally means 'outward movement'. We retain a sense of this in the idiomatic expression of being 'moved' by an experience. A ceremony or a film or a funeral might all be described as 'moving'. But what, if anything, is actually on the move? The answer begins, but does not end, in the soul.

The legacy of antiquity when it comes to human feelings is this: the affective character of human experience depends, essentially, on what a human *does*, and what a human does is dependent in turn on what a human *is*. Aristotle's theory of passions and virtues tied everything to action and to habit, which conditioned the soul. But the soul itself, and its nature, predisposed humans to suffer passions, to be virtuous and vicious, to seek the good and to fail. Much of classical philosophy, and much of the centuries of intellectual thought that came after the ancients, was based on the negotiation of the different parts of the human soul: of the primacy of the rational soul and the imperative for this part of the soul to master the desiring or sensitive part. Animal function – the nutritive soul – lay beneath these two levels and was held in common with beasts and plants. While there are fine-grained debates about the nature of the human through the centuries, the essential Aristotelian and Platonic schemes were preserved intact, such that theories about the passions were automatically limited because the range of things that a human could do were also circumscribed by what a human was.

Enter René Descartes (1596–1650). It is impossible to understand the import of Descartes' work on the passions without first understanding the way in which he turned the human upside down. Descartes' human depended only upon a rational soul. This alone separated the human mechanical apparatus from every other kind of life. One way to get to grips with the profundity of this revolutionary thought is to think through pain with Descartes. To use his own example, picture a man whose foot has been left dangerously near a fire:

> Thus, for example, if fire A is near foot B, the tiny parts of the fire – which as you know move very rapidly – have sufficient force to move with them the area of skin that they touch, and in this way they pull the tiny fibre *cc* which you see attached to it, and simultaneously open the entrance to the pore *de*, located opposite the point where this fibre terminates: just as when you pull on one end of a cord you cause a bell hanging at the other end to ring at the same time.
>
> Now when the entrance to the pore or small tube *de* is opened this way, the animal spirits from cavity F enter and are carried through it, some to the muscles that serve to pull the foot away from the fire, and some to the muscles that make the hands move and the whole body turn in order to protect itself.[26]

Put simply, the action of pulling the foot from the fire depends on nothing but a kind of pulley system of bodily mechanics. Pleasure and pain, according to such mechanics, are a product of the same system of moveable parts. The difference between warmth and burning is only one of degree, the bodily responses to each being automatic. Yet this is already to move on a stage, for in this description of mechanics there is neither pleasure nor pain, but only movement of the body. An animal's body would respond in much the same way, automatically retracting a foot as if yanked by a rope. To have an affective response to the movement of the body requires a superadded substance. Animal spirits alone will not suffice.

Descartes explains all this in the *Discourse on Method* (1637). On the one hand, he makes an argument for human exceptionalism, the human being the only being that can think (and therefore feel), and on the other hand he connects humans to animals and inorganic matter in the most striking way. He claims to have discovered 'everything that can exist without thinking' and found that all these 'functions are the same as those in which the unreasoning animals resemble us'. What follows is a demonstration of the import of contemporary medical knowledge about the movement of the blood in humans and animals. He suggests that readers unfamiliar with anatomy acquire for themselves 'the heart of some large animal cut open before them, for the heart of an animal with lungs is quite similar to that of man'. Assuming the reader has returned with said heart, he continues to explain that the motion of the heart, its continual beating, is the result of nothing but the 'mere disposition of the parts'.[27] It could only beat thus and no other way. He compares it to a clock, the motions of which follow from the weight, location and configuration of its counterweights and wheels. Moving from an understanding of William Harvey's discovery of the circulation of the blood in 1628, Descartes compares this movement, as well as the nature of the nerves and muscles that are animated by 'animal spirits', to a machine, an automaton. The burning foot comes out of the fire not because of pain, but because of an automatic sequence of movements set in motion by the fire's own moving parts:

> This will hardly seem strange to those who know how many automata or machines can be made by human industry, although these automata employ very few parts in comparison

to the large number of bones, muscles, nerves, arteries, veins, and all the other component parts of each animal. Such persons will therefore think of this body as a machine created by the hand of God, and in consequence incomparably better designed and with more admirable movements than any machine that can be invented by man.[28]

What is the point of this sequence: animal heart, clock, circulation of the blood, automaton? It reduces nature to mechanics, animals to machines, bodies to mechanisms. A human, without a soul, would be a mere machine. All its movements could be explained simply

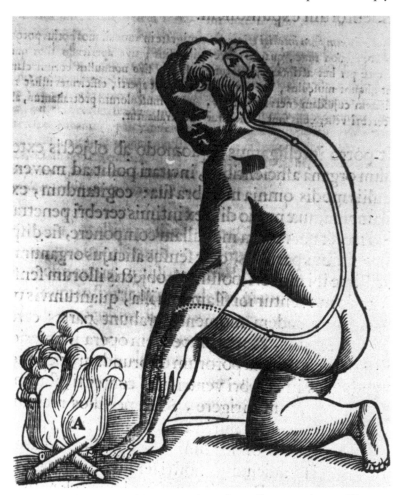

Woodcut illustration of the pain pathway, from a Latin translation of René Descartes' *L'homme . . . et un traité de la formation du fœtus* (1664).

by the function and disposition of its parts, heated by the fire of the heart and the movement of 'animal spirits'.

Yet whereas the body is mechanical, the human being taken as a whole cannot be considered a mere machine because Descartes joins to it a rational soul that distinguishes it entirely from other animals and automatons. Nevertheless, in essence, the functions of a human being are mechanical. Descartes asserts that humans are more than machines by stressing *cogito*, normally translated as 'I think'. This thinking existence, which is not corporeal, is evidence for Descartes of a rational soul, put there by God. God is the first cause.

Descartes' definition of the soul, its function and nature, is encapsulated in this passage:

> I soon noticed that while I thus wished to think everything false, it was necessarily true that I who thought so was something. Since this truth, I think, therefore I am, was so firm and assured that all the most extravagant suppositions of the sceptics were unable to shake it, I judged that I could safely accept it as the first principle of the philosophy I was seeking.
>
> I then examined closely what I was, and saw that I could imagine I had no body, and that there was no world nor any place that I occupied, but that I could not imagine for a moment that I did not exist . . . Thus it follows that this ego, this soul, by which I am what I am, is entirely distinct from the body and is easier to know than the latter, and that even if the body were not, the soul would not cease to be all that it now is.[29]

Before pursuing this further, let us pause a minute to reflect on 'I think, therefore I am', *cogito ergo sum*. We retain the Latinate form in English, in our words 'cogitate' and 'cognition', but the easy translation of *cogito* into 'I think' covers over one of its essential components. *Cogito* is itself a contraction of *con agito*, where *agito* refers to putting into motion. 'I think' is therefore, more literally, 'I put into motion.' This more accurately describes Descartes' understanding of the *movement* of the soul. What Descartes called the *res cogitans* is usually translated as the 'thinking thing' that demarcates human exceptionalism. A more literal and for us a more useful translation would be 'moving matter'. Motion was at the heart of everything that set humans apart. Not only human passions but human thought was related to the literal movement of the soul, and this form of motion stood in direct contrast to all other forms of motion, which could be reduced to mechanical operations.

Because of this, Descartes could reject the tripartite division of the soul according to Plato and Aristotle and the generations of theology that followed them in Europe. For it was not necessary, in order to explain mechanical functions, 'to conceive of any vegetative or sensitive soul, or any other principle of movement or life, other than its blood and its spirits which are agitated by the heat of the fire that burns continuously in its heart, and which is of the same nature as those fires that occur in inanimate bodies'.[30] These animal movements were no more than simple *motion*.

Usefully for us, Descartes went to considerable lengths to describe the movement of the soul in humans. In the *Treatise of Man*, eventually published posthumously in 1664, Descartes describes the man machine and its soul in great detail. He understood where the soul was seated and how it related to or communicated with the body. Descartes placed the soul in the pineal gland, so called because it looks like a pine nut. The way animal spirits move in this gland corresponds to movements of the body in the world, either as primary cause of movement, or as the effect of some disturbance outside the body, since the 'tiny tubes' inside the surface of the brain are connected here and link back to the various parts of the machine. When a soul is attached to the gland, the soul gains an awareness of the significance of these movements and attaches understanding to them. It is also able to extrapolate understanding without the body moving. This is how he explains both human movement and human understanding (movement of the soul). The description accompanies the image:

> Here for example, we can assume that what makes tube 8 turn towards point *b* rather than toward some other point is simply that the spirits that issue from this point tend toward it with a greater force than do any others. And the same thing will cause the soul to sense that the arm is turned toward object B, if it is already in this machine, as I shall later suppose it to be. For we must imagine that all the points of the gland toward which tube 8 can be turned correspond to

Woodcut illustration of the movement of the soul, from a Latin translation of Descartes' *L'homme . . . et un traité de la formation du fœtus* (1664).

places toward which the arm marked 7 can be turned, so that what makes the arm turn toward object B now is simply that this tube is facing point *b* of the gland. But if the spirits, changing their course, turn these tubes toward some other point on the gland, say toward *c*, then the tiny fibres 8 and 7, which emerge nearby and proceed to the muscle of the arm, in changing position by the same means, would close up certain pores of the brain near D, enlarging others. This would make the spirits, which would thereby pass into these muscles in a different way from that they do now, promptly turn this arm toward object C. Reciprocally, if some action other than that of the spirits which enter through tube 8 were to turn this same arm toward B or C, this would make this tube 8 turn toward points *b* or *c* of the gland. As a consequence, an idea of this movement would be formed at the same time . . . Thus in general we should take it that each tiny tube on the inside surface of the brain corresponds to a bodily part, and that each point on the surface of gland H corresponds to a direction in which these parts can be turned: in this way, the movements of these parts and the ideas of them can cause one another in a reciprocal fashion.[31]

So much for the machine and its movements. The mechanics are more complex than the simple bell pull, perhaps, but they are essentially the same. What difference does a soul make? The accompanying image depicts the soul's sympathetic movements, and is described thus:

And when a soul has been put in this machine, this will allow it to sense various objects by means of the same organs, disposed in the same way, and without anything at all changing except the position of the gland H. Here, for example, the soul can sense what is at point L by means of the two hands holding sticks NL and OL, because it is from point L on gland H that the spirits entering tubes 7 and 8 issue. Now suppose that gland H leans a little further forward, in such a way that points *n* and *o* on its surface are at the places marked *i* and *k*, and that as a consequence it is from them that the spirits entering 7 and 8 issue: the soul would sense what is at N and what is at O by means of the same hands without them being changed in any way.[32]

The soul's reasoning and functioning pertain to its *movement* of the gland independently of the motion of the body's material. All understanding, all the passions – all the motions projected outwards, including *emotions* – are here in the soul, which moves, or can move, independently of the body. Without the soul none of these things can be. To return to our example of the burning foot, *pain* could only be ascribed to a being with a soul because without it, the bodily movements that seem to indicate pain, and even the cry that issues from the mouth, are merely automatic mechanical responses. There is only a degree of difference between pain and its associated movements and pleasurable sensitivity and its movements. In other words, what is sensed as delightful or as noxious is translated by the soul as joy and sadness respectively. Pleasure and pain only attain their affective qualities through the movement of the soul. The soul gives them their human subjective significance. The body *represents* to the soul through its movements and the soul *understands* them through its own. Noxiousness in the absence of a soul is the mere breaking of a machine. The passions, available only

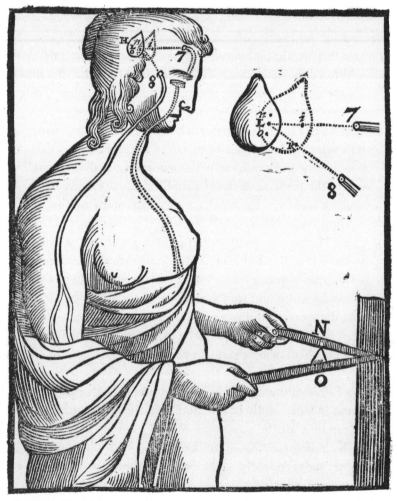

Woodcut illustration of the movement of the soul, from Descartes' *L'homme . . . et un traité de la formation du fœtus* (1664).

to humans, were themselves evidence of divinity and an essential quality of the immortal soul.

Descartes' influence cannot be overstated, especially as it pertains to the consequences of human exceptionalism. While Descartes broke abruptly with theological and philosophical traditions about the nature of the soul, he nevertheless doubled down on a human tradition of dominance over nature, and in fact swept away all ethical concerns about such dominance. He said that there was no error greater, with the exception of denying God, nor one 'so apt to make weak characters stray from the path of virtue as the idea that the souls of animals are of the same nature as our own, and that in consequence we have no more to fear or to hope for after this life than have the flies and the ants'.[33] Indeed, the path of virtue lay through an absolute mastery and possession of nature. On the basis of Descartes' beast-machine ideas, Malebranche is said to have kicked a pregnant bitch in front of the shocked writer Bernard le Bovier de Fontenelle, who was told with some contempt: 'So what? Don't you know that it has no feeling at all?'[34] The Jansenist theologian Antoine Arnauld had quickly taken Descartes on board and persuaded the solitaries at the Abbey of Port-Royal that they might beat their dogs with indifference since the cries of the animals were 'the mere creaking of animal "clockwork"'.[35] An eyewitness recorded the tenor of experimental work in the monastery, as the solitaries 'nailed the poor animals to boards by the four paws to dissect them while still alive, in order to watch the circulation of the blood, which was a great subject of discussion'.[36] We might see in such acts a kind of terrible cruelty, or else a callousness that has awful implications for civilization. Yet we should entertain, most seriously, that these actors acted in good faith. Descartes, they thought, was correct and they acted accordingly and without scruple. After all, if Descartes was correct, there were no scruples to be had. To think and to feel all depended on the presence of soul and its capacity to *move*.

The Map of Tender

In the early Enlightenment salons of Paris, talk of reason was also inflected with movement: of passions, doubtless, but inextricably bound with the niceties of social mobility. The elite *précieuses* who clustered around Madeleine de Scudéry (1607–1701) at the Hôtel de

Rambouillet were famed for their romantic tales and witty exchanges, and their fascination with polite practices. While the salon was a major marker of the importance of women in the intellectual life of the French elite, its point of interest for us lies in its mapping of the vagaries of love onto the topography of the female body. Scudéry's novel *Clélie* (1654–60) contains an engraving of a map, originally designed as a salon game, showing the potentially perilous route towards different types of love.[37] At least, that is how the *Carte de Tendre* is usually characterized, but 'love' is at best a loose translation of *tendre*, and there are good reasons to revisit this fantastic place.

A nearer translation of *tendre*, rather obviously, is 'tender', but there are some difficulties to negotiate if we are to understand the various routes towards tenderness among close friends that the map describes. The reluctance among commentators on the map to talk of a tender feeling or a tender emotion is born out of a lack of understanding as to what this might mean, hence the utilization of love as an analogy. But even in English until the early twentieth century there was common knowledge and experience of the 'tender emotion', which received its own special treatment in early works of comparative psychology. I shall turn to these in due course. A mix of sympathy, love and affective other-orientation, 'tender' could not be encapsulated by any other emotion word. It is a lost emotion requiring careful reconstruction.

A dictionary definition will not prove particularly helpful. In the eighth entry for 'tender' as an adjective or adverb in the *Oxford English Dictionary* (1989), we find that a 'tender' person's feelings are 'characterized by, exhibiting, or expressing delicacy of feeling or susceptibility to the gentle emotions; kind, loving, gentle, mild, affectionate'. This goes some way to describe the tender emotion itself, but by no means does it encapsulate the complexity of that feeling. Indeed, the only mention of something like this in the dictionary concerns 'the tender passion', or 'tender sentiment', which are equated quite simply with 'sexual love'. The existence of a discrete and observable phenomenon called the 'tender emotion' is absent from our modern reference guides, which is all the more surprising when one considers its central importance in theories of both civility and civilization, up to the twentieth century.

Let us return, therefore, to the *Carte de Tendre*. The Map of Tender combines the topography of social customs, the ideal of Platonic

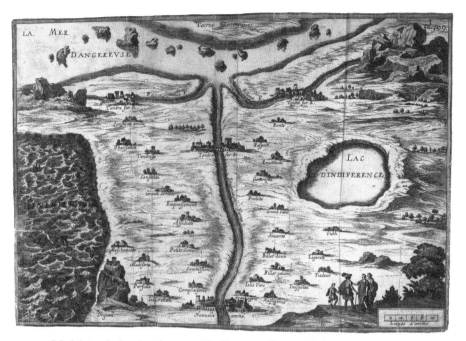

Madeleine de Scudéry (engraved by François Chauveau), the *Carte de Tendre* from her novel *Clélie* (1654–60).

relations, and the perilous internal anatomy of the human female: not so much a machine as an untamed landscape. This land descends from a high point of new friendship, through a river plain towards a dangerous sea. The flood plain is dotted with towns that encapsulate both the character of affective relations as the new friendship develops for better or for worse, as well as the social practices that signify the affective dynamic between two friends. There are three principal routes to three major cities of Tender. A land route to the west of the River of Inclination leads to Tender on Gratitude, named for one of two minor rivers that flow into the Dangerous Sea. East of the Inclination, another land route leads to Tender on Esteem. Most direct of all, the River of Inclination itself leads directly to Tender on Inclination, but the apparent breadth and speed of the river suggest caution. Overshoot, and one flows straight into the Dangerous Sea. Either side of the land routes are other ways to go awry, falling into the Sea of Enmity to the west and the Lake of Indifference to the east.

The whole place is structured loosely around a crude representation of the female reproductive system. The River of Inclination is the vagina, flowing directly into the uterine Dangerous Sea, beyond which lie Unknown Lands. The two minor rivers resemble fallopian tubes, also flowing into the Dangerous Sea, but their principal towns offer a comparative safety of approach. The significance of the anatomical topography is clear. Any attempt to reach Tender by Inclination – that is, any attempt to follow one's felt desire to cement a friendship through feelings alone – risks turbulent and hysterical consequences. Women following their desires, thereby bypassing the social niceties designed and policed so as to restrain and direct those desires, has the potential of rich reward but also the prospect of perilous consequences. By emphasizing the risk of following one's 'inclination', the Map of Tender delivers a familiar warning about the passionate instability of the female sex, guaranteed by her mysterious reproductive anatomy.

The 'wandering womb' – the literal meaning of *hysteria* – was hardly reducible to mere hearsay and everyday chauvinism. Indeed, it had been part of medical knowledge since at least the time of Galen. The medical (and political and educational) establishment regularly recapitulated the 'facts' of female deficiencies with respect to the passions, locating the instability of the 'weaker sex' in the womb, uterus and reproductive system in general until the close of the nineteenth century. Colloquially, this knowledge endured beyond that date and still abides idiomatically in our civilization. Whenever a person, male or female, is told today that they are 'hysterical', we understand the valuation loaded into the term. That person is 'irrational' and has lost emotional control. For centuries upon centuries, the charge indicated that the behaviour was 'womanish'.[38]

If the uterine apple cart was reputedly so easy to upturn, no wonder that society women in the Parisian salons were wary of those who followed their heart's desires. After all, intellectual life itself was generally considered a risk to female stability, exposing them to passions that they could not accommodate or manage. How much more risky, therefore, for a member of this intellectual set to simply follow her sentimental inclinations. The risk presumably also encompassed the licentiousness of lust and sex that lay 'beyond the final limits of friendship'.[39]

It is this context that makes sense of the land-based routes on the Map of Tender. Rarely does a single document provide such rich clues to both a theoretical understanding of passions per se and a clear summary of the moral economy designed and implemented in order to make sure that passions are kept in check.[40] As an extra bonus, this map also indicates what happens when that moral economy is breached or transgressed. It perfectly encapsulates the umbilical connection between feeling and practice, between affective expression and social prescription, and between the feelings of individuals and the communities of feeling that contain, define, form and inform them. In *Clélie*, the heroine draws the map in order to check the passions of suitors because, according to one critic, the passionate 'agitation beneath the sociable surface is so palpable'.[41] The word choice here should not escape us. Passions touched and were touched, felt and were felt, in a sensational way. Their presence, especially in a complex social dynamic, necessitated a strict system of conventions and observations. While the *précieuses* became somewhat nonsensical figures through the age of reason, and while the map 'has come to stand for all that is ridiculous in the enterprise of the group of salonières', it nevertheless is a frank expression of the intertwining of affective feelings and affective behaviour, emotions and emotional practices in contemporary parlance, that defines all social relations.[42] We do not always, or even usually, have a map. But that does not mean we could not conceive of one.

The route towards Tender on Gratitude is defined by service, clearly demonstrating that the cultivation of a platonic friendship depends on a power dynamic between individuals that is acquiesced in by the inferior and not abused by the superior. The small towns on the way from New Friendship included Deference (*Complaisance*), Submission (*Soumission*), Lavish Attention (*Petits Soins*), Constant Attention (*Assiduité*), Willingness (*Empressement*) and Great Services (*Grand Services*), only then reaching the more affectively orientated staging posts of Sensibility (*Sensibilité*) and Fondness (*Tendresse*). These in turn lead to Obedience (*Obeissance*) and Constant Friendship (*Constante amitié*), which gives way finally to the tender emotion, built on the dynamic of gratitude (*Reconnoissance*) for services given and opportunities afforded. Tenderness is, on the one hand, an other-oriented feeling arising from a sense of condescension, or benign superiority, that mixes something positive (something like joy) with something negative (something like pity) that opens the person up to feelings of tenderness. The feeling of gratitude emphasizes not simply the services rendered or the work done, but the fact that the services and work were done *for* a superior. Feelings and expressions of gratitude contain and recapitulate the hierarchy that was all too evident at the beginning of a friendship, but which has now become personalized. On the other hand, tenderness is an other-oriented feeling arising from a sense of submission, of comparative lowliness, and from a tacit acceptance of this inferior position. Gratitude in this sense is a deferent acknowledgement of grace dispensed purposefully. The two positions in the dynamic complement each other perfectly.

On the other side of Inclination, the route towards Tender on Esteem is defined by formal modes of courtship and demonstrations of good character. Again, the emphasis is on practices delimited by convention. From the common departure point of New Friendship, the traveller passes through Wit (*Grand esprit*), Beautiful Verses (*Tolis Vers*), Amatory Note (*Billet galant*) and Love Letter (*Billet Doux*) before character is revealed through Sincerity (*Sincerité*), Kind Heart (*Grand Coeur*), Honesty (*Probité*), Generosity (*Generosité*) and Precision (*Exactitude*). This gives way to the kinds of affective dynamic that lead to a mutual tender emotion built on the recognition of such qualities: Respect (*Respect*) and Goodness (*Bonté*). The quality of esteem seems perhaps to be more egalitarian than the relationship defined by gratitude, but it remains the case that there is a directional flow of friend building (courtship, perhaps) that indicates the status differential between lover and beloved, for want of better terms.

The only variable in the development of the tender emotion seems to be time, for beyond a certain point on the route, the destination seems inevitable. It is only at the beginning of the journey, when the friendship is relatively new, that a wayward path might be followed. As with the virtuous paths, they depend on practices that mark out the presence of sentiment, but in an altogether negative sense. On one side, the wayward traveller first hits Indiscretion (*Indiscretion*), from which follows Perfidy (*Perfidie*), Scandal Mongering (*Medisance*), Wickedness (*Meschanceté*) and the forbidding peak of Vanity or the Sin of Pride (*Orgueil*). From here it seems straightforward to fall into the Sea of Enmity, a relational dynamic built upon the interplay of suspicion and unrestrained passion. On the other side, the shaky foundations of New Friendship lead to Negligence (*Negligence*), Disparity (*Inesgalité*), Tepidity (*Tiedeur*), Thoughtlessness (*Legereté*) and Neglect (*Oubli*). From here, one enters the Lake of Indifference, the summation of a road defined by the gradual erosion of any kind of other-oriented affective feeling or behaviour. Through careless neglect of social convention, passion itself becomes desiccated.

The tender emotion, in its seventeenth-century Parisian incarnation, is not one lost emotion, but three, each built on different platforms of social practice or on giving in to desire. If we are the heirs of any of this, it is only to this pursuit of pure feeling that we tend to gravitate. We should dwell, however, on the ways in which meaningful relationships were built upon sociality and custom, and on the importance of performances that could be recognized as tending in a certain affective direction. There is no distinction between these social practices and their accompanying feelings. In fact the feelings cannot exist without the practices, nor can the practices be carried out with the feelings. In matters of tenderness, but especially in matters of love, such social practices defined the management of the passions for centuries before love was pursued as a matter of choice. Just as with the dangers of *tendre d'inclination*, *amor d'inclination* was considered just as risky individually, but also as a threat to the whole social fabric.[43]

Indeed, the observation and performance of social practices that produced the tender emotion among friends and perhaps lovers was no less complex in matters of love itself. If one digests the scholarly literature on love in early modern France, one finds this passion buried under a politics of status, reciprocity and the intricacies of marriage. What is clear is that love itself was a hotly contested topic, with some considering the pursuit of it for its own sake a dangerous and destabilizing activity. Marriage, among the elite at any rate, was to be a strictly controlled and carefully negotiated process of social dynamics. A newly married couple represented their families' social status and together signalled something about their own rank in society. Affective ties, if they were to come at all, were to come over time. Perhaps such ties could be called 'love', but they scarcely fit a model of love that we would readily recognize. One did not 'fall' into it so much as one carefully contracted it.[44] By no means were such arrangements any guarantee of success. If loveless marriages were a risk of rituals of arrangement and dynamics of social and political power, some thought the risk of pursuing love itself was far greater. While the pursuit of love could also be no guarantee of a successful marriage, any match based on passion alone risked rending the social fabric.

The influence of the Map of Tender can be seen as far away as late eighteenth-century Prussia and mid-nineteenth-century England, but the tender emotion was in for a hard time on its slow route to oblivion. In Immanuel Kant's (1724–1804) *Kritik der Urteilskraft* (1790), known in English as the *Critique of Judgement*, tender feelings (*zärtliche Rührungen*) are condemned, when they rise to the level of an expressed emotion (*Affekt*), as completely useless sentimentality (*Empfindelei*).[45] From the late 1850s Alexander Bain (1818–1903) was England's most prominent psychologist. He made his name establishing a place for 'emotions' in common English usage and for 'psychology' as an academic discipline. He went into great detail about the tender emotion in his *The Emotions and the Will* (1859). Structurally, the description of the tender emotion largely follows the seventeenth-century map. It is uncertain whether or not Bain knew about it, but I would argue that he did not need to be aware of late Renaissance French literature on the matter, for the parameters and qualities of the tender emotion would have been well known across broad sections of society, especially among the cultured and the educated.

Bain's particular knack was to demonstrate, from a social psychological standpoint, exactly how the tender emotion came about, and what its effects were. The peculiarity of the tender emotion lay in two unusual aspects. It was 'an outgoing' emotion connected with sensation, pleasure and pain. The 'outgoing' aspect placed the origins of the tender emotion in 'objects' outside of the self, and especially in other human beings. Animals and even inanimate matter could incite it, but Bain was somewhat disparaging of these manifestations. In keeping with Bain's general appreciation of the historicity of emotional expression, he was sure that the tender emotion could only be activated once a person had sufficient experience to interpret emotional expressions of others, though he made a special case for the universality of the 'pathetic wail' of grief or pain and for the 'watery eyeball', where lachrymosity was 'primitive, although extended by subsequent associations'.[46] Somewhat later, Herbert Spencer's (1820–1903) description of pity (about which more in Chapter Five) made the tender emotion an epiphenomenon, or a branch, of pity, with pity as the root of all such feelings. Since it was so often misplaced in objects that did not command such emotional attention, it was condemned as being an evolutionary atavism. Emotional evolution, so went the dogma, would see the back of this kind of sentimentality.[47] Sometime shortly after that, people stopped talking about the tender emotion altogether. A love's labour: lost.

FOUR

THE AGE OF
UNREASON

The period between roughly 1600 and 1800 is often character-ized as the 'age of reason'. Encapsulating the Enlightenment in its various centres, from Descartes to the birth of utilitar-ianism at the end of the eighteenth century, it is typically marked by a will to master or conquer nature. That which is wild, including that which is wild within humanity, is tamed. Passions of the soul are framed outside of the realm of reason, and judgement is grounded in measured, distanced and controlled *thought*. Doubtless, such a characterization applies only to those select philosophers, economists and politicians whose names define the age, not to the general mass of populations, whose lives continued much as they had before. Yet even within the works of those eminences who spearheaded the age of reason, there remains a sometimes awkward relationship to the passions, to the affections and to the sensibilities and senses that drive judgement.[1]

A focus on the rational might gloss over the centrality of the passions to Enlightenment thought. Descartes, as we have seen, had a well-developed understanding of the senses and of the passions, his emphasis on rational thought encapsulating movement. But others emphatically rejected the isolation of reason and insisted that body and soul were one, driven by the relationship of passions and reason. Spinoza, for example, understood the vast importance of the passions. Into the eighteenth century, Adam Smith (1723–1790), David Hume (1711–1776), Edmund Burke (1729–1797) and others all focused on the centrality of sympathy, a feeling of emotional identification, to the functioning of a moral modern state. If the high point of the Enlightenment was the wave of revolutions that institutionalized its ideas in nation states, those revolutions nevertheless depended upon an emotional outpouring.[2] It is a period defined more or less explicitly as one of anger, or terror: a great release of sentiments suppressed by old regimes. The pillars of these new revolutionary nations were affective states and practices – liberty, equality, fraternity, the pursuit of happiness – driven by notions of 'common sense': not an intellectual understanding, but an understanding that was readily *felt*.

The episodes in this chapter exemplify the focus on feeling in the age of reason, beginning with Spinoza's *Ethics*, and the argument that reason and passion cannot coexist. Anybody who experiences passions has not yet fully attained a true understanding of the world, yet anybody who truly has attained such an understanding can know both the end of sorrow – its *telos* – and the end of sorrow – its termination.

The character of the Age of Revolutions has been revised and revisited by historians who have ably demonstrated the limits of liberty and equality, not least because fraternity implicitly excluded half the population. They have, with great success, put women back in the picture of the revolutionary triumph of right reason, while condemning their marginalization.[3] An inversion is possible here, however. It can be shown that the male protagonists of the revolution depended on affective practices and arguments for their success, though they were often implicit. What was it about male passions in this period that allowed them to be veiled, concealed and applied to the revolutionary cause, whereas women's passions were deemed beyond the pale? If we assert that affect is part of cognition and cognition is part of emotion, then to be sure even the most arid revolutionary rhetoric has its affective content. But how was it gendered, and what difference did it make?

The chapter concludes with a remarkable account of inductive medical reasoning, of feeling and groping towards a breakthrough, that ended in failure and personal tragedy. It is a short retelling of the life of Edward Jenner, one of the most celebrated doctors in history, who is famed for the discovery of the smallpox vaccine and credited with its propagation. In my recasting of Jenner's life, we will see a story of assumption, uncontrolled experiment and affect, of the intertwining of the abstract understanding of disease and the experience of disease, since forgotten in the wake of a triumph of reason, research and progress through vaccination.

The End of Sorrow

Baruch Spinoza's (1632–1677) most celebrated work, his *Ethics*, was published posthumously in 1677. In it, Descartes' philosophy is swept away in a breathtaking flurry of propositions and proofs. In particular, the notion that there is a body and a mind (soul) as two separate – if conjoined – entities is discarded as mere ignorance. For

> when men say that this or that action of the body springs from the mind which has command over the body, they do not know what they say, and they do nothing but confess with pretentious words that they know nothing about the cause of the action, and see nothing in it to wonder at.[4]

The notion of *I* as distinct from its body was completely anathema to Spinoza, who posited that

> The first thing that constitutes the essence of the mind is the idea of the body actually existing, the first and chief thing belonging to our mind is the effort to affirm the existence of our body, and therefore the idea which denies the existence of the body is contradictory to our mind.[5]

Those who, like Descartes, 'devise seats and dwelling-places of the soul, usually excite our laughter', he wrote.[6] Moreover, there could be no 'doubt that brutes feel', for they had body-minds analogous to humans.[7] So much for Descartes.

At the core of Spinoza's reappraisal of what it is to be human is a long disquisition on the subject of the origin and nature of the affections (*affectuum*). In most modern translations, this is rendered, with hopeless inappropriateness, as 'emotions'.[8] Spinoza does not talk about emotions. Indeed, his *affectuum* are unlike anything that had come before, and, while highly influential, scarcely like anything that has come since (though there are tendrils of influence, especially in sociology).[9] In *The History of Emotions* I challenged that we would do Spinoza a major injustice if we treated him as a commentator on the emotions.[10] Here I try to meet that challenge by explicating what Spinoza had in mind by affections (*affectuum*) and passions (*passionum*).

I resist the temptation to call affection (*affectus*) 'affect', as some have, because of the semantic confusion this might cause with what contemporary psychologists know as affects. In Spinoza's general definition, affection – an *animi pathema*, passion of the soul – is 'a confused idea by which the mind affirms of its body, or any part of it, a greater or less power of existence than before; and this increase of power being given, the mind itself is determined to one particular thought rather than to another'.[11] We should not be misled by the phrase 'confused idea' into thinking that Spinoza was himself unsure what an affection was. On the contrary, he makes clear that 'the mind suffers only in so far as it has inadequate or confused ideas'.[12] Affection is only possible as a failure to be entirely rational. It is opposed to understanding. Moreover, passions do not reside in the soul, or rather, it is not in the nature of the soul to have the capacity for passions. Rather, passions and affections are confused ideas about external objects that affect our bodies.

All of the things that we might label 'emotions' are, in Spinoza's scheme, epiphenomena of a primary action and two core affections. The primary action is *cupiditas*, defined as self-conscious appetite (*appetitum*), and is usually translated as 'desire'. Spinoza remarked that appetite 'is the essence itself of man in so far as it is determined to such acts as contribute to his preservation', and desire falls under a similar definition. Desire 'is the essence of man in so far as it is conceived as determined to any action by any one of his affections'.[13] The two affections are *laetitia* and *tristitia*. Modern translations, looking for consonance with modern philosophical preoccupations, often translate these terms as 'pleasure' and 'pain' respectively, but these bald categories do not seem to capture the qualities of master *affective* categories. 'Joy' and 'sorrow' come nearer to the mark, and help understand how all of the other affective categories, including love (*amor*), hate (*odium*), hope (*spes*), fear (*metus*) and so on, are derived from either joy or sorrow directed to a particular object, or else with the accompaniment of attendant ideas specific to a context. Hence fear (*metus*) is 'a sorrow not constant, arising from the idea of something future or past, about the issue of which we sometimes doubt'.[14]

These confused ideas that inflect joy and sorrow fall under the category of 'external bodies'. The ideas a person can have of an external body, as they encounter it, do not say anything about the nature of that external body, but only about the body of the person explicitly.

Decoded, it sounds like this: if I poked myself in the eye with a stick I might see a flashing light. The light has nothing to do with the stick and everything to do with the way the eye works. Spinoza's ultimate aim was to have reasonable people come to an adequate idea of the stick itself, but first he set out to explain the nature of the stick's affection of the body and the passion associated with it. As we go through our lives, our encounters are particular to us. Our desires vary according to the passions aroused by contact with objects outside us and the degree to which our ideas of those objects are confused.

As indicated above, Spinoza ultimately has adequate ideas in mind, whereby the nature of things external to us would be truly known. This state of perfection, of reasonable knowledge of nature, would not include passions of any kind. In general, he posits that every kind of joy is good and every kind of sorrow is evil, and that joy is towards reason. But it is possible also to be mistaken about our desire for what we call good, and in such cases joy can lead to sorrow. Indeed, 'we neither strive for, wish, seek, nor desire anything because we think it to be good, but, on the contrary, we adjudge a thing to be good because we strive for, wish, seek, or desire it'.[15] Goodness and evil are, with the passions, evidence of imperfect or confused ideas about the world.

In Spinoza's scheme, therefore, reason and affection (including all the passions) are not so much opposed as mutually exclusive. The experience of passions is a sign of falling short of reason, which is to say that one's ideas of nature are not adequate. This involves a further explanation about the meaning of 'nature' in Spinoza and its relation to God. Spinoza infamously conflates the categories of God and nature, so that the phrase 'God or nature' is held to be a peculiarity of Spinoza's thinking. God's immanence makes him indistinguishable from nature, but the converse is also true. Nature – the objective world – is indistinguishable from God.

Ultimately, the ideal end of existence is the elimination of all passions, of the master affections of joy and sorrow, and of all ideas of good and evil. Insofar as we desire or are led by affections we are enslaved, even if we have an idea that we are free. True freedom only arises when we have adequate (true) ideas of our body and of objects (and therefore of God). These ideas lead to actions based on reason. Insofar as our desire accords with reason we are free. But what is the nature of that freedom? A free man, led only by reason, does not know sorrow or joy; and therefore he does not know good or evil. A reasonable man will be amoral because God or nature is amoral. God could not have created sorrow or any of the things that follow from sorrow (though he may have caused it) since once the causes of sorrow are understood it 'ceases to be a passion' (*ipsa desinit esse passio*).[16] Understanding removes the affection of our bodies caused by confused ideas of external objects. Understanding is categorically incompatible with any passion. Freedom – true freedom – is therefore a state of transcendence, above feelings and above morals. It involves understanding the nature of things beyond the self and beyond the human. Since nature was only one substance (God), then humans already had knowledge of God (insofar as they could know themselves), and this meant that the end of sorrow and joy was possible.

To many, this short precis of Spinoza's *Ethics* will be painful to read, and may challenge the understanding. It challenges mine. Think, however, of the ramifications of this scheme, boiled down to its essential elements, and reflect on the seismic and shattering effects of such a treatise in late seventeenth-century Europe. God is demystified, and knowable, and is not merely *in* all things, but *is* all things. Many saw this as a denial of God himself. All claims to reasonable thought and reasonable acts could, in this high age of reason, be shown to be mere charades. People's idea of reason was actually affection, poorly understood as such. Wherever Spinoza could see people affected by desire, by shades of joy and sorrow, and by pursuits of good and evil, he could see a failure to have attained to reason. So, not only is the moral economy of major established religions demolished, so too are the foundations of political discourse and institutions. It was all affection, not reason. Precious few, in Spinoza's estimation, ever attained the state of wisdom he described.

Paine and Happiness

In the century after Spinoza's death, understanding in popular politics was all feeling. In the American colonies, as Nicole Eustace has brilliantly shown, competing ideas about what and how to feel and competing notions of the self (the modern, individual self and the earlier, social configuration of the self) lay at the heart of the flux and doubt that defined the instability and uncertainty of years of war and political and religious upheaval.[17] Americans had to work out who they were, what and how to feel and how best to feel for and about their emerging nation and the people in it, according to Eustace, either in the name of loyalty or the spirit of liberty. Feeling rules – those emotive scripts 'written' by the powerful – were in flux on the emotional frontier, with the pressure to emote pulling people in different directions at the same time.[18] Eustace paints a picture of instability, disrupting any supposition of a natural affinity or emotional co-dependence of the modern self and civil society. Indeed, society before the revolution in America had seemed to depend on a collective and contractual management of love and anger, a politics of affect that had long underwritten social stability. Individualism – the rights of 'man', as it were – risked a torrent of unbounded passion. When Thomas Paine (1737–1809) anonymously published *Common Sense* in early 1776, therefore, it definitively formulated a new script that would unite the individual American self with a modern notion of civil society and its form of government. Importantly, however, for all that this script delivered in the name of rights, and of reason, it was an affective script and it appealed explicitly to a sense or kind of feeling.

We absolutely cannot overestimate the impact of *Common Sense*. There are various ways to play with the prodigiousness of the circulation of Paine's pamphlet, but one biographer calculates that the pamphlet is the 'greatest best-seller ever' if viewed proportional to the size of the population at the time. In 1776 alone it sold perhaps 100,000 copies, and circulated far more widely than this. Hardly anybody can have escaped noticing it and, importantly, it also sold in huge quantities in Britain and in France (in translation).[19] It was the first piece that dared to be publicly explicit about the promise of republicanism, and as such its influence was profound.

To begin, let us observe the tenor of Paine's introduction. The contents of his work on 'Common Sense', he tells us straight off, are 'sentiments' that work against 'custom'. That the sentiments are right will be acknowledged in 'time', which 'makes more converts than reason'.[20] Here then, programmatically, we have an assertion that the feeling of what is right is ultimately that which is persuasive, not what is right in the abstract. And the feeling of what is right takes time. It is a pamphlet written because the 'Affections' of all 'Lovers of Mankind' are interested in such a cause as America, which, Paine avers, is a universal cause. It is directed against tyranny, which he says 'is the Concern of every Man to whom Nature hath given the Power of feeling'.[21] *Common Sense*, let it be understood from the outset, was an affective appeal to a feeling audience in the language of sentiment. It is reason and rights pitched at the *sense* of its readers, requiring not so much an understanding as an intuition of its correctness. The first chapter of the pamphlet also begins in this register, for it frames the nature of government and of society in terms of how they safeguard – positively and negatively respectively – *happiness*. Paine has us avert our eyes and cover our ears to protect against the bedazzlement of colonial Kingship, noting that governments are for 'freedom and security' – a qualification of the definition of happiness, then – which is confirmed by 'the simple voice of nature and of reason'.[22] A lot of weight gets put on the voice of reason, but what is the 'simple voice of nature' but an affect, a sense, a conscience, a feeling? It is the wellspring in Paine's later work – entitled, appropriately enough, *The Age of Reason* (1794) – of the pure belief in God (Paine had read Spinoza, at least, and seems to have been heavily influenced by him). Not for nothing did Paine open his account of *The Age of Reason*, a sustained attack on established religion, with a profession of faith. It was written both to destruct and to limit destruction, for much as it pointed the way for freethinkers to abandon national churches, so it also sought to protect that 'morality . . . humanity, and . . . theology that is true'. These things were held by the 'mind of man' in communication 'with itself'.[23] In his profession of faith Paine hoped for 'happiness beyond this life', expressed a *belief* in equality, and a *belief* that religious duties involved 'doing justice, loving mercy, and endeavouring to make our fellow-creatures happy'.[24] Paine's whole outlook, based as it was in rights derived from 'nature', was about affective practices for affective ends, in this life and the next. If there is reason in the destruction of biblical texts and of churches as political schemes, such reason is ultimately bounded by belief: personal belief, projected and scripted so as to persuade; and by affect: the desire for and the projected means to acquire and disseminate happiness. Later in *Common Sense* that 'voice of nature' is said to be 'weeping' at the continued relationship of Britain and colony.[25] To be sure, there is God in this nature, for Paine actually argues that America's discovery was vouchsafed by God just in time for the Reformation, so that the persecuted might have an open sanctuary to which they could flee.[26]

Cover our eyes and ears as we may, Paine is nevertheless reaching out to the human sensorium. 'Common sense' is not, as we might now style it, a sort of quotidian intelligence; it is not *just what gets done*; it is not custom; it is a shared *feeling*. Who partakes in it? Well, nobody, at first, and then, with guidance, everybody. It is the wonderful irony of a work like Paine's that in claiming to demonstrate what is popularly felt it in fact creates that popular feeling. It is a sense that becomes common after the reading of the script. If it is asserted that it is the reasoned content of the script that gets adopted as feeling right, then it is only so effective because of the affective packaging of that content. Paine was telling Americans, showing them, how to feel.

The first part of this was to show them that any prevailing attachment to the British crown was an aspect of 'national pride', not one of reason. It had to be put aside to get at 'modes and forms, the plain truth', for 'any prepossession in favour of a rotten constitution of government will disable us from discerning a good one'.[27] Step one in learning how to feel like a republican, therefore, is to control or shut off pride in the monarchy, for monarchy, as he goes on to point out, is not the 'means of happiness' in the world, but the means of 'misery to mankind'.[28] Thus the orientation of thinking on this issue is explicitly affective. If pride is thrown off, what is to replace it? In describing the state of affairs in America, Paine motions towards 'simple facts, plain arguments, and common sense', but in bidding his reader to cast off the pride of prejudice against revolt, he appeals not merely to the reader's reason, but to 'his reason and his feelings'.[29] Those feelings encapsulated a universal claim of Christian brotherhood and 'triumph in the generosity of the sentiment'. Those who could not grasp the truth of Paine's argument were said to be blind: 'weak men, who *cannot* see; prejudiced men, who *will not* see'.[30] Seeing, feeling and reasoning are, in Paine's understanding of common sense, all one. For he bids his readers to 'examine the passions and feelings of mankind' and asks how a man – explicitly a man – wronged by tyranny, could 'hereafter love, honour, and faithfully serve' that power.[31] Those who, having suffered losses at the hands of British power, could nevertheless reconcile with that power, were 'unworthy of the name of husband, father, friend, or lover, and ... have the heart of a coward, and the spirit of a sycophant'.[32] These are explicit claims that the right path is unavoidable to the right-feeling individual, the wrong path being the domain of those deranged by passions. Paine was 'trying' the situation 'by those feelings and affections which nature justifies, and without which we should be incapable of discharging the social duties of life, or enjoying the felicities of it', and yet in the next breath he claims that the subjection of America is 'repugnant to reason'.[33] Perhaps there is a clue in this, for the experience he implies is one of disgust, not one of rationality. Rationality sits in the background. Its contravention is highlighted by a feeling of recoil. Americans could no more forgive Britain than a lover could 'forgive the ravisher of his mistress'. The set of 'unextinguishable feelings' aroused by such horrors were, said Paine, 'implanted in us' by the 'Almighty' for 'good and wise purposes':

> They are the guardians of his image in our hearts. They distinguish us from the herd of common animals. The social compact would dissolve, and justice be extirpated from the earth, or have only a casual existence were we callous to the touches of affection. The robber, and the murderer, would often escape unpunished, did not the injuries which our tempers sustain, provoke us into justice.[34]

It was not *reason* that set men apart, that inspired their quest for justice, but *feelings*, and, in particular, *hurt feelings*. For all this, the new American constitution was to be formed 'in a cool deliberate manner', so as to guarantee 'the greatest sum of individual happiness, with the least national expense' (here Paine quoted, and ringingly endorsed, the words of radical Italian jurist Giacinto Dragonetti).[35] Here was a preliminary affective orientation to nation building. Forged on the rancour of dishonour and wounded affections, the new polity would assert itself not through pure reason, but through controlled affect. The tyrant having been expelled, this too was only common *sense*.

One of the Calmest Acts of Reason

Paine had asserted that 'Male and female are the distinctions of nature.'[36] They were different not by degree, but in kind. Politically and socially, when considering the construction of a new polity, they simply did not figure. Hence *The Rights of Man*, which Paine had published in 1791, really was about the rights of *men*, as they were given by nature. Women were assumed to lack reason and to be guided by passions, and they had therefore been excluded from the freedoms won by the French Revolution of 1789. Female physiology – afflicted with wandering wombs and nervous weakness – made them unfit for education. Their place in the revolution, therefore, as was implicit in *Common Sense*, was as wives and daughters, not as human beings. As the revolutionary impetus took root in Europe, so France's new republic was founded, like the American one before it, on the natural rights of *men*, the unique holders and arbiters of reason. As the Jacobins swept all before them, the Rousseauian notion of educating women only for the pleasure of men held sway.[37]

Yet rereading the revolutionary texts that propped up those new regimes, one cannot escape their affective pleading. Reason, such as it was, was irrevocably entangled in the bundle of passions and feelings that came with appeals to 'nature'. The breach in logic, in reason itself, did not escape notice. In her dedication of *The Vindication of the Rights of Woman* (1792) to Talleyrand, Mary Wollstonecraft warned that, unless women's lack of reason be proven, the first constitution 'founded on reason' would be nothing if not tyrannical. It would be unjust and inconsistent.[38] Yet the challenge, a challenge she accepted, was actually Wollstonecraft's, for women appeared to lack reason because their minds were in such an unhealthy state. To demonstrate that they could and should be educated was, in the 1790s, no small task. Females, she asserted, were not treated as 'human creatures', but as 'women', a term that derogated them to something distinctly other. Men were 'anxious to make them alluring mistresses' rather than 'rational wives', and had succeeded in normalizing this effort to a degree that women themselves 'are only anxious to inspire love'.[39] Women's pathetic minds needed to be educated. Men's attachment to reason needed to expand.

In John Opie's depiction of Wollstonecraft from about this time, therefore, she is shown doing that which few would have countenanced. She is at study, a face of concentration. There is a steely gaze at the viewer, as if perhaps slightly irritated by the distraction from work that will be picked up again momentarily. The posture is bent forward, as if immediately prior she had been poring over the pages of the book in front of her. Those pages appear blank, which is perhaps a political expediency. Nevertheless, above it lie the inkwell and

quill that were Wollstonecraft's making. The blank page may in fact
be waiting for Wollstonecraft to fill it. The portrait therefore shows
a pause in something otherwise active and intellectual. In its want
of affective pretension or posture, and in the absence of any kind of
romanticism in its composition, this is a perfectly targeted projection
of the female reason for which Wollstonecraft argued. Hers is not
a countenance to be dismissed as being in any fashion overwrought
by the activity of her mind, nor by the tumult of her emotions. It
bespeaks the potential of the woman of reason in a sensible age.

Wollstonecraft's private life did not afford her the opportunity to
realize her hopes, or to live in the manner of Opie's representation.

John Opie, *Mary Wollstonecraft (Mrs William Godwin)*, c. 1790–91, oil on canvas.

A public statement of the importance of engendering reason in the female mind, and with Wollstonecraft as the exemplar of the advantages of so doing, was undermined by lived experience of the passions. She herself became entrapped in anxiety to inspire love, and was repeatedly scorned. She was in Paris during the Terror and had backed the 'wrong' side, putting her life at risk from those who were only too ready to police political thought with the guillotine. She had fallen in love, in Paris, with the American Gilbert Imlay, and had conceived a child by him. In difficult circumstances, he declared them to be married, even though they were not, in order to afford her the protection of American citizenship. She was utterly deceived by a man who, Wollstonecraft's advanced political views on the rights of women notwithstanding, used her to satisfy his desires, without fidelity and without the commitment that she had shown him. Her hopes dashed and dashed again by Imlay's philandering, Wollstonecraft attempted suicide twice. Wollstonecraft's life and her writings are so well known that I do not propose to enter into her biography in great depth or to any great extent. Her particulars, in extraordinarily personal detail, are available for anyone to read at leisure.[40] Instead I wish to offer a forensic examination of two of her letters to Imlay, her estranged lover.

The first is a suicide note. The second, the letter she wrote after having been resuscitated. They are of amazing value, not merely for their drama and pathos, but for exemplifying the distinctive affective style of Wollstonecraft herself, and her entanglement of sentiment or emotion and reason. They are a snapshot of the embodied Enlightenment: of sensibility as a vehicle for rational thought and rational action. Yet they are also filled with a profound sadness that afflicted Wollstonecraft despite her best efforts. In a prior letter, she had told Imlay that 'Every emotion yields to an overwhelming flood of sorrow.' The tide of affection was drowning her. 'I am unable to tear up by the roots the propensity to affection which has been the torment of my life,' she wrote in October 1795. But, she warned portentously, 'life will have an end!'[41]

The suicide note follows. I include it in full before going back to analyse it closely:

> I write to you now on my knees; imploring you to send my
> child and the maid with —— , to Paris, to be consigned to

the care of Madame ——, rue ——, section de ——. Should they be removed, —— can give their direction.

Let the maid have all my clothes, without distinction.

Pray pay the cook her wages, and do not mention the confession which I forced from her – a little sooner or later is of no consequence. Nothing but my extreme stupidity could have rendered me blind so long. Yet, whilst you assured me that you had no attachment, I thought we might still have lived together.

I shall make no comments on your conduct; or any appeal to the world. Let my wrongs sleep with me! Soon, very soon, shall I be at peace. When you receive this, my burning head will be cold.

I would encounter a thousand deaths, rather than a night like the last. Your treatment has thrown my mind into a state of chaos; yet I am serene. I go to find comfort, and my only fear is, that my poor body will be insulted by an endeavour to recall my hated existence. But I shall plunge into the Thames where there is the least chance of my being snatched from the death I seek.

God bless you! May you never know by experience what you have made me endure. Should your sensibility ever awake, remorse will find its way to your heart; and, in the midst of business and sensual pleasure, I shall appear before you, the victim of your deviation from rectitude.[42]

On first reading, one seems automatically to look for the affective content, that is, for the overwhelming emotional upheaval that would lead to self-destruction. And one finds it. Wollstonecraft's mind is in 'a state of chaos'. Her existence is 'hated'. She implicitly separates mind and body in her fear that her body will be rescued in the attempt to drown herself. It is as if it is an innocent vessel for a mind already deranged beyond hope. She tries to impress on Imlay the experience she has had to 'endure'. This allusion to suffering suggests a patience long smashed by chronic passion. She describes herself as 'victim', the object of injustice, the result of which is a breaking of mind and of heart.

One could write it like this. It would be, perhaps, the Hollywood version, but it would be only half of a more complex story. Examine the preamble of the letter. It is of practicalities, though it comes in the form of a supplication, or else absolute defeat, 'on my knees'. Wollstonecraft is not so lost to her chaotic mind that she has not thought through arrangements for the care of her daughter. She bequeaths her personal effects. She looks after the cook (who has confessed knowledge of Imlay's new mistress). There is, in this, an attachment to the world she is set to depart; a sense of duty or obligation that is suggestive of a reasoned appreciation of the social contract being broken by her actions. Perhaps such arrangements are not so unusual, but opening the note as they do, they set an incongruous tone to what follows, which is in turn made complex by the way Wollstonecraft shapes her passion.

That Wollstonecraft had been unable to detect – to *see* – Imlay's new transgression against her love, she calls 'extreme stupidity'. Stupid, in 1795, did not mean what stupid tends to mean today, referring as it does to a person's wits or level of knowledge. In the 1792 edition of Johnson's *Dictionary*, to be 'stupid' was to be 'dull, wanting sensibility, wanting apprehension, heavy, sluggish of understanding'.[43] From the Latin *stupere* – to be stunned or benumbed – stupid has more of stupor about it than of a lack of intelligence. Insofar as it was a hindrance to understanding, it was nevertheless couched in a dulling of sensibility. When Wollstonecraft says she was 'blind', this metaphor for the loss of a sense is in perfect accord with her 'stupidity'. She is not reproaching herself for being slow witted, but is expressing dismay at the long-term impact of her suffering on her sensibilities.

Wollstonecraft implies her feverishness – a sense of dis-ease caused by passion – will be cooled by the Thames. She wishes to be at peace, yet professes, incongruously, already to be 'serene'. It is the foreknowledge of the 'comfort' she will find in death that makes her so, perhaps, but – going by Johnson's definitions – it is difficult to see how Wollstonecraft can be 'calm, placid, quiet' or 'unruffled, undisturbed, even of temper', while also being in a 'state of chaos'. It seems to me that Wollstonecraft is here making a claim to proportionality. Her projected act – to drown herself in the river – is presented not as an act of madness or desperation. It is not a cry for help. It is an act made inevitable by circumstance, namely, betrayal of the heart. At the peak of Wollstonecraft's distress, her actions were undertaken with an even assurance that they were the correct actions.

The letter concludes with a gesture towards the justification for her impending death: Imlay's 'deviation from rectitude'. She is mortified by having become that against which her whole intellectual life had been set. She is the jilted mistress. She is deceived in love. She is the pleading heart. And he, the callous cad. For all her appeals to the value of reason, it is to sensibility that Wollstonecraft ultimately appeals. She does not demand that Imlay reflect on what he has done in an abstract, reasoned way, but hopes that his 'sensibility . . . awake', that he might feel 'remorse' in his 'heart'. There is something substantial about the remorse she conjures up, for she wishes it to afflict him in the coolness of his business practices and in the gratification of his senses, that is, in the act of having sex with his new mistress. It is not a superficial quality that Imlay is said to lack, but a qualitative lack of feeling. If these had been the last words ever to spill from the hand of Wollstonecraft, we should have had to decipher the importance of a strident advocate for the extension of male reason to women making an uncanny appeal for a man to learn how to feel.

These were not her last words, however. Pulled from the river, Wollstonecraft was reanimated. Her next letter to Imlay is as follows:

> I have only to lament, that, when the bitterness of death was past, I was inhumanly brought back to life and misery. But a fixed determination is not to be baffled by disappointment; nor will I allow that to be a frantic attempt, which was one of the calmest acts of reason. In this respect, I am only accountable to myself. Did I care for what is termed reputation, it is by other circumstances that I should be dishonoured.
>
> You say, 'that you know not how to extricate ourselves out of the wretchedness into which we have been plunged.' You are extricated long since. – But I forbear to comment. – If I am condemned to live longer, it is a living death.
>
> It appears to me, that you lay much more stress on delicacy, than on principle; for I am unable to discover what sentiment of delicacy would have been violated, by your visiting a wretched friend – if indeed you have any friendship for me. – But since your new attachment is the only thing sacred in your eyes, I am silent – Be happy! My complaints shall never more damp your enjoyment – perhaps I am mistaken in

supposing that even my death could, for more than a moment. – This is what you call magnanimity. – It is happy for yourself, that you possess this quality in the highest degree.

Your continually asserting, that you will do all in your power to contribute to my comfort (when you only allude to pecuniary assistance), appears to me a flagrant breach of delicacy. – I want not such vulgar comfort, nor will I accept it. I never wanted but your heart – That gone, you have nothing more to give. Had I only poverty to fear, I should not shrink from life. – Forgive me then, if I say, that I shall consider any direct or indirect attempt to supply my necessities, as an insult which I have not merited – and as rather done out of tenderness for your own reputation, than for me. Do not mistake me; I do not think that you value money (therefore I will not accept what you do not care for) though I do much less, because certain privations are not painful for me. When I am dead, respect for yourself will make you take care of the child.

I write with difficulty – probably I shall never write to you again. – Adieu!

God bless you![44]

The beginning of this letter is striking in its naming of the act that saved her life as 'inhuman'. To understand it, we have to take seriously her firm conviction that she should die. In the rather strange reflective moments of a period after one's own death is supposed to have occurred, we might expect something like remorse or even more evidence of chaos. Wollstonecraft is defiant, in the full extent of her feelings, that her act was *reasonable*. Not only was this a 'fixed determination' that endures, Wollstonecraft also cuts off any possibility of being reduced to her emotions. It was not a 'frantic attempt' (*frantick*, in Johnson's *Dictionary*, means 'mad; deprived of understanding by violent madness; outrageously and turbulently mad', or 'transported by violence of passion'). On the contrary, it 'was one of the calmest acts of reason'. Here we see the qualification of the word 'serene' in her previous letter. It recapitulates the notion that suicide, though couched in terms of a feverishness and a broken heart, was a rational and proportional act. The dishonour of having attempted suicide has no meaning, for she has already been dishonoured in life by Imlay to an order of magnitude far greater than anything she can bring upon herself.

It is implied in Wollstonecraft's letter that Imlay has not visited her because it would be considered 'indelicate'. Here Wollstonecraft plays on the ambiguity of the term, for Imlay clearly has referred to delicacy as 'politeness, gentleness of manners', but Wollstonecraft, by referring to her 'wretchedness', demands delicacy meaning 'tenderness, scrupulousness, mercifulness' (definitions six and eight of 'delicacy' in Johnson's 1792 *Dictionary*). She is again accusing Imlay of lacking heart, of prioritizing social form over interpersonal substance. Having chided him and invoked his new mistress, she declares 'I am silent', even though she has already said plenty. The imperative 'Be happy!' must not be misconstrued. It would be a sardonic demand in the context, if we take it to be Wollstonecraft's wish for Imlay to be *pleased* or *glad* with his new woman, and in his life in general. These might be our understandings of 'happy', but cannot have been hers. Happy in Johnson's *Dictionary* refers us to 'felicity', which in turn refers us to 'blissfulness'. We find an important qualification of this in Johnson's definition of 'happiness': 'Felicity; state in which the desires are satisfied'. This, then, is what Wollstonecraft scornfully implores Imlay to do. She might as well have said, referring to his 'new attachment', his 'sacred' *thing*: fill your boots! As the following line attests, this is about his 'enjoyment', which is all surface and no feeling.

Wollstonecraft then refers to her 'magnanimity'. Again, we should be mistaken to read this as a kind of generosity in forgiveness on Wollstonecraft's part. In the 1790s the word was much closer to its literal meaning: 'elevation of soul'. It was a 'greatness of mind' akin to 'bravery'. It was an elevation of sentiment. It was a quality that, once again, calls forth an admixture of reason and emotion, of mind and soul. When she says that it is 'happy' for Imlay to have such a degree of this quality, here she is surely being sarcastic, for he has, in her opinion, showed precisely none of this quality. The misdirection, 'happy', is a way of referring to Imlay's opinion of himself as magnanimous. He is mistaken, for he mistakes the gratification of desire for bravery of action.

The penultimate paragraph refers to Wollstonecraft's absolute distaste for appearing to be a kept mistress, essentially a prostitute, living on and for the money of a heart that is lost to her. In calling this 'an insult which I have not merited' she draws attention to the incommensurability of their view on the relationship. She was in love and wanted Imlay's heart. He knows only the fickle and fleeting needs of desire. If he now wishes to send money, it is not for her sake, she avers, but out of 'tenderness for your own reputation'. This is another affective inversion; another pointed barb at Imlay's faulty sensibilities. For, as we have seen, tenderness was always predicated on the other. To be tender for oneself is a perverse anxiety for one's own well-being. It is, ultimately, selfish, but also superficial. Wollstonecraft is clear that it is *reputation* that is at stake here, an outward-facing representation of himself, not his own conscience. It is this, and this alone, that will oblige him in his fatherly duties, not any sense of genuine parental affection.

In this letter Wollstonecraft exemplifies a radical Enlightenment understanding of the relation of body and soul, reason and emotion, thinking and feeling. She demonstrates the callousness of living by reason and sense alone, forcefully expressing a belief that the mind is lost without heart, even as the heart is still ultimately governed by the mind. Her tumult is irrevocably emotional, but no less a part of reason for that. She was, as Syndy McMillen Conger put it, 'a disciple of sensibility', but never lost entirely to it. Sensibility was the vehicle of her reason, as inseparable from the workings of her mind as her soul from her body.[45]

In a Sad, Sad State of Decomposition

If the 1790s were full of turmoil for Wollstonecraft, situated in an extraordinary political landscape and centred in the great European metropolises, for others the decade was entirely bucolic, though perhaps nonetheless animated on a personal level. Edward Jenner (1749–1823) is one of the world's best-known historical medical figures.[46] A student of the renowned Scottish surgeon and anatomist John Hunter (1728–1793), Jenner is famed for his pioneering work in smallpox vaccination, serving to set in motion the processes and institutions that would ultimately eradicate smallpox from the earth (but not until 1980). Jenner's first son was born in the year of the French Revolution, 1789. By 1796 Jenner had performed the first human-to-human inoculation with cowpox (the first vaccination). And by 1798 he had made his findings known to the world. All of this from rural Gloucestershire. It is a story that tends, typically, to promote certain progressive exemplars of medical reason. Jenner's vaccine experiments have become the rhetorical starting point for the development of the 'controlled trial' in pharmacological research. Jenner's victory – of successfully establishing the practice of vaccination, of the endorsement of Parliament and the institutions of medicine – is touted as a victory of reason over a rampant quackery that wished to preserve smallpox because of pecuniary interest. I have major doubts about such narratives, not least because Jenner did not actually understand how or why vaccination worked, and neither did anyone else. The success story of medical reason is easy to tell from the point of view of how things eventually turned out. Time has told, as it were. Yet even the vaccine work was nothing like as reasonable as it appears. Nevertheless, this is not the story I want to tell here.[47]

Jenner's life provides us with an alternative narrative: one of inductive reasoning, hope, failure, despair, pain and grief. It ends in the derangement of the senses and in an inglorious death. One of the true medical luminaries of the age of reason was a deeply anxious, melancholic and pained man, by his own account. His testimony concerning these lows and emotional wounds, filtered through the working knowledge of a medical expert, gives us some clues about the affective style available to a country surgeon working in the decades either side of the year 1800.

Jenner's knowledge of the heart and of the self, of understanding and of the world, was of a different order entirely to that of Wollstonecraft. The world of sensibility was not open to him in anything like the same way as it was for those political and literary figures in the world of Wollstonecraft and Paine. Knowledge, for Jenner, was both a precondition for and a product of medical practice. Understanding was a complex cocktail of empirical work and prevailing custom in professional practice.

Jenner's greatest failure in life was his work on tuberculosis. In terms of time spent in research and experimentation, Jenner spent longer on this than on vaccination in the early part of his career. By 1790 he was already presenting his theories on the causes of tuberculosis to his peers in Gloucestershire, to little acclaim. In his spare time when not traversing the countryside visiting patients, he was up to his elbows in the carcases of various animals, including humans, looking for evidence of tuberculosis across the species barrier. He was convinced that the cysts he found inside the lungs of pigs, sheep, cows and people were the product of hydatids – wormlike parasites – and all of his attention was put on proving this to be the cause of the disease and thereafter finding a cure. He was, of course, hopelessly wrong. His peers in the medical community thought his ideas ridiculous, his vaccination fame notwithstanding, and his findings went nowhere, as did their influence.

All this would be nothing to the purpose if it were not for the personal consequences of this failure. From a reputational point of view, Jenner (eventually) accrued enough honour from vaccination to not have to worry about other failures. But the question of tuberculosis was at the very centre of Jenner's life and well-being. His wife likely already had the disease when they married. His first-born son, Edward, would contract the disease when still a boy. And his son's tutor, who lived with the Jenners, also died of TB. The Jenner household was afflicted with this mysterious disease while Jenner laboured in his rooms to try to unravel and defeat it, to no avail. His wife, his son and his son's tutor all predeceased Jenner from TB. Even the subject of that famous first vaccination eventually died of TB. For all the lives Jenner saved, directly or indirectly, from smallpox, he felt his own losses with greater acuity, coming as they did from a different and stubbornly vexing disease. It is the emotions surrounding these diseases and deaths in Jenner's family, as well as the emotions evoked by his own terminal decline, that interest me here. They are personal, but in their expression revealing of the affective style of a thwarted medical hero.

The assumption that Jenner carried into his TB research was similar to that he carried into his smallpox research: it was a disease caused by 'our familiarity with an animal that nature intended to keep separate from man'.[48] The connection of the etiology of disease with the transgression of a divine natural law – essentially, a moral failing of humanity – was par for the course in the late eighteenth century. It gave to disease an affective quality connected to sin. The presence of disease did not mark out the individual as guilty so much as confirm the condition of humanity as sinful. For many in this period, preventing a disease was a form of blasphemy, for it went against divine intention. Jenner was far too pragmatic for this. The communion of men and beasts was a fact that could not be undone. As a doctor it was only reasonable to try to come to terms with the consequences.

Edward's tutor, Worgan, died first, in 1809, by which time Edward was already ill. In London on business, Jenner made his way home with 'a heavy Heart'.[49] Between May and the following February, Jenner wrote regularly of his spirits. He complained, once his son's haemorrhaging became regular, that he had 'but very little ground to rest my hopes upon', knowing from experience exactly where the disease would lead. We find in Jenner a curious mix of terror and fatalism: 'Death is a terrible [that is, most frightening] visitor in whatever shape he approaches us, and this is a frightful one indeed,' he wrote, adding 'But God's will be done!'[50] There is, throughout Jenner's correspondence, a resignation about divine intervention that mitigates his earthly sorrow. It is a common enough rhetorical device for the period, and one might pursue the extent to which the uttering of acquiescence to God's will actually worked as a salve for painful emotions, but given Jenner's background such religious fatalism is surprising. He spent his life arguing against those who, with regard to smallpox, taunted him with 'God's will'. The vaccine, for many, was precisely a subversion of God's will. I speculate that Jenner saw his success with the vaccine experiments and his failure with TB as also signs of God's will. Were he meant to save his son, it would have come to pass. As Edward declined, therefore, we see Jenner locked in an emotive process where he strove to submit to religious feelings that could justify and explain his son's disease, and in which he largely failed. Jenner's store in God's will notwithstanding, his spirits were earthly, his emotions fitting for a grieved and then bereaved man of the early nineteenth century.

He told his friend that he was always within earshot of Edward's 'hollow cough', and the experience left him 'most miserably depress'd'.[51] Of course, *depression*, as a medical diagnosis, did not exist, so we must take Jenner at his word.[52] He was pressed down, dejected, humbled by helplessness. It is a physical description of his emotional state. We must imagine Jenner literally feeling the weight, the heaviness, of his son's disease. To another correspondent he called it 'a melancholy prospect' – referring now to an outlook of gloom rather than anything to do with black bile – scarcely knowing 'how to bear it'. Thus, another allusion to a heavy weight. Again, immediately following on: 'The decrees of Heaven, however harsh they may seem, must be correct, & the grand Lesson we have to learn is humility.'[53] To another correspondent – a fellow doctor – Jenner complained he was 'as moping as the Owl, and all day long sit brooding over Melancholy' as his 'poor Boy' wasted 'inch by inch'. Yet here Jenner raises himself above the common lot and confides that 'The ray of Hope is denied only a medical Man when he sees his Child dying of pulmonary Consumption; all other Mortals enjoy its flattering light.'[54] Experience checked any emotional delusion. In the figure of his ailing son there was no hope to cling to for a man who knew the course of the disease.

Jenner's inner torment reached its pitch when Edward finally died. The death – a 'melancholy event' – took from Jenner 'much of my earthly comfort'. It was an event the coming of which was clearly seen, and yet when it did come 'it was dreadful [that is, it filled him with fear] to me, & my reason almost forsook me'. He could not understand, when death made 'such gradual approaches', why his mind was not reconciled to the event. But, he said, separating reason and understanding from feeling: 'the edge of sensibility is not thus to be blunted'.[55] Jenner did not lose his reason in grief, but found it through grief's moderation. The emotional salve that cleared his mind was faith. Edward's death 'fix't my eye more steadfastly than ever on that Being in whose hands is omnipotence, and whose infinite wisdom *must* direct every thing for the best purposes'. Saying again, 'God's will be done!', Jenner was ready to 'kiss the rod with submissive reverence'.[56] He was, in the end, but one of God's creatures, subservient, unknowing, but trusting. Here was relief of the physical burden he carried on the death of a son from a disease he knew but could neither explain nor cure.

Jenner's wife, who had long suffered with pulmonary problems, died five years later. Even though she had suffered with consumption for their whole married life together, her death came upon Jenner as a 'severe shock', the terminal decline being rapid. Though 'Her departure was mark'd with that sweet serenity' of one being 'blessed' with a termination of suffering, Jenner felt the 'irreparable loss', a 'privation' that he could scarcely describe.[57]

Two months later Jenner was making an effort with that description, trying to understand what was happening to himself. His friend wished to visit, but Jenner told him he 'will find him not, but only a part of him, and that part, in a sad sad state of decomposition'.[58]

The double 'sad' is worth a moment's focus, for few words have been emptied of meaning in recent times to a similar extent. A contemporary reading of sad finds little of pathos in it, and hardly a meaningful reflection on grief and the physical withering away of the body. Yet Jenner intended to convey just this. Examine the definitions of 'sad' at the end of the eighteenth century and one will find a long list of particularly unpleasant feelings and physical qualities. Sad is, following Johnson's *Dictionary*, 'sorrowful; full of grief'; 'habitually melancholy; heavy; gloomy; not gay'; 'serious; not light; not volatile; grave'; 'afflictive; calamitous'; 'bad; inconvenient; vexatious'; 'dark coloured'; 'heavy, weighty, ponderous'; 'cohesive; not light; firm; close'. Judging by the context and contents of Jenner's correspondence, his use of 'sad' conveyed all of this, but doubled. A darkness and a heaviness shrouded Jenner's being such that he was losing himself. Why? Because 'The mind & body act reciprocally on each other. In me, the qualities of both have undergone a considerable change; consequently their union, forming the Animal, differs essentially from that compound you once knew, when this union was more correct.'[59] The somewhat lyrical style belies a general despondency that informed Jenner's own resignation. As he told another medical correspondent, the 'doleful event' of his wife's death had caused Jenner to seclude himself at home: 'a public place by no means harmonizes with the present state of my feelings'. Regarding his 'privations', Jenner was wont to use metaphors of a surgical bent, perhaps unsurprisingly given his work. Yet when he says they 'cut deep' we should take him at his word, for 'in a mind possess'd of sensibility, [they] produce sensations of the most painful kind'.[60] Jenner felt physically wounded by grief. It was as much sensation as emotion, and the pain he felt was literal.

As Jenner's grief was moderated by time, with the sharpness of pain diminishing, so his 'miserably low' spirits abided, enveloping him in 'mists & clouds'. In solitude he was sinking 'into the Earth'.[61] Eventually, Jenner did so sink, though not before a stroke brought on a case of hyperaesthesia that left him unable to bear the sound of clinking plates and glasses. His domestic retreat, which was identified with his burden, became a torture. In sum, Jenner's language of emotion, his use of figures and medical imagination, mark out his affective style as particularly afflicted by grief, consoled in part by faith, but frustrated likewise by a shortcoming of human knowledge.

This celebrated country doctor never shied away from discussing the precise nature of his emotional pain, never put on a front of stoical imperturbability. A man defined by history as an embodiment of medical reason and the value of new knowledge was, in the final analysis, defined by his 'sensibility', however far removed his life has seemed from the epicentre of that particular age.

FIVE

SENSELESSNESS AND INSENSIBILITY

J ane Austen published *Sense and Sensibility* in 1811. It marks the apogee of what has become known as the 'age of sensibility' among historians. In different ways, men and women alike, especially among Britain's elite, were known for their finely tuned nerves, their propensity to succumb to fits of tears and melancholy, with elite women in particular being renowned for their tendency to be overcome by hysteria, 'vapours' and melancholy.[1] The sentimental novel, a marker of eighteenth-century literary innovation, was at the forefront of both praise and criticism for this nervous era, where the passions were supposed to be easily disturbed by flights of fancy, and where English reserve could be upset by tales of romance. Key to the understanding of this 'sensible' age is the conflation of nerves, senses and passions, so that feelings – literally, that which is detected by the senses – were translated into practices that defined both public and private life, from discourses of illness and disease, to the politics of courtship and marriage, to the very identity of the polity. All of this has become familiar, even commonplace, among historians. When looking for emotional change over time, the eighteenth-century age of sensibility has become a common departure point, leaching steadily into romanticism and sentimentality, which often serve to characterize the nineteenth century.

In this chapter I want to overlook all of this and examine the passage from long eighteenth century into the long nineteenth afresh. My reasons for so doing arise from a suspicion that much of the copious literature on sensibility focuses disproportionately on the smallest class of people. That the aristocratic elite left behind the best traces of their existence is compellingly attractive for the historian looking for something substantial to dig around in. But the rest of the population, whose experiences may not have been so conveniently recorded, especially for the historian of emotions, does not necessarily fit the characterization of the time as one of sensibility. On the contrary, my encounter with the eighteenth century has tended to foreground callousness, cruelty, aloofness and depravity. It is not that the age of sensibility is a myth, for such an age certainly existed for some. It is rather that it fails to characterize the age in a broad sense. Looking again at Austen's *Sense and Sensibility*, even here we find a surfeit of cold-heartedness and 'unfeeling behaviour'. It is only in contrast to coldness, as it were, that sensibility derives its meaning. It is sensibility's other, and examples of it are legion.[2]

My focus here, therefore, is on the absence of feeling, and the extent to which this lack defined social practices in the long eighteenth century. In truth, getting to the heart of the age of insensibility also relies heavily on sources left by the elite, but focuses on their outward gaze at the social other, rather than on their internal reflections on elite experience. In particular, I will examine the connection between insensibility or callousness and moral decay.

This leads, in due course, to a reappraisal of the embrace, among certain members of the nineteenth-century elite, of calculation, coolness and equanimity for the sake of the public good, especially in matters of public health. The appropriation of callousness as a kind of affective state, with its own set of emotional practices, is shown to depend, once again, on a certain classist gaze that justifies unfeelingness in the hands of the 'civilized' but condemns it when it is expressed by the masses. Yet the culture of insensibility in the eighteenth century is umbilically connected to that of the nineteenth, and indeed the latter depends entirely on the dark unsaid of the age of sensibility for its justification. The strands of the chapter are brought together to explain the burgeoning cultures of science, utility and experiment in the second half of the nineteenth century.

Four Stages of Cruelty

In William Hogarth's (1697–1764) well-known series of engravings *The Four Stages of Cruelty* (1751), we follow the career of Tom Nero, from youth to death, in a downward spiral of wantonness. At its heart is an apparently simple thesis, recapitulated over the centuries since the time of Thomas Aquinas, that cruelty to animals perpetuated as a child will harden the heart, and lead to cruelty to humans in adulthood. Immanuel Kant is famed for having said much the same thing, arguing that the animal served as an analogue of the human in the formation of a child's sense of relationships, and that the heart-hardening process began in puerile cruelties. Rather less well known is that Kant was referring directly to Hogarth's prints.[3] Yet I have long maintained that there must be a problem with the attachment of this thesis to what Hogarth depicts, for there is an unreconciled tension between cruelty and the hardened heart.[4]

Cruelty, as commonly understood throughout the eighteenth and nineteenth centuries, was connected to the wantonness of an action or practice. Put another way, for an act to be cruel it had to be carried out in full knowledge and awareness – despite the feeling – that it was wrong. Recent research into the complexities of psychopathic pathologies has upturned the standard view that such people are dangerous because they are incapable of empathy. Rather, some psychopaths at least are shown to be able to enter quite readily into the emotional suffering of others, but their empathy does not hold them back from hurtful actions. In this sense, the practices of these psychopaths have been termed 'empathic cruelty', to demonstrate that they are carried out in full cognizance that they cause pain and suffering.[5] It is this kind of cruelty that early campaigners in the eighteenth and nineteenth centuries tried to stamp out. There was a deeply held concern that certain sections of society, including both the indolent poor and the indolent rich, were cruel for kicks, putting greater weight in the gratification of their own desires than in the harm caused to others. Cruelty was wrong, in these terms, because it was immoral. Immorality, in turn, presupposed something awry with the feelings – the sensibility – of the immoral; for the moral sense was a person's guide through civilized life. Cruelty was not a deadening of the moral sense, but a wilful practice of ignoring it.

Distinct from acts of cruelty was the state of being callous. Callousness implies an absence of feeling, a lack of moral sense. It is, in essence, what people have commonly understood of the psychopath: an inability to enter into the emotional condition of another and therefore to act with consideration for the other's suffering or plight. While Hogarth's series depicts four stages of 'cruelty', the notion of a hardening heart has more in keeping with a drift towards callousness.

William Hogarth, the 'First Stage of Cruelty',
from *The Four Stages of Cruelty*, 1751, engraving.

Indeed, only do the actions of Tom Nero in the first stage of cruelty
appear to be cruel. Everything else in this image and everything that
follows after this point appears to be callous.

The question I pose here is whether cruelty or callousness was
considered the greater threat to civilization. I have argued elsewhere
that concerns about cruelty to animals centred on concerns about
civilized behaviour among humans, which is to say that reformers
wanted to punish those who would not or could not listen to their
moral sense.[6] By making the moral transgression of cruelty a crime,
potential perpetrators would have to think twice about the ease with

which they could cast off moral concerns. Much of the debate that was generated about whether a government should legislate against cruelty resided precisely on the question of whether or not it was within the scope of any parliament to interfere in moral questions, or to superadd the penal code to the human conscience. Those who opposed legislation against cruelty to animals – and they were legion – pointed to both the pulpit and to the example of societal betters as more appropriate locations of the model civilized conscience. A faith in the march of the mind, and in the progress of civilization, seemed at odds, to these opponents, with fatalistic legislation that seemed to imply that government had given up hope about the natural improvement of society. Those who argued for legislation, as well as those who formed charitable societies to help enforce it, tried to find a middle way, prosecuting where they found deviance, but educating as a general function of institutionalization. Those prosecuted would serve as ready examples of the consequences of ignoring one's conscience, to be endlessly recapitulated in pamphleteering campaigns.

That we know so much about the importance of the moral sense and its transgression seems to point to the status of cruelty as the paramount concern in the age of sensibility, gaining new ground in the age of utility that followed. Yet I am persuaded that callousness was a more sinister problem, not the least for its intractability. The callous, the properly hardened, could appear anywhere, among the dregs of society or at its apex. The threat they held was twofold. On the one hand, one could not hope to educate feeling back in once it had departed. A callous individual was lost to society. Conscience was calcified. Yet, on the other hand, the callous could spread their hardness to others, educating the feeling out.

In the 'First Stage of Cruelty' a variety of puerile activities involving animals is on display. The dominant tone of the piece is fun. Children delight in their activities, which nevertheless seem to have the curiosity of harm as one of their defining motivations. The eyes of a bird are delightfully burnt out. Two cats are hung upside down to fight it out, to the gleeful expressions of an assembled crowd. A boy takes aim with a stick at a cock in a concentrated expression of skill and traditional manly prowess (the sport of throwing at cocks was a long-standing English pastime, particularly associated with Shrovetide). A boy in the front right ties a bone to the tail of a dog, so as to revel in its endless spinning – an image lent pathos by Hogarth by having the faithful dog lick the hand of its master. The key group of figures include Tom Nero inserting an arrow into the anus of a dog, with the help of two accomplices. Their faces are obscured, in favour of a focus on the face of the one opponent to the activity, who tries both to restrain Tom Nero and offer him food as an alternative to fun. In the verse below the image, this boy is described as 'Pity', which 'charms the sight'. The implication, as will become a common thread in the series, is that the other characters have no pity and therefore lack something of humanity. The animalistic behaviour of these children is mirrored in the lower left by the dog devouring a cat. Nobody would have ascribed cruelty to the dog, but merely brutality. Its lack of reason and lack of feeling define its actions, which are based purely on animal desire and instinct. Though Hogarth emphasizes the cruelty in the scene, it actually draws attention only to the wantonness of Tom Nero, who alone is singled out for the noose in the portentous gallows graffito on the wall adjacent to him. The rest of the scene suggests no awareness of wrongdoing. There is no feeling in the scene at all, save for pleasure, and for the pity of the single dissenter.

The second stage continues with the theme of tension between wantonness and unfeeling. While Tom Nero is again identified in the act of being cruel to an animal, driven in this instance by 'rage', the rest of the scene is marked by its lack of care or feeling. The verse under the image refers to the sheep driver in the bottom right as an 'Inhuman Wretch', a double emphasis on his animal-like nature, given a third emphasis by reference to his 'barb'rous deeds'. Hogarth asks where this 'coward Cruelty' is leading, answering only in the most negative terms. The very question suggests optimism, for a label of cruelty implies *human* intention, whereas all indications point to a brutalization of society: literally, to people becoming brute animals. The bills posted on the walls advertise boxing matches and a cockfight, while in the distance a bull-running event ends in gore as much as sport. Tom Nero himself is a cab driver, and the fact that a motley assemblage of magistrates are prepared to employ him suggests both the unfeeling state and the meanness of the law. An overburdened mule is driven without care. A drunken dray driver runs over a playing child without even noticing. Again, the final analysis is of a scene bereft of feeling, of pity, of humanity. Where, in a scene of animals, can one find cruelty?

William Hogarth, the 'Second Stage of Cruelty',
from *The Four Stages of Cruelty*, 1751, engraving.

Again, the answer seems to lie solely in the figure of Tom Nero,
whose beating of the horse comes with an understanding of the
horse's suffering, driven as it is by rage. The attribution of an unrestrained anger to Tom Nero at least marks him out as capable of
human passion, and this alone gives him the capacity for cruelty.
Hence the action in the next scene, 'Cruelty in Perfection', focuses
primarily on him as he progresses from wanton cruelty to animals
to murder. The victim is his mistress, who has been manipulated to
steal for him. His humanity is again highlighted, for the sight of the
body, slit open at the throat and wrist, at last shocks 'his trembling
soul'. His path of wanton cruelty has brought him to this, but in the

final breach of human morality, his humanity is exposed. It is too late for Tom Nero to be redeemed and he will succumb to the noose. This is, on a superficial reading, the narrative line of Hogarth's series of prints. Yet Tom Nero is only one character among many. What becomes of the rest, we are asked, in a society in which a man like Tom Nero can come to be?

Ultimately it is the threat of a spread of callousness that Hogarth alerts us to. The final stage of cruelty – cruelty's 'reward' – is, on the face of it, an ignominious desecration of the body. Given up to science, Nero's heart is fit for nothing more than food for dogs. The reward of his cruelty is death, dissection, objectification. Yet as with

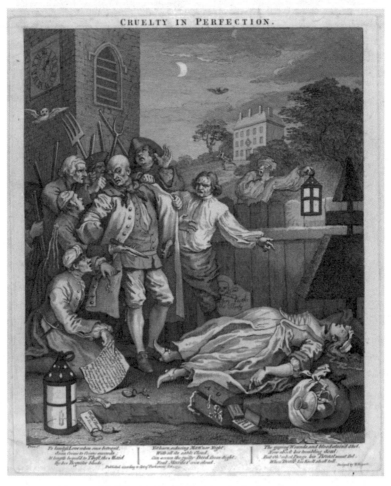

William Hogarth, 'Cruelty in Perfection',
from *The Four Stages of Cruelty*, 1751, engraving.

William Hogarth, 'The Reward of Cruelty',
from *The Four Stages of Cruelty*, 1751, engraving.

the other scenes in the series, Hogarth is not simply depicting the actions of Tom Nero, and in the final scene in particular Nero – as a dead body – is doing literally nothing, save posthumously gesturing to the process of skeletonization that awaits him. All of the action revolves around the others in the room, who are themselves reaping the reward of cruelty, which, I aver, is callousness. Tom Nero, though an extreme example, is Everyman in the final analysis. He is part of a steady degradation of civilization in which all those who partake of it are moving towards a numbing of the sensibilities. That which is marked as progress – here, the field of anatomy as an important component of scientific practices of knowledge acquisition – is shown in fact to depend on the unfeelingness of its participants. It is therefore a progress marked by inhumanity. A sacrifice of conscience, of heart, to knowledge. And in this sense it is the abdication of any hope for the soul of humanity.

Hogarth is referencing here the practice of claiming the bodies of murderers for dissection by surgeons. A year later, in 1752, this practice received legal sanction in the Murder Act. The enthroned president is John Freke, at the time Governor of St Bartholomew's Hospital, and renowned for having been instrumental in beginning the process of professionalization of surgery. While Hogarth counted him as a friend, the scene over which Freke presides is critically composed. In fact, the 'reward' of cruelty is supposed to show society at its most morally corrupted. All the people in the room, save one, are already completely callous, unfeeling, their senses benumbed by morbid curiosity. Tom Nero's fellows in crime adorn the walls as skeletons. James Field, the boxer-cum-robber, whose violent exploits caught up with him when he was sentenced to death by Henry Fielding in 1751, hangs to the left. James MacLaine, the famous highwayman who was hanged in 1750, is mounted to the right. The inclusion of MacLaine is particularly pointed, for his career as a robber was reputedly conducted with the veneer of civility, to the point that he became celebrated for his politeness. That so many society figures romanticized this villain is further evidence of public dissimulation of sensibility that thinly covered a growing hardness: for who in their right feelings would celebrate such a criminal? The one good soul in the image stands under the skeleton of Field and points, looking anxiously into the room, as if to say 'do not we all tend in this direction?'

I contend, however, that it is not the fate of criminals that is most alarming in this print, but rather the implicit condemnation of professional medicine. The verse appended to the print ends with a reference to the exposed heart of Tom Nero, which 'to pity has no claim'. The assembled surgeons (in wigs) and physicians (in mortar boards) are more or less engaged in a *procedure*, involving an *object*. The facial expressions are marked by dispassion, a lack of solemnity and occasionally a kind of determined focus. To call out the assembly as having no pity is to make a serious charge. Pity, in the eighteenth century, said more about the sensible qualities of the pitier than it did about the plight of the object of pity. Pity was an openness to suffering in others, being synonymous with compassion and, importantly, with *humanity*. The species label and its defining affective feature – a sort of other-orientated sociality – are conflated in a single word. The person who pitied was thought not merely to take on the suffering of another, but to transform it in his or her mind and heart, into an impetus to action – charitable or otherwise – and into a subspecies of pleasure, the sublime, or luxury, that hinged on a distancing practice, whereby the suffering of another is acknowledged but is nevertheless definitively located outside the self. Pity is a pleasurable pain, a heartache, a compound of complex sensibilities that reminded the pitier of his or her own humanity while at the same time ensuring that the suffering of others would be alleviated. Pity was humanity itself.

This assemblage of physicians and surgeons has no pity. It is not that they have no pity for Tom Nero in particular, but rather that they are incapable of pity in general. The image draws on a longstanding perception that those who deal with blood and gore in an habitual fashion become desensitized to its power to move. The myth that surgeons and butchers (otherwise odd bedfellows, but forever conjoined in their reputation for callousness) were not allowed to serve on juries in England was enshrined by Bernard Mandeville in *The Fable of the Bees* in 1714. 'Every body knows', he wrote:

that Surgeons in the Cure of dangerous Wounds and Fractures, the extirpations of Limbs, and other dreadful Operations, are often compell'd to put their Patients to extraordinary Torments, and that the more desperate and calamitous Cases occur to them, the more Outcries and bodily Sufferings of others must become familiar to them; for this Reason our *English* Law, out of a most affectionate Regard to the Lives of the Subject, allows them not to be of any Jury upon Life and Death, as supposing that their Practice it self is sufficient to harden and extinguish in them that Tenderness, without which no Man is capable of setting a true value upon the Lives of his Fellow-creatures. Now if we ought to have no Concern for what we do to Brute Beasts, and there was not imagin'd to be any cruelty in killing them, why should of all Callings *Butchers*, and only they jointly with *Surgeons*, be excluded from being Jury-men by the same Law?[7]

How much worse had things become in the decades since Mandeville wrote, with the attachment of pecuniary motives to surgical and anatomical exploits? To be sure, dissecting the dead did not involve inflicting suffering per se, but the principal sensory organ of civilization – the eye – was nonetheless afflicted by the sight of the opened and disembowelled bodies of the dead to the same degree as of the living. When the sensibilities ceased to be disturbed by such sights, then hardness was complete.

While Hogarth had clearly referenced the politics of the production of meat in the 'Second Stage of Cruelty', the butcher hardly represented the same level of social threat as the physician or the surgeon. These, after all, were gentlemen, societal leaders, men of influence. Where they led, others would follow. If knowledge – surgical, anatomical, physiological – were to take precedence over pity, humanity or a simple aesthetic reaction of disgust, then into what kind of brutal existence would the young followers of such teachers be led?

This concern would resurface repeatedly over the century and a half after Hogarth's *Four Stages of Cruelty*, and I think there is a persuasive argument to be made that the tail end of the so-called 'age of sensibility' and its sequel, 'the age of sentimentality', were both defined by an ever-present threat of their opposite. The emphasis on feeling for others throughout this period was often explicit about the concern that such feelings were being lost, and where the concern was not explicit, it nevertheless loomed large in the subtexts of sentimentality. I do not mean to upend the historiographical focus on sense and sensibility entirely, but only to make a claim that the emphasis on *feeling* in the eighteenth and nineteenth centuries only really makes any sense in the light of those things against which it was expressed in opposition.

Of course, another worthy definition of the period from the late eighteenth century, through to at least the late nineteenth, would be the 'age of utility'. It is, at first blush, a philosophy of feeling par excellence, for its preoccupations are pleasure and pain, its goals to maximize the former and minimize the latter. Yet there is a great distance between suffering, a phenomenon defined by emotional pain, and a calculus of suffering, which might be worked out in a study, or a laboratory, or simply in one's head. Utilitarianism thought about pain in the abstract, and in the aggregate, not as individuated experience. The father of utilitarianism, Jeremy Bentham, is widely known for having written the rallying cry for animal activists of the late twentieth century, down to our own day. Philosophical traditions were apparently turned on their heads when Bentham threw out the importance of *logos* in his ethics: 'the question is not, *can they reason*, nor *can they talk*, but *can they suffer?*', he wrote, the 'they' in question being animals, of course.[8] I have, in various other places, pointed out the almost wilful misreading that needs to take place to make Bentham into the prophet of animal rights, including a rather pointed analysis of his use of the word 'suffer' in this context.[9] But I raise Bentham again here because his actual arguments, that is, the arguments he made to clarify the axiom above, were the arguments that proved definitive for the next century, at least for scientists and medical researchers.

The part of utilitarianism that gets overlooked quite often is the element of *usefulness*. Pain, in particular, had to be weighed against its purpose in order to establish its level of evil. Bentham was explicit about this. The commission of pain was not cruel if it was done for 'a useful purpose'. This might be something as straightforward as disciplining an animal to make it 'moderate'. Or else it might be towards the wholly justifiable end of 'making the animal subservient to the necessities or conveniences of man', as food, medicine, clothing, transport or manufacture. In the name of protecting another human, an animal could be hurt. There was no entertainment that humans were anything other than superior beings. And, in the name of peace, animals might be pained for being annoying to humans. Crucially, Bentham also condoned vivisection, if it promoted 'medical and other useful knowledge'.[10] From Bentham onwards, utilitarians practised a cool rationalism that actually placed them at some distance from the contexts of suffering that they sometimes described.

If pain in other animals was not the be all and end all that it has seemed to be to some scholars, what was? Bentham, for his part, was clear enough: 'habits of cruelty or insensibility, which when indulged are apt to lead one into the worst of crimes'.[11] He was thinking, explicitly, of the example taught by Hogarth's *Four Stages of Cruelty*. Yet humanity was safe, in the final analysis, so long as its insensibility was purposeful and useful. Almost a century later, we find the echo of Bentham's outlook in a passage that was added to the second edition (1874) of Charles Darwin's *Descent of Man* and so is often omitted when the first edition is quoted instead:

> In the agony of death a dog has been known to caress his master, and every one has heard of the dog suffering under vivisection, who licked the hand of the operator; this man, *unless the operation was fully justified by an increase of our knowledge*, or unless he had a heart of stone, must have felt remorse to the last hour of his life [emphasis added].[12]

Purpose trumped sensibility. With the rise of anaesthetics, all such scruples about the commission of pain were jettisoned, including by Darwin.[13] The risk of a 'heart of stone' was averted, first, by the quest for knowledge and, later, by the chemical removal of feeling. By the time the fierce opponent of vivisection, Frances Power Cobbe, asked 'what shall it profit a man if he gain the whole world of knowledge and lose his own heart and his own conscience?', such men had already safeguarded their hearts in chloroform and ether.[14] In numbing the object of their research, it allowed them, justifiably, to feel nothing in return.

Insignificant Grimaces

Part of that physiological impetus that saw a great rise in animal experimentation was borne on the back of a new research interest: the emotions themselves became the purview of medical and scientific research, with a new ardour to extend human understanding of what emotions actually were, and an equal zeal to uncover how they worked, physiologically, anatomically and psychologically. There are analyses of this movement elsewhere, including my own, and I do not want to rehash it here, but rather to focus particularly on one aspect of it, literally.[15] Scientists increasingly focused on the face, of humans and animals alike, in researching and documenting what emotions looked like. New technologies of stimulation – galvanic means of administering electricity, for example – combined with new technologies of recording (most notably photography) to allow scientists to *fix* the faces of emotion. I deploy that verb consciously, for it can be shown that in attempting to capture and preserve the otherwise fleeting signs of emotions on the face, those emotions had to be fabricated, forged, *fixed*. The famous grimaces of the nineteenth-century research subject, so important and influential in the formation of a theory of facial affect that still exerts a profound influence in emotion sciences today, actually signified nothing at all.

Let us begin with the electrocution of the dead. In 1819 Andrew Ure (1778–1857) acquired the dead body of an executed criminal, hooked him up to a battery, with a conducting rod at his heel and another to the eyebrow, and shocked the body. The result: 'every muscle in his countenance was simultaneously thrown into fearful action: rage, horror, despair, anguish, and ghastly smiles, united their hideous expression in the murderer's face'. Such was the effect on the assembled audience in the anatomical theatre that 'several of the spectators were forced to leave . . . from terror or sickness, and one gentleman fainted'. Hogarth's Tom Nero was not alone in pointing suggestively from the slab, for 'when the one rod was applied to a slight incision in the tip of the fore-finger, the fist being previously clenched, that finger extended instantly; and from the convulsive agitation of the arm, he seemed to point to the different spectators, some of whom thought he had come to life'.[16]

All the emotions in the room belonged to the spectators, yet those same spectators' emotions were aroused through a perception that the reflex movements of the dead body actually signified something. The grimaces, the pointing, the scowls of rage and anguish – emotions befitting a murderer, perhaps – were all attributed to the dead body, even in full knowledge that such a body was incapable of feeling anything at all. Somehow, the sign of the emotion was sufficient, in people's imaginations, to indicate the presence of the emotion.

Doubtless by the time Ure inserted his device into the dead and simulated the corpse's reanimation, some of those in attendance had already read Mary Shelley's *Frankenstein* (1818).[17] The very idea of the making of a feeling subject out of an inanimate object was alive. While Ure was among the first to propose that such electrical techniques might actually resuscitate the recently passed-on, for the most part anatomical and physiological research in this vein aimed to show that the muscular reflex actions of the body could be simulated, even in the dead, to prove that grimaces of horror and, especially, pain could not be trusted as signs of an emotional event. As the nineteenth century progressed – 'progress' was the watchword of the century – medical scientists in particular became highly motivated to disassociate the signs of pain and emotion from the phenomena of pain and emotion. The ethics of physiological research, which relied on vivisection for its advances, increasingly depended on being able to prove that animals did not suffer, their howls and grimaces notwithstanding. As a corollary, those scientists had to respond impassively or in a manner contradictory to the expression on the face of the experimental subject. That Ure's corpse caused some of the onlookers to flee in horror was already, by 1819, a source of regret for the scientific rationalist. In 1875 David Ferrier (1843–1928) performed 'Experiments on the Brain of Monkeys' with similar effects to the experiment of Ure's.[18] Most of the audience had understood that there was supposed to be an interruption between the expression of the experimental animal and the sympathetic response of the audience, because the animal itself could not feel anything. But it pushed the boundaries of taste. One of the witnesses, a committee member of the Royal Society for the Prevention of Cruelty to Animals (founded 1824), had 'left the room in consequence of the pain with which he saw the laughter of the young people'. That Society's secretary told a Parliamentary Commission inquiring into the question of animal cruelty in vivisection that he could not complain about animal pain, since it was evident the animal in question could not suffer. He went on the record as saying it was 'a departure from good taste', 'a case of levity, likely to produce a bad effect', and an event that lacked 'decorum'. The jocund responses to the facial expressions of the monkey caused *him* pain, or perhaps, a feeling of social awkwardness or uneasiness.[19] This 'spirit of jocularity' similarly lay at the heart of the complaint in the Old Brown Dog Affair of 1903, where vivisection seemed to lack the necessary gravitas.[20] The principal female anti-vivisectionists who brought the case to light complained about the teaching room that 'there is nothing of the serene dignity of science about the place, everybody looks as if he expected an hour's amusement'.[21]

The scientific community howled in protest at such sentimentality, which seemed far from any concern for the animal, but instead expressed anxiety about the state of a society that could see a pained face and yet laugh. The rationalist argument, as put forward by G. M. Humphry (1820–1896), anatomy professor at Cambridge, that the 'violent contortions of the worm' on a hook were no indication of pain, 'for there may be violent contortions and no suffering whatsoever', seemed nothing to the purpose. If the sign of pain was not reliable, what else was there to prevent society from becoming completely callous in all its dealings with others? James Crichton-Browne (1840–1938), neurologist at the West Riding Asylum, wrote of the ability to reproduce the outward signs of pain in animals 'in the deepest state of anaesthesia', or even in those without a brain at all, by 'stimulation of the motor centre'. Whatever appeared as 'intense and protracted agony' was in fact 'not greater than that of a pianoforte when its keys are struck'.[22] After the passage of centuries, the automaton of Descartes was alive and well (or dead, or at the very least unwell) in the high Victorian age.

Yet here we reach an impasse, or a contradiction, that sits awkwardly in a narrative of deceptive signs and apparently painless pain. Crichton-Browne was a principal correspondent of Charles Darwin in the period immediately prior to Darwin's publication of *The Expression of the Emotions in Man and Animals* in 1872, and indeed supplied Darwin with many of the photographs and notes used to develop a thesis of universality of expression of emotions.[23] Crichton-Browne ultimately demurred from sharing authorship of the *Expression*, perhaps because he could not quite endorse the argument. Indeed, Crichton-Browne appears to be the source of Darwin's knowledge of Ferrier's monkey experiments, but Darwin's line of thinking was not immediately down the route of automaticity in facial affect. He asked Crichton-Browne if the electrical stimulation excited an idea that caused expression, or whether the motor nerves were acted on directly.[24] That he entertained the former is highly suggestive of the work Darwin was doing with photography. Despite the general scientific air of mistrust about any connection between emotion and expression, especially under artificial stimulation, Darwin jumped the shark.

Darwin's *Expression of Emotions* is predicated on the idea that expressions of emotions are not communicative devices, transmitting inner feelings into the world, but rather are vestiges of habitually conditioned behaviour that have become associated with inner emotions. The whole thing hinges on the inheritance of acquired habit – a fact most contemporary Darwinists do not care to hear – with the relegation of the theory of natural selection to the background, almost to the point of obsolescence. While Darwin was working to overturn the earlier work of Charles Bell (1774–1842), whose thesis on emotional communication depended on intelligent design (a divine creator), he nevertheless fundamentally confirmed Bell's notion that the expression of emotions was naturally and absolutely limited by the physical anatomy of the face, and that emotional expressions were therefore universal across humanity. It is a thesis of profound influence.

Darwin's interest in Crichton-Browne's photographs of insane people stemmed from a belief that the insane had no emotional inhibitions. What one could capture photographically was, so the thinking went, likely to be *authentic*. Unlike the other photographs of emotional expressions that Darwin could muster, which were acted, strained or feigned, these would be *real*.[25] Crichton-Browne, much that he supported Darwin's endeavours, could scarcely have agreed with such a notion, for he knew the deceptiveness of outward signs. Yet the two eagerly exchanged Darwin's copy of another profoundly influential work of scientific photography, which seemed to go further still into the realms of both simulation and, paradoxically, authenticity.

In 1862 Guillaume-Benjamin-Amand Duchenne de Boulogne (1806–1875) published *Mécanisme de la physionomie humaine ou analyse électro-physiologique de l'expression des passions*. It was, in principle, not so different to those early-century experiments of Ure and others, who animated the faces of the dead. Duchenne's departure was significant in two ways: first, he mastered the art of photographing the expressions of the passions he produced on the faces of his experimental subjects with his galvanic apparatus; second, those subjects were alive. This would have presented some severe difficulties, since the electrical current would doubtless have produced great discomfort in a conscious person. Duchenne, however, managed to find a subject who 'suffered' from a lack of sensitivity in the face. This was, for want of a better description, an anaesthetic man.

What Darwin and his correspondent Crichton-Browne discovered in the pages of Duchenne was an unmatched series of photographs that *seemed* to prove Darwin's point. Here, on the face of a neutral human test subject, were all the expressions that were possible, given the limitations of facial anatomy. Handily, Duchenne named the emotions his subject was electrocuted into expressing. And who could disagree that here was *souffrance* (Duchenne's fig. 19), or *souffrance profonde, avec resignation* (his fig. 20), or there *surprise* (his fig. 56) or *effroi* (his fig. 63)? The imagery, the allure of the new technology, was most persuasive. Except, everybody missed the three massive flaws in putting these images to a universal application of human emotional expression. First, not everything Duchenne managed to conjure on the face of his subject was recognizably an emotion. Where this was the case, Duchenne wrote '*expression incomplète, fausse*' (incomplete expression, false), as if the face had in fact assumed something Duchenne could not recognize. But in labelling it incomplete or false he eliminated those examples that did not fit an a priori scheme of emotional signs. This implies the second flaw, that in fact all the categories of emotion (*passion*) were decided beforehand, and Duchenne experimented with the electrodes until the face matched the expression he *desired* to see. And third, most damningly, far from being evidence of universal signs of human passions, the subject here explicitly did not feel *anything*, let alone the emotions these facial expressions were supposed to portray. By technological means, Duchenne had *forged* the emotions on the face. The camera was designed to lie from the outset.

This was compounded, and Darwin was complicit in this, by the use of actors who tried to assume the expressions of emotions prescribed for them. Darwin famously remarked that such was the effort, sometimes only half of the actor's face got the expression *right*, while the other half betrayed a completely different emotion altogether. In this case, the *wrong* half of the face was eliminated from the photograph displayed. The absolute rejection, out of hand, of facial expressions that did not fit preconceived notions of what emotions looked like, ought to have condemned the work. Yet since the presentation ably and conveniently confirmed assumptions, these flaws went by without comment.

In the end, Darwin drew heavily on the photographs of Duchenne, producing woodcuts of Duchenne's images that intentionally eliminated those aspects that showed the artificial manipulation of the face. By comparison, Darwin did not draw on the asylum photographs of Crichton-Browne to any great degree. Looking at those photographs, in comparison to Duchenne's, it is not hard to see why. Whereas Duchenne strove to make emotion faces, labelling them as he went, Crichton-Browne took candid portraits of his patients. Their expressions, though often doleful, betray very little. (Not that this prevented Crichton-Browne reading emotions into them. See if you can spot either the laziness or the quizzical look in the image shown here, that was so labelled.) Without prompting, an observer would be

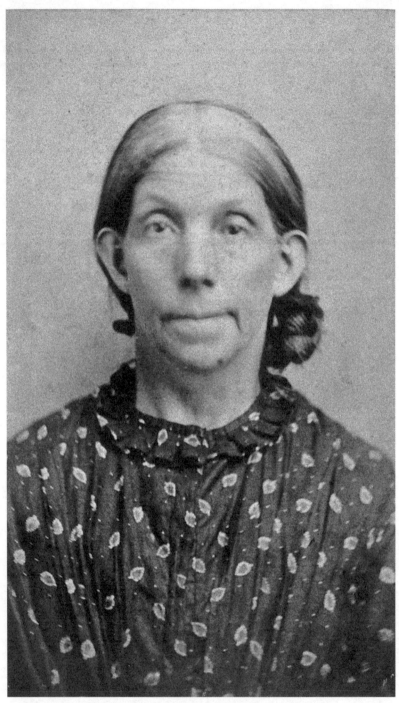

James Crichton-Browne, photograph of a woman
'with quizzical mouth and lazy eyes', 1869.

hard-pressed to pinpoint any nameable emotion at all. Would the conclusion be that some expressions were *neutral*, or emotionless? Is it possible, at any point, to be feeling nothing? Since the answers to these questions are probably negative, and since the photographs did not conveniently play to Darwin's (and Darwin's correspondents') confirmation bias, they were left, as it were, on the cutting room floor.

We are left, therefore, with a paradox of scientific discourse. The picture of facial affect was, in discourses of scientific and medical *practice*, mistrusted, automatically signifying nothing at all without further substantiation; but in discourses of scientific *theory*, it was a universal key, signifying emotions in common across humanity.

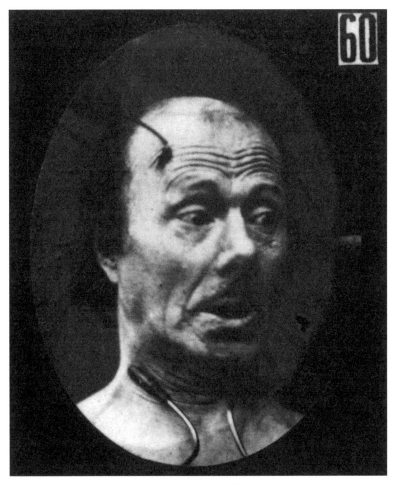

Duchenne de Boulogne, photograph of 'Fright' personified, 1862.

Ultimately, however, despite the tenacity of the latter strand of thought that lives on in the work of affect theorists, and of Paul Ekman in particular, there were few emotions in Darwin's book on expression, which was dominated precisely by *expressions*.[26] What they meant, especially in the case of the human subjects photo-graphed for the purpose, was either not what they were supposed to portray, or else *nothing at all*.

Aequanimitas, or the End of Sympathy

The impact of anaesthesia on the affective practices of surgeons and physiologists, in particular, is wonderfully depicted in two famous paintings by Thomas Eakins (1844–1916). The first, *The Gross Clinic*, was painted in 1875. The second, *The Agnew Clinic*, is from 1889. Both depict surgical operations under anaesthesia and they share much by way of formal content. Both essentially herald modern surgery as a wonder of progress, with the surgeon as a sort of modern hero.[27] Much has been written on the way the two images capture key changes in the practice of surgery, not least in the way that the assembled surgical team are dressed. While the earlier painting was widely celebrated as a modern American masterpiece, the later one challenged public taste in its depiction of the nude female subject, the focus of the gaze of a room full of men. Yet the interval of four-teen years between them also had a dramatic impact on the kind of visual tension that Eakins could employ in the images, and the affective context of the two has not been well explored. While both capture the cool demeanour of experienced surgeons working with benumbed and unconscious patients, *The Gross Clinic*'s drama hinges on a palpable horror that hangs a contemporary moral question over the whole scene. *The Agnew Clinic*, by way of contrast, completely lacks this tension. Both scenes show surgery in a teaching environ-ment and are faithful records of space, personnel and procedure. The so-called 'realism' or 'objectivity' of the style nevertheless tele-graphs a moral concern, in *The Gross Clinic* at least, and attempts to address it.

To be able to read the emotional dynamic of *The Gross Clinic* we first have to go back. Call to mind, to begin, that apocryphal tale from *The Fable of the Bees*, mentioned earlier, about the hardened character of the surgeon. For better or for worse, the surgeon carried

Thomas Eakins, *Portrait of Dr Samuel D. Gross* (*The Gross Clinic*), 1875,
oil on canvas.

with him – always *him* – a certain mark of insensibility. This general reputation was part of the received representation of surgery throughout the eighteenth and much of the nineteenth centuries. It was, as Michael Brown in particular has shown, something of a myth.[28] Surgeons were moved by their practices, felt compassion and fear, but proceeded determinedly. They saw themselves, no doubt, as being distinguished by their capacity to do what was necessary, where others would have been overcome by the prospect of pain and by the burden of risk. Yet their reputation for hardness and coldness preceded them.

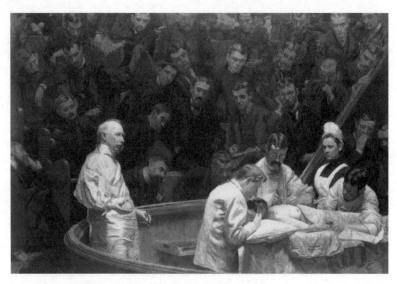

Thomas Eakins, *The Agnew Clinic*, 1889, oil on canvas.

Next, call to mind the emotional atmosphere of surgery, specifically relating to the way in which pain was anticipated. The concept of 'atmosphere' is becoming increasingly important in the history of emotions in its intersection with social geography. The theory, coined by Gernot Böhme, defines an atmosphere as an 'affective mood which spatial arrangements stir in the sensual bodies of their users'. It is particularly fitting to apply this to the changing mood of the surgical clinic or theatre. As developed by Andreas Reckwitz, affective moods are formed 'when a space is practically appropriated by its users', being 'always already connected to a specific cultural sensitivity and attentiveness on the part of the carriers of practices, a specific sensitivity for perceptions, impressions and affections'. What I document here is the disruption of an atmosphere when cultural sensitivities are in flux. The atmosphere becomes tense, dynamic, before re-forming according to newly prevailing cultural sensitivities.[29] How does the suffering of a patient present itself to the mind of the observer? David Hume, the Scottish Enlightenment philosopher, was under no illusions about the impossibility of directly knowing the affective state of another person. The room, or the scene, filled in the atmosphere that signalled the magnitude of pain ahead:

> Were I present at any of the more terrible operations of surgery, 'tis certain that even before it begun, the preparation

of the instruments, the laying of the bandages in order, the heating of the irons, with all the signs of anxiety and concern in the patients and assistants, wou'd have a great effect upon my mind, and excite the strongest sentiments of pity and terror. No passion of another discovers itself immediately to the mind. We are only sensible of its causes and effects. From *these* we infer the passion: And consequently *these* give rise to our sympathy.[30]

There are two implications: first, anybody who knows the signs of the causes of pain should have his passions aroused directly. Sympathy rides upon, or emerges from, pity and terror. Second, anybody who does not have his passions aroused, even though he knows the signs of the causes of pain, must be callous. Imagine, for example, being witness to Fanny Burney's mastectomy (her account of it is from 1812): As 'the dreadful steel was plunged into the breast – cutting through veins – arteries – flesh – nerves', she 'needed no injunctions not to restrain [her] cries'. She 'began a scream that lasted unintermittingly during the whole time of the incision'.[31] How could anyone, goes the rhetorical question, remain unmoved at the sight and sound of this ordeal? This puts the surgeon in a dubious category of one who has the power to save life, and one who cannot access the normal passions of the soul: a humanitarian in practise; a monster by nature. Hume's contemporary Adam Smith fundamentally agreed. The 'remote effects' of the 'instruments of surgery' might be 'agreeable', he said. Their end, or *telos*, is the 'health of the patient'. But their 'immediate effect . . . is pain and suffering', which means the 'sight of them always displeases us'.[32] The surgeon, it is supposed, is able to overcome this displeasure and focus fixedly on the remote effects. Everyone else recoils in terror. The questions that arise are these: what happens to the signs of pain and suffering if the reality of pain and suffering changes? If the surgical patient no longer has to endure any pain in the surgical procedure, how quickly do the *signs* of pain change to accommodate the new reality, if at all? These are not hypothetical queries, but essential lines of inquiry in both the history of emotions and the history of medicine. With the advent of anaesthesia in 1846–7, the possibility of painless surgery emerged, and with it thoughts of a painless age.[33]

The implications of painlessness involve both those who other-wise would be in pain and those who bear witness to it. As I have argued elsewhere, pain is not meaningfully *painful* unless attended by affective experience.[34] The immediate causes of physical pain – things like injury, a surgical incision, an internal lesion of some kind – are actually stimuli not necessarily experienced as painful. Certainly there is no way to predict how painful an incision might be. In theory, at least, the amount of pain experienced in surgery is propor-tional to the degree of fear and anxiety the patient feels, the perception of the fear and anxiety of the surgeon, the degree of control and assurance the patient derives from the setting, and the perceived risk of consequences in the context of the patient's life. It is well known, for example, that surgical procedures have been performed painlessly without anaesthetic, under some form of hypnotic technique, whereby any affective activity associated with the physical disruption of the body is effectively shut down or controlled. In surgery in pre-anaesthetic days, however, where the risks were known to be high, outcomes were by no means predictable. Where pain was assumed to be inevitable, we must assume that the experience was unpleasant – noxious – in the extreme.

Pain, then, might be considered a cluster of emotions. At the very least it is affectively complex. What is more, as the testimony of Hume and Smith indicates, the perception of pain does not depend on being the person being cut, but also dwells in the brain-body of the witness to the person being cut. Pity, terror, the very act of sym-pathy itself, are experiences of pain, at one stage of remove from the disruption of the physical body, but nonetheless pain in its own right in the observer. Anaesthesia promised not merely to take away the pain of the patient, but implicitly also the pain of the witness. Moreover, the suspicion concerning the insensibility of the surgeon could also be lifted, since he would not need to feel anything in the anaesthetized atmosphere of the new operating theatre.

Several factors made the reality less clear cut. First, anaesthetics were not universally used once they were discovered. In fact they were purposefully withheld for a whole host of reasons: there were lingering doubts about *how* to administer them safely; if pain was God's will, then eliminating it was an act of sacrilege; some people, notably racial and class others, as well as women, children and ani-mals, were not considered to be sufficiently sensitive as to require anaesthetics; cost also limited their spread. This meant that the reality of pain in surgery was maintained, for many, until well into the twentieth century. This is certainly true if we count the *memory* of painful encounters with the institutions of medicine.

Second, the logic that the alleviation of pain in the patient would necessarily alleviate the pain of the witness did not accord with the way things were experienced. If pity was the passion that moved Hume on seeing the instruments of surgery, thinking of the pain ahead, nineteenth-century research on pity itself recorded the strange projection of feelings onto objects that could not have carried them. Pity was considered to be a sort of affect of mothering, driving an individual to want to coddle and care for a *thing*, which might be a person in pain, but might also be an inanimate object. In current parlance, such things are considered 'cute' and elicit the utterance '*aw*', and include such things as baby seals, pictures of baby seals and toy baby seals. Some have called it the 'Disneyfication' of sentiment, whereby we are enjoined to fawn over Bambi while we ignore the plight of less aesthetically alluring animals.[35] Yet the observation is far older than this.

In 1872 Herbert Spencer wrote that 'pity implies . . . the representation of a pain, sensational or emotional, experienced by another; and its function as so constituted, appears to be merely that of preventing the infliction of pain, or prompting efforts to assuage pain when it has been inflicted'. Significantly, however, there was a 'certain phase of pity' in which 'the pain has a pleasurable accompaniment; and the pleasurable pain, or painful pleasure, continues even where nothing is done, or can be done, towards mitigating the suffering', or when there is not any suffering to mitigate in the first place. This 'parental instinct', as Spencer styled it, was excited

> always [by] relative weakness or helplessness. Equally in the little girl with her doll, in the lady with her lap-dog, in the cat that has adopted a puppy, and in the hen that is anxious about the ducklings she has hatched, the feeling arises in the presence of something feeble and dependent to be taken care of.

This rather cloying sentimentality, which Spencer derided, was extended to 'weakly creatures in general, and creatures that have been made weakly by accident, disease, or by ill-treatment'.[36] The seeds of Disneyfication were all there in the late nineteenth century.

Regard the explicit gendering of this affective disposition and its timing. Increasingly, social activism was becoming defined by its sentimentality – a charge brought by its critics – and its femininity. From the late 1860s the anti-vivisection movement surged in importance and was known as a particularly female-led campaign. Other groups, such as the Royal Society for the Prevention of Cruelty to Animals, had been longer running, but were also known to depend on the patronage of women. The National Society for the Prevention of Cruelty to Children was founded only in 1884 and shared many of the female patrons and activists of animal charities. All of this developed in the context of the sentimental novel, the rise of charity and the 'lady bountiful', so as to appear as a wave of misdirected and miscalculated humanity to those who would rather have reformed society on altogether more 'rational', scientific or utilitarian grounds.

Pity, therefore, by the time Thomas Eakins set about painting *The Gross Clinic*, was often mocked among men of science and medicine as a wayward emotion peculiar to women. It conceived of pain in objects that could not be in pain. Insofar as Hume's observation about the instruments of surgery inspiring pity still held good for such people, so too did the arousal of pity by the surgical patient, irrespective of whether the patient actually experienced any pain. The same was true of those experimental animals at the heart of the anti-vivisection campaign, where the perception of *torture* remained stubbornly in place irrespective of any and all appeals to the effect and attendant affects of anaesthesia. The surgeon as a kind of cold monster remained in the popular imagination, even though the essential emotional difficulty was (theoretically at least) swept aside by chloroform and ether.

Eakins had himself set out to become a surgeon, and he knew his way around the anatomy theatre. In his depiction of Dr Samuel Gross at Jefferson Medical College, Philadelphia, Eakins at once celebrates the impact of anaesthesia on the affective practice of surgical genius and the cultural lag that still saw pity and terror aroused in the uninformed witness of pain, even when pain itself was literally not in the picture. At the heart of the image, at the point where all surgical arms point and intersect, is the incision in the leg of a young patient, being operated on for osteomyelitis.[37] There is an air of procedure, of the banal, about the surgical team surrounding the patient: it is difficult to discern an expression that signifies any emotion in their concentration. The figure of Dr Gross is said by Goodrich to possess a 'marmoreal imperturbability'.[38] Immediately above the surgical wound, the means of administering anaesthetic is clearly depicted. The patient is immobile, expressionless, needing only the lightest of precautionary restraint. He is a surgical object, devoid of those terrors that would otherwise signify to those in attendance that their own pity and terror should be aroused.[39] The assembled students look appropriately interested and bored by the scene. The overwhelming atmosphere of ennui speaks to the degree of banality that anaesthesia and refined surgical technique brought about. Whereas the patient would, not long before, have been facing an excruciating amputation, here there is calm, cool, apparently emotionless work. It is a case to study in a detached mode, as Eakins himself did.

Yet there are deliberate challenges to the public gaze. The instruments of surgery, those objects with the power to arouse terror, are situated in the immediate foreground of the picture, as if the viewer has to literally *get over* them. As Gross looks away from the patient, his bloodied scalpel-wielding hand comes into view of what is usually thought to be the patient's mother, who recoils in horror at the sight. She is alone in the image in her emotional response, and is also the only woman present. Eakins captures the medical critique of an outmoded sensibility concerning pain, with surgical instruments and, in particular, blood as its signs. Eakins also captures the implicit gendering of this out-of-place horror, this misplaced pity. To the rest of the room, there is no reason to recoil, but only to come closer, to look more carefully, to *see* the operation without any qualms about the bygone aesthetics of suffering.[40] Goodrich has come closest to understanding the context, observing 'there is no lack of humanity; not the sentimentality that hides its eyes and shrinks from the less pleasant aspects of life, but the robust understanding of the scientist who can look on disease and pain, and record them truthfully. The work has the impersonality of science, and its humanity.'[41] Yet this all too readily accepts the 'robust understanding of the scientist' as *correct*, as opposed to a historical product of scientific affect, and rather misses the point that, in looking on at this scene, there *is no pain*.

Insofar as Eakins praised medical progress, and implicitly the affective disposition of those who embodied it, he also uncannily captured the public mood in the figure of the distressed mother. Reception of the painting was hostile, with strong reactions to the sight of blood. One critic condemned it on the basis that it would do damage to those 'men and women of weak nerves'. Another opined that 'even strong men find it difficult to look at long'.[42] Another criticized the attention placed 'so entirely . . . on that reeking hand' of Gross, as if somehow the blood did not merely offend the eye, but also the nose.[43] That the blood referred to was actually *paint* gets lost in the suspended disbelief of the viewer, all too ready to be allured and repelled in equal measure by the spilling of blood. As one reviewer lamented, 'If we could cut this figure [Gross] out of the canvas and wipe the blood from the hand, what an admirable portrait it would be!'[44] The presence of the horrified woman also drew ire, for in highlighting 'a melodramatic element' in order to tell a 'horrible story – horrible to the layman at least', Eakins was directly charged with showing the public to itself.[45] The public, defined by an affective response to surgery and the surgeon that harked back to more painful days, 'have no need of hearing' such a story, for it challenges their understanding and attacks the foundations of their feeling for what is moral, what is sacred and what is *gross*. Eakins, tapping into the medical scientific discourse of controlled emotions and far-reaching humanity, told a story that was incomprehensible to anybody outside of that discourse.[46]

Turning now to *The Agnew Clinic*, something crucial has changed. Painted in a hurry in 1889, the picture marks the retirement of David Hayes Agnew. Commissioned by some of his students, it was, as with *The Gross Clinic*, the recipient of critical reception for its *butchery*. Agnew himself apparently demanded that all traces of blood be removed from his hands, lest that particular shade of red give offence (Eakins did not altogether comply with the wish).[47] Yet despite these similarities, the overall tenor and affective tone of the scene is transformed.

The painting is usually noted for marking the sudden rise and adoption of an aseptic environment for surgery. The appearance of professional white clothing signifies that the operation is being conducted fully cognizant of germ theory. It is also common to remark on criticism of the painting's use of the female nude under the gaze of a room full of men, such did this offend art-critical sensibilities at the time. The depiction is of a breast-cancer operation, and shows one of the surgeons both holding and cutting the female breast. It pushed the limits of taste. Yet it was expressly not a celebration of artistic taste, but of medical prowess and heroism. The very lack of any indication that the public might recoil at such a scene is key. The painting is marked by the absence of female sentimentality and horror. The only woman other than the patient in *The Agnew Clinic* is a professional nurse. In being the only person wearing black, and the only one wearing any headgear, she refers back to the lone woman in *The Gross Clinic*, but stands in stark contrast to that figure of recoil and revulsion. Here the woman stands stoically at attention, expressionless of face, and looking directly at the surgical subject. Agnew himself is captured, as with Gross, turning away, perhaps addressing his students, who again take on the countenance of the respectively engrossed and sedated.

The fact that Eakins no longer felt the need to represent public horror, pity or disgust at the blood and perceived pain of surgery – even though it was no less in evidence in 1889 than it was in 1875 – shows that the kind of humanity and imperturbability that could overlook the instruments of surgery and the significance of gore had become more entrenched. Moreover, the surgeons themselves were by that year beginning to appropriate the charge of callousness often levelled against them and were spinning it into a positively desirable state. Most notably, in the same year and in the same city, the famous physician Dr William Osler (1849–1919) enshrined the affective qual-ities of the surgeon in lore, before a graduating class in medicine at the University of Pennsylvania. The subject of his speech has become the watchword of Oslerians ever since: *aequanimitas*. In English 'equanimity' is a state of 'mental calmness, composure, and evenness of temper, especially in a difficult situation', if one goes by the *Oxford Dictionary* definition (1989).

I have argued elsewhere that Osler's speech before the graduating class marked a genuine departure in the affective practices of doctors, surgeons and physiologists, in its explicit appropriation of the charge of callousness, reconceived as a virtue available only to those with the correct training. The essence of the speech was an exhortation to rise above the atmospheric inertia of the clinic: to rid oneself of any trace of pity, sympathy, fear or anxiety. He forecast disaster for an operation if the surgeon felt his patient's pain, not least because in modern surgery the perception of that pain was a phantom. Any wave of compassion in the clinical setting was a projection of the practitioner, an atavistic response to signs of suffering that in fact no longer signified anything but the patient's hope. As such, he told the assembled graduands to have their 'nerves well in hand' and to resist betraying any sense of alarm by facial expression, even when 'the most serious circumstances' were at hand. A surgeon must have his 'medullary centres under the highest control': the brain could no longer be carried away by unpleasant sights, but was to come under the active, conscious control of the body. The ensuing 'imperturbability' would be a 'bodily endowment' that would guarantee the 'coolness' and 'calmness' of the surgeon, allowing for 'clearness of judgment in moments of peril'. Lest this *phlegmatic* demeanour not be explicit enough, Osler went even further into the ownership of an affective disposition that had, throughout history, been evaluated as a suspicious flaw in the character of the surgeon:

> Now a certain measure of insensibility is not only an advantage, but a positive necessity in the exercise of a calm judgment, and in carrying out delicate operations. Keen sensibility is doubtless a virtue of high order, when it does not interfere with steadiness of hand or coolness of nerve; but for the practitioner in his working-day world, a callousness which thinks only of the good to be effected, and goes ahead regardless of smaller considerations, is the preferable quality.

In sum, Osler demanded of medical practitioners an ability to turn their sensibilities off, in certain contexts, but not to harden 'the human heart by which we live'. Theirs would be 'a judicious measure of obtuseness' to 'meet the exigencies of practice with firmness and courage'.[48]

This profound redrawing of the lines of compassionate or humanitarian practice took modern surgery into new affective realms, far from the hardened and brutal dispositions that history had reputed surgeons to carry, but into hardness all the same. In fact, Osler's speech tacitly confirms that, before the rise of anaesthesia, the surgeon would have had a difficult job being so cool and calm in the face of pain, for the signs of pain would have been a furious assault on the senses. Osler, in fact, seems to be pointing medicine into the realm of callousness as if for the first time, and in a laudatory way. There is an implicit acknowledgement that the patient and the public may not be able to understand or sympathize with this new concentrated affective practice, but no quarter is given. And it is this, above all else, that Eakins captures in *The Agnew Clinic*, which distinguishes it from *The Gross Clinic*. The only discernible emotions in the room are in the face of the man immediately to Agnew's left, who looks on with a wry smile of admiration. Insensibility, of the patient and of the cast of medical practitioners and students, had won the day. In this society, and in this precise context, there was no higher mark of humanity than the feeling of nothing at all. Equanimity was not the end of sympathy, but sympathy's displacement to a better end, a higher purpose, a more noble *telos*.

SIX

THE MINISTRY OF
HAPPINESS

I have lately experienced a most personal sense of the historicity of emotions. A friend explained it thus: Generation X struggles to put a label to the peculiar cocktail of emotional experience; Generation Y only wants to express the order of magnitude of feeling. Extremely moving experiences are said to encompass 'all the feels', which, to me, is completely meaningless. That it is meaningful to those who claim to go through such a thing gives me pause. I am, as a confirmed member of Generation X – an almost neo-astrological category of apparent emptiness that, nevertheless, seems to encapsulate me to a tee – witnessing a distancing intergenerational motif. I do not know how to access 'the feels', or know the peculiarities of emotional management when emotion concepts have themselves been boiled down to an all-encompassing generality. I do not find any utility or any depth in communicating by emojis, though these pictographic representations of affect seem to have supplanted substantial modes of feeling by reducing them to the crudest of displays. Needless to say, I am :-(about this to an extent hardly conveyed by such a sign. Yet I overlap with the moral economy of millennials. I am friends with some of them. I have interacted, candidly, confessionally, with them, and they with me. I do not know if we correctly empathize with one another or if we miss each other despite our good intentions.

Equally perplexing, and even more idiomatically everyday, is the phrase 'it's been emotional', or variations thereon. The announcement that an experience has been 'emotional' is supposed to convey a meaningful appreciation of something momentous, but the label itself lacks all specificity. It is as if people can no longer identify, on any level, exactly what kind of affective experience they have had, but only that they have been moved. On the one hand, the clichéd abundance of such statements suggests a profound openness to emotional experience, and on the other, a bewildering emotional aporia: a sort of affective illiteracy. Yet, appearances to the contrary, this vapid generalization seems to carry a great weight with many people. To say that something was 'emotional' makes *sense*, even without further definition or clarification. Even the scholarly literature on the history of emotions has been marked – and perhaps this is also a marker of the generation that predominates in such writing – by an overuse of the adjective 'emotional', as if it is analytically useful to say that a certain historical encounter or situation was an 'emotional experience'. The history of the emotions surely has to do more than beg the question.

Not too long ago, people used to say that they were 'moved' by experiences that 'touched' them. Perhaps this was no more specific than today's *sui generis* 'emotion', but on the face of it such expressions had more traction. At the very least, being moved grounded an experience in the body, connected it to an expression – being moved *to tears*, for example – and implicitly connected both to a kind of solemnity in the object that caused it. Films, funerals, memorial processions, ceremonies: such things had the power to move. In some way the experience was connected either to sadness or to an appreciation of the sublime, of the effect of a kind of grandeur.

If this sounds anecdotal, the following pages should substantially demonstrate the extent to which the category 'emotion', while being ever more tightly defined and delimited by psychological sciences, has been increasingly emptied of experiential meaningfulness. People talk of the emotions all the time, but I am concerned that emotions have been appropriated by institutions and situated outside the body to such an extent that the palette of emotional life has become less colourful for people. Ironically, perhaps, this lack of depth can be indicated by apparently grandiose public displays of emotion that would seem to indicate a much more comfortable and prevalent sense that people are in touch with their emotions. My interpretation, on the contrary, is that such public displays of, say, grief, have only emerged because of a general superficiality of feeling on the one hand, and an ever more powerful inducement to emote publicly on the other. This chapter looks at what I want to call the low stakes of emotion in modernity, which is to refer to the degree of people's engagement with their affective lives. This correlates, unhappily, with the high stakes of emotion as seen from the perspective of corporate and government worlds. Our emotions have long been up for grabs. As Eva Illouz has put it, 'never has the private self been so publicly performed and harnessed to the discourses and values of the economic and political spheres'.[1]

Uniform Happiness

The twentieth century has been defined, by many scholars, as an age of pathological emotions. A raft of new nervous disorders that seemed to be tied to the electricity of modern, relentless urban living was distorted and magnified by the horrors of the First World War and its devastating effect on the minds and bodies of its participants.[2] Conterminously, a new intellectual, pseudo-medical discourse of emotional normativity gave pathological terms and diagnoses to those whose emotions deviated from established boundaries. Increasingly, this seemed to encompass us all. Economic depression and *depression* as a diagnosable form of mental illness seemed to go hand in hand, though the meaning of 'depression', a distinctly twentieth-century coinage to take the place of mania and melancholy, has hardly been stable.[3] Nonetheless, the twentieth century was marked by an overwhelming push – both in medical and psychoanalytical circles and in public discourse – to categorize the negative, afflicted feelings that defined an era characterized by war, violence, loss, grief and rapid social change and displacement.

Contrast this bleak assessment with the British Parliamentary Recruiting Committee poster from 1915, inciting men to enlist. The depicted soldier is ruddy, smiling, at ease. The caption reads, 'He's happy & satisfied – Are you?' With hindsight we might wonder incredulously that anybody might fall for such a scheme, given the unlikeliness of either happiness or satisfaction in any of the various theatres of war. Yet it was, in the grand scheme of recruitment propaganda, both in keeping with the rest and plausibly persuasive. What work does it do?

Implicit in the rhetorical question, 'Are you?' is an answer in the negative, on two levels. First, the government's orchestration of the war effort involved making sure that stigma was attached to those

'He's happy & satisfied – Are you?': First World War British Army recruiting poster from 1915.

who resisted involvement or, worse, protested or objected. A sense of shame was projected by those who appropriated this top-down message, and was doubtless felt by those who looked at enlistment with reluctance. Despite all the images of gleeful pals battalions marching off together in camaraderie, there can have been no uncertainty that war involved danger and death and fear and loss. A generation of children prior to the war had been raised on both the importance of home and family and fantasies of military adventure, such that love of the former may have inspired both fear of leaving and a commanding sense of duty to express that love in service.[4] The shame of being seen out of uniform is almost a cliché. It is something that people seem to know about. The implicit conclusion is that a man out of uniform could not have been happy. That his condition was itself made by the government's orchestration of an emotional regime was overlooked.

The second point is that life, especially among the working classes across the country, was assumed to be bleak, miserable, squalid and deeply dissatisfying. The turn of the century had seen the completion of surveys on the condition of the poor (notably that by Charles Booth, 1840–1916) that painted grotesque pictures of poverty and wealth disparity. These had been compounded by the government's own findings of general unfitness for military service in the South African War around the turn of the century. A broad programme of 'national efficiency' had sought to look after the health of the nation, especially the nation's men, for the sake of the nation's status as the world's leading industrial power. But little attention was paid to the well-being of the nation in a broader sense. The question 'are you happy?' was not on the political radar. Putting it there, in the context of war, was an explicit gearing of emotional and affective qualities to political ends. The beginnings of a state-orchestrated machinery of happiness creation was nothing more than a sham: a light shone on real misery for the sake of putting bodies on the front line.

The thing about emotional regimes, however, is that their successful implementation does lead to experiential change. As noted above, men out of uniform by 1915 doubtless felt the shame, or at the very least a sense of overwhelming pressure, that the authorities had intended them to feel.[5] Likewise it seems safe to assume that the process of enlistment, the putting on of a uniform, the camaraderie of departure and so on, did inspire happiness, or satisfaction, arising from a sense of higher purpose or duty fulfilled, in many. Whether it lasted long in the mud, or in the desert, is another question. The First World War, therefore, saw the rise of a politics of emotion that was explicitly made part of government policy. *Making* people happy, or ashamed, was government business, but it was also government business to set out the terms and conditions of happiness and shame.

To a degree, it worked, though the management of societal shame ultimately seemed to be a more effective means of recruitment than promises of happiness. The realities and horrors of war, both in the heat of battle and in the mangled and maimed aftermath, thrust an unavoidably visible problem into the rhetoric of patriotic duty. As the war poets were fond of pointing out, in the gruesome trenches the glamour and romance of war, of duty and of country soon wore off. Wilfred Owen could not bring himself to say it in English (was it less shameful in Latin?), but he said it nevertheless: Horace's axiom that it was sweet and fitting – oh how close these affective categories are to 'happy and satisfied' – to die for one's country was a lie.[6] Death, and the manner of death, were ignominious. That men were treated to such deaths was a national shame. Moreover, after the war, when men were out of uniform again, those battlefield scars, war wounds and lost limbs that had been marks of heroism became signs of emasculation.[7] The war had constructed rhetorical heroes out of real bodies, but its cessation had unmanned them. Shame and happiness – government business in wartime – assumed different proportions in the aftermath in the shifting context of what was an inherently unstable emotional regime.

If we can look back on war recruitment propaganda from a century or more ago and easily *see through it* to the institutions of power that were attempting to manage both the terms and the experience of happiness and shame, what prevents us from doing the same today? How aware are we of the governmental attempts to delimit the terms of our own happiness, and what are the stakes involved in resistance?

The Happiness Agenda

On 20 March 2017 the weather in Montreal was partially cloudy with a low of -7°c and a high of 5°c. At least it did not snow. I do not remember anything specific about this day. March is generally a forgettable month. According to my email inbox, nothing much happened. A glance at the news summaries from most of the major news outlets for that day also suggests that nothing much happened.

Except 20 March was International Day of Happiness. A more meaningless tag is difficult to imagine, and it seems in general the world failed to notice this momentous day. Yet on this day, at the United Nations, the fifth *World Happiness Report*, for 2017, was issued, following on from a World Happiness Summit in Miami. The first *World Happiness Report* was published in 2012, 'in support of the UN High Level Meeting on happiness and well-being'. 'Since then,' the 2017 *Report* continues gleefully, 'we have come a long way. Happiness is increasingly considered the proper measure of social progress and the goal of public policy.' By way of substantiating this extraordinary remark, the *Report* begins by noting that the Organization for Economic Co-operation and Development (OECD) has 'committed itself "to redefine the growth narrative to put people's well-being at the centre of governments' efforts"'.[8] The OECD has 35 member states and commands a budget of €374 million.[9] Thus happiness and well-being are intertwined, connected to 'progress' and made the subject of economic policy in particular. As a field of academic research, happiness is a hot topic that commands enormous amounts of funding. Indeed, International Day of Happiness is not about being happy per se, but about 'spreading the influence of global happiness research'.[10] Happily, interested readers can refer to the *Journal of Happiness Studies: An Interdisciplinary Forum on Subjective Well-being* (behind a paywall), which is 'devoted to subjective well-being'. It looks for contributions that address 'the conceptualization, measurement, prevalence, explanation, evaluation, imagination and study of happiness'.[11]

The *World Happiness Report* is not alone in offering an index of human happiness and well-being. One might look to the Social Progress Index, run by the Social Progress Imperative, which aims to 'empower leaders and change-makers from business, government, and civil society by providing them with the data they need to understand where their actions will have the greatest impact'. Their Index 'provides difference-makers around the world with an unparalleled tool to target their efforts and track their successes'. And it perhaps goes without saying that one of the major indicators of 'what life is really like for everyday people' is a 'dimension of social progress' called the 'Foundations of Wellbeing'.[12] The elements of the Foundations of Wellbeing are 'Access to Basic Knowledge', 'Access to Information and Communication', 'Health and Wellness' and 'Environmental Quality'. My overriding concern with such studies, apart from the fact they do not in any way illuminate how people actually feel about their lives, is that their targets are explicitly political and capitalistic. According to a post on the Social Progress Imperative's website, 'people who live in a world of social progress are likely to be happier, and it very well may be that happier people are advocates for better lives and higher social progress'.[13] It may very well be. Or not. The vacuity of phrases like 'higher social progress' makes for a difficult assessment, but the politics of such a formulation are clear. Given the emphasis on personal rights and freedoms, access to education, access to information, and so on, we can clearly see that 'social progress' means tending in the direction of liberal democracy. Such a tendency is all very well if you like liberal democracy, but not everybody does, and certainly not everybody likes having liberal democratic change foisted upon them from outside agents. Equating happiness with social progress in such terms basically allows 'change-makers' in the rich, white West to declare other people to be unhappy. The implication is a kind of liberal democratic colonialism, sponsored by entrepreneurs of various stripes. Intentions might be laudable, but the effects *may very well* not induce happiness.

In practice, what does such an index show? Denmark, for example, ranks 5th out of 128 countries when it comes to 'Foundations of Well-being', with a 'score' of 90.86 across the four elements. Yet Denmark has a suicide rate of 10.35/100,000 people, placing it 61st out of 128. Data from another study from 2015 shows that among the little over 2 million Danes and residents of Denmark born between 1 January 1971 and 31 December 2002, and residing in Denmark on their tenth birthday, 46,943 people had attempted suicide, while 1,414 people had actually committed suicide, giving a suicidality rate of 2,337/100,000 people over part of the whole life course, not including those people who have had suicidal thoughts.[14] We might well ask, if 'well-being' – a largely but not entirely economic category – is being conflated with happiness, then why are so many Danes trying to kill themselves?

If the *World Happiness Report* leaves more questions than it answers, how about other surveys? The OECD Better Life Index claims that

> Measuring feelings can be very subjective, but is nonetheless a useful complement to more objective data when comparing quality of life across countries. Subjective data can provide a personal evaluation of an individual's health, education,

income, personal fulfilment and social conditions. Surveys, in particular, are used to measure life satisfaction and happiness.

It goes on to say that 'life satisfaction' is a measure of 'how people evaluate their life as a whole rather than their current feelings', but if you hover your cursor over the link to the 'life satisfaction' data, a little pop-up appears asking 'how happy are you?', showing a clear intent to correlate happy feelings and overall satisfaction.[15] The data is compiled from people's answers to surveys and opinion polls, but it is not immediately apparent how inclusive the data are, though it gives the index a gloss of real-life plausibility. To stick with the Danes as our example, Denmark came in third overall. The language of 'satisfaction' is the key marker of this index, which is given a number rating out of 10. The Danes gave themselves 7.5 out of 10 for 'general satisfaction', showing that they are 'more satisfied with their lives than the OECD average'.[16] Does satisfaction equate to happiness? What does it mean to be 7.5/10 satisfied? And what extremes does such a number conceal?

Gallup's Well-Being Index similarly combines 'objective' measures of well-being and 'subjective' measures. 'Objective' measures include GDP, employment and poverty, as well as health and literacy. Such measures may be indicative of *something* on a national scale, but the tendency of statistics in these categories to average out across populations always risks hiding or overlooking those outliers in a country – minorities or indigenous people, for example – for whom there might be markedly different numbers. Similarly, the 'subjective' ratings of life evaluation and life experience will, when aggregated, tend to flatten out the numbers. What does it mean to rate the well-being of a whole country? Is the nation state really the unit of measurement for happiness? Doubtless there are arguments in favour of it, not least because of its statistical convenience, but there is nothing 'natural' about it. The nation state and this particular well-being agenda are no less 'objective', and no less historical than any of the other accounts I have examined in this book. Big data, allusions to economics as a science, and the implicit trust that people's own evaluations must be reliable, all work to hide the emotional regime(s) that such indexes serve and help form.[17]

The Happy Planet Index, for example, coordinated by the New Economics Foundation (a 'People-powered think tank'), claims to measure 'what matters', providing an implicit definition of happiness as 'sustainable wellbeing for all', again at the level of the nation state.[18] The results look somewhat surprising, however, with the top five happy countries listed as Costa Rica, Mexico, Colombia, Vanuatu and Vietnam. Sweden ranks 61st out of 140. Canada ranks 85th. The usually unimpeachable Danes rank 32nd. The reason, despite the higher life expectancy and high self-evaluation of well-being, is that the former countries appear to be environmentally sound, with sustainable environmental management and low 'ecological footprint'. Despite the massive income inequality, poverty, human-rights abuses and low self-evaluation of well-being of some of these places, the perceived long-term 'happiness' of the planet itself upends the typical happiness scale. People in Scandinavia might live a long time and might think they are happy, but their ecological footprint makes the world a less happy place considered as a whole.[19]

Taken together, these things fall under the head of 'happiness economics'.[20] The reality is that none of these surveys, reports or indices tells us very much at all about what it is like, experientially, to live in these places. They do not say how it is to be marginalized in these places – by race, gender, age, ability, sexual orientation – and what the causes of a statistically manifest unhappiness might be. One might even argue that such things are part of the problem, for in couching happiness in political and economic terms and in promoting political and economic solutions to unhappiness (lack of well-being), they implicitly operate with the neoliberal capitalist agenda. And it is unfulfilling work, high debt, stress, lack of community, loneliness and so on – all symptoms of the neoliberal capitalist agenda – that make people unhappy. Eva Illouz has famously coined the phrase 'emotional capitalism' to describe the appropriation of emotions by economic processes, which in turn have come to define social relations. In emotional capitalism, she explains, 'affect is made an essential aspect of economic behaviour, and emotional life, especially that of the middle classes, follows the logic of economic relations and exchange. Market-based cultural repertoires shape and inform interpersonal and emotional relationships.' Hence, economic relationships become irrevocably bundled with prescriptions for emotional practices. In her terms, phrases like 'cooperation' and 'teamwork' have promoted the language of psychologists and 'the corporate language of efficiency' to the extent that people now *feel* through these scripts, conceptualizing corporate relations as relations per se.[21] I would add that when happiness and well-being (conceived as a single category) are defined in purely economic terms – for example, work–life balance, health (conceived of as a question of work efficiency), fulfilment (at work, in one's career) and education (to prime one for one's best work) – then the reach of emotional capitalism becomes total. So what specifically is being done to happiness to make it, at this historical juncture, the purview of economists? Following on from this, I am concerned to lay out the political implications of the colonization of happiness and well-being by policymakers. What difference does it make that governments might refer to such indices and reports to *tell us* that we are happy? What is happening to the experience of happiness when the terms of happiness are being explicitly prescribed so as to conform to politicized metrics?[22] This is a most pressing political concern for all of us, and leads us to the process of critical and contextual reflection that I signalled in the introduction to this book. Can we, or do we want to, break free of the limiting terms of happiness under emotional capitalism? Or is it sufficient that we simply recognize how the terms of our happiness are being appropriated in order to disrupt and resist them?

Politicking Happiness

Happiness has long been political. As we saw in Chapter One, Aristotle considered *eudaimonia* to be the aim of the good life, with the best example of goodness being the life of politics. In the American Declaration of Independence, the 'unalienable Rights' to 'Life, Liberty and the Pursuit of Happiness' are asserted in distinctly political terms. The Declaration institutionalized the right to pursue happiness (not the right to *be* happy) in American life. The 'pursuit of happiness' has inspired many scholars and authors to try to nail down precisely what could be meant by this phrase, which has had personal, philosophical, sociological, neuroscientific, psychological and economic implications. Everything hinges on a definition, the slipperiness of which provides the political dimension.[23]

Jeremy Bentham, the famous father of utilitarianism, was referring to the French variety of revolution when he referred to 'natural and imprescriptible rights' as 'rhetorical nonsense, – nonsense upon stilts', which were dangerous because they provoked unrest and discord against governments.[24] In his own way, Bentham understood the constructedness of rights and their connection to a historical and political moment, which implied also that they could dissolve and disappear. To make the 'pursuit of happiness' a natural right seems to be a variety of this kind of rhetorical nonsense, for happiness is neither stable enough to be able to build a polity around it, nor flexible enough to allow for changes in society, culture, political ideals and so on. Happiness, as with any of the other affective labels we have been exploring in this book, is not a fixed category. It cannot be defined for all time. There are major reasons to doubt that the happiness currently being pursued by Americans, if indeed they are exercising that right, has any resemblance to the happiness the drafters of the Declaration had in mind.

To return to the most cursory but definitive of examples, Johnson's 1755 dictionary defined happiness as the 'state in which the desires are satisfied', connecting the pursuit of happiness to the satisfaction of other desires (see the section on Wollstonecraft in Chapter Four). In other words, happiness was not an end in itself. Even then, one of Johnson's usage examples showed some complexity, and was portentous about the kinds of practical difficulties involved in making the pursuit of happiness a right. For, according to Locke, since the 'same thing is not good to every man alike', so 'every one does not place his *happiness* in the same thing'. Johnson's other entries for happiness made it synonymous with 'good luck' and with 'unstudied grace'.[25] While the affinity between luck and happiness is perhaps preserved (especially in German), the mapping of the two is by no means straightforward. As for unstudied grace, or 'fortuitous elegance', surely this meaning is lost. In any case, when the authors of the Declaration invoked happiness, they could not have been referring to a right to pursue luck or grace, but rather were honing in on the satisfaction of desire, on attaining an ease and contentment in life as a whole that comes with the realization of one's wishes. This is a far cry from *eudaimonia*, but it is equally far from what happiness has come to mean in our world. As we shall see, the satisfaction of desire has transformed into a kind of striving: for work–life balance, for meaning-making, for well-being. Happiness in the twentieth century became an end of certain strands of medicine, which remain entangled with intentions to instrumentalize happiness for political ends.[26]

What are the current global stakes of happiness, in a world that often looks to be in poor supply of it?

Few politicians have been more explicit about the 'happiness agenda' than David Cameron, who launched an initiative in Britain in 2010 to get beyond GDP as a measure of the nation's well-being. He quoted Bobby Kennedy, who once said that GDP 'does not allow for the health of our children, the quality of their education, or the joy of their play. It measures neither our wisdom nor our learning; neither our compassion nor our devotion to our country; it measures everything, in short, except that which makes life worthwhile.' Cameron endorsed these sentiments, while branding them an overstatement. Nonetheless, he asked the Office for National Statistics 'to devise a new way of measuring wellbeing in Britain'. He pointed out his own examples of how GDP itself can tell a misleading story: GDP increases after an earthquake, because of reconstruction; GDP increases 'when a city is torn apart by crime and disorder', 'because we spend money on locks'; a person falling seriously ill 'can increase GDP, because of the cost of buying drugs and paying for care'. GDP goes up, well-being clearly goes down. Yet the specific politics of his 'happiness agenda' addressed social conservative concerns about 'progressive' social policies that had negatively impacted well-being from a specifically conservative point of view. In other words, the measurement of well-being was de facto in place in the speech calling for new instruments of well-being measurement.

The examples are explicit: 'We had, in Britain, something of an immigration free-for-all justified by the argument that it [sic] supposed to be good for growth, but without enough thought about the impact on public services and social cohesion.' Cameron's happiness agenda was anti-immigration, based on an assessment that well-being was adversely affected by immigration. 'We've had something of a cheap booze free-for-all – again, supposed to be good for growth, but were we really thinking about the impact of that on law and order and on wellbeing?' His happiness agenda was anti-social, pro-law and order, and implicitly expressed a desire to appropriate people's personal health under government policy. 'We've had something of an irresponsible media and marketing free-for-all – again, this was meant to be good for growth, but what about the impact on childhood?' The specifics of this statement are less clear, though the connection of the happiness agenda to a curtailment of media freedoms is implicit. In sum, Cameron's happiness agenda looked a lot like Conservative Party policy.[27]

By 2014, in the depths of austerity politics and an apparent tide of misery and dissatisfaction across the country, the happiness agenda looked lost. But Brian Wheeler for the BBC reported that it was very much alive, if in apparent disarray. His editorial on the happiness agenda and the testimony of the man responsible for it, Nick Hurd MP, before a parliamentary committee, is evidence of critical scepticism about its usefulness. Nick Hurd, 'for a man in the happiness business', Wheeler wrote, 'does not smile very much'. According to Hurd's testimony, 'happiness is a very difficult concept to measure. You are constantly "tip-toeing" towards "stating the bleeding obvious".' The ineffectiveness of the happiness agenda in influencing policy is summarized in the following key points: 'Why . . . are people in Stoke-on-Trent less content with life than those in other towns? It's something to do with their personal "characteristics" apparently. And what about Swansea? Why are its inhabitants so miserable? (No one seems to know.)'[28] The journalistic scorn aside, the substantial point is that the happiness agenda, despite the efforts of those who try to measure well-being, does not actually make much difference beyond rhetoric.

This is not, however, to belittle rhetoric. Rhetoric is the politician's main weapon. Thucydides understood its power. Rhetoric makes emotions, if it is constructed well. When Cameron set out the happiness agenda it was a way of attaching an affective, qualitative and life-affirming set of labels to an otherwise fairly typical Conservative platform. It was branding, attempting to make Tories feel good about being Tories. Perhaps it worked. If so, it did not so much measure happiness as make it. For those who suffered from the raft of cuts in social and benefit spending, however, the happiness agenda was nothing but empty rhetoric, an emotive bite with no teeth.

Elsewhere, the happiness agenda has been institutionalized at the level of high politics in no uncertain terms. In February 2016 the United Arab Emirates appointed its first Minister of Happiness. Readers will be forgiven for thinking the office sounds somewhat Orwellian. The office holder is Ohood bint Khalfan Al Roumi, who also acts as the Director General of the Prime Minister's office and is a member of the Global Entrepreneurship Council of the UN. This, coupled with her background in Business Administration, suggests the subtext of the happiness agenda. 'What is the purpose of government if it does not work toward the happiness of the people?' she has asked rhetorically, even though scores of scholars might actually come forward with substantial alternative answers.[29] 'It's the duty and role of the government to create the right conditions for people to choose to be happy,' she says. If that construction seems to put quite some distance between her office and the actual creation of happiness, perhaps this is apt. The focus, as with the happiness indices, is actually on well-being, and that ultimately makes the office economically orientated. In the politics of happiness, these policies have an irresistibly positive appeal: 'We have no intention as a government to impose happiness, or mandate it, or force it,' she says. 'We're just doing the right thing for our people . . . so they can have a better life.' Quite how it might be imposed, mandated or forced if a government chose to do so is perhaps moot. Then again, the emphasis on simply altering conditions so that people can 'choose' happiness understates the government's intentions. For Roumi has also said that cultivating happiness is 'a science. It touches on medicine, health, social sciences. We're trying to bring it from a broad framework into a daily practice in our society.'

What are the specific measures in the UAE that are designed to make the conditions for happiness? It is still early days. As one of her advisers, Meik Wiking of the Happiness Research Institute in (where else?) Copenhagen, Denmark, said in 2017, 'They don't know yet how they're going to increase happiness . . . First they're trying to work out what drives wellbeing in the country.'[30] Still, Roumi has installed 'happiness meters' in offices, much like those one sees outside bathrooms and security lines at some airports. In 2018 Dubai will roll out happiness meters to the public as part of its aim to make 'the happiest city in the world'.[31] Punch an emoji in the face to register your happiness, unhappiness or neutrality about the experience you have just had. She launched a campaign for '100 days of positivity': students and teachers are pledged to 'practise positive behaviour'. There are 'happiness patrols' in Abu Dhabi. Good drivers get rewards, rather than bad drivers getting tickets. It is surveillance with a positive twist. It nevertheless depends, for its success, on drivers carrying an awareness that they are being watched. Roumi has sent her 'Chief Happiness and Positivity Officers' off into the world to 'be trained in how to create a more positive workforce and, ultimately, a more joyful nation', though it is unclear whether the Greater Good Science Center at uc Berkeley, or the Mindfulness Centre at the University of Oxford, will be able to impart specific policy advice. The former aims to study the 'psychology, sociology, and neuroscience of well-being, and teaches skills that foster a thriving, resilient, and compassionate society', whereas the latter has a 'vision' of the 'world without the devastating effects of depression, where mindfulness enables people to live with awareness, wisdom and compassion', again with a focus on clinical and neuroscientific research so as to develop and teach 'new approaches to mindfulness-based interventions'.[32] When mindfulness becomes government policy, and when business and economics are top of the mind, the word 'intervention' has the potential to raise ethical concerns. Are the politics of happiness really about individual feelings of well-being, or are they about instrumentalizing happiness to business efficiency? After all, depression costs money, directly and indirectly. Absenteeism is a major drag on profitability. Illouz notes that psychologists were invited into the corporate realm of 'management' precisely to 'find solutions to the problem of discipline and productivity'.[33] It is not so much that the worker's emotions have to go away, so much as that they have to be re-focused and newly delimited so as to operate within the framework of the corporation's needs, of its employees as workers, and of workers as consumers.[34] The sociologist Arlie Russel Hochschild showed long ago that corporate emotional prescription *makes* the emotions of employees.[35] Being compelled to smile is formational of happiness, yes, but the happiness we are talking about is defined and delimited by the context of the forced smile. It is not happiness in the abstract. Indeed, it seems to have shown that there is no such thing as happiness in the abstract. If emotional states are always subject to instrumentalization, then corporate emotions are only a more conscious form of control. With these things in mind, how likely is it that happiness as a government project conjures with happiness as an end in itself?

If my narrative sounds cynical, it should be pointed out that the uae's record on making people unhappy has been particularly noted by such groups as Amnesty International, who are on record as recently as June 2017 pointing out the uae's involvement in torture campaigns both domestically and in Yemen. Amnesty has reminded the uae that it became party to the un convention against torture in

2012, and that it is a signatory to the global Arms Trade Treaty, which obliges them to 'refrain from acts that defeat the Treaty's purpose, which includes reducing human suffering'.[36] The U.S., also implicated in this torture report, noted in its State Department Report on Human Rights Practices for 2016 that the UAE's chief problems were 'the inability of citizens to choose their government in free and fair periodic elections; limitations on civil liberties (including the freedoms of speech, press, assembly, and association); and arrests without charge, incommunicado detentions, lengthy pretrial detentions, and mistreatment during detention'. These are compounded by 'lack of government transparency; police and prison guard brutality; government interference with privacy rights, including arrests and detentions for internet postings or commentary; and a lack of judicial independence'. The list goes on, noting that non-citizens, women and people with HIV/AIDS come in for particularly rough treatment in society.[37] It is highly unlikely that the jurisdiction of the Minister for Happiness is far-reaching enough to allow UAE citizens to 'choose happiness' under such conditions.

We must be careful, while emphasizing that torture should be contraindicated on any happiness agenda, that happiness and freedom (or 'rights') are not unquestioningly and axiomatically connected. It is a conceit of the liberal democratic West that anti-democratic or secretive regimes make all of their citizens miserable. We know, from substantial research on the German Democratic Republic (East Germany), for example, that the happiness agenda there worked to a large extent where it was employed among children. It did not work for everyone, and one should not understate the degree of suffering that the regime brought about, but practices of happiness, wrought by government prescriptions and enforcement, did undoubtedly raise happiness. In the GDR, its particular expression was love of country and fealty to party ideology: the greater the extent to which an individual could be nurtured genuinely and *authentically* to feel such things, the happier that individual would be within that system. Juliane Brauer has carefully documented practices of childhood collective singing to show that not all the smiles under communism were forced, and not every practice conducted in fear.[38] This does not preclude criticism of the regime. It is merely to point out that happiness is not limited to a pre-defined set of external conditions. Humans are emotively adaptable. We can be 'happy', for whatever worth the label retains, seemingly anywhere.

This, one suspects, is the aim of the Ministry of Happiness in the UAE, although contentment at work, not love of country, is its expression. It does not intend to reach everyone and it does not need to. It only needs to apply to those people whose daily lives unquestioningly reinforce state power. For those people, the government's happiness agenda might well prove to be a real boon. Certainly I am in no position to gainsay anybody who says 'I am happy,' however implausible it sounds from my point of view. Nevertheless, the example of the UAE is perhaps a cautionary tale of the kinds of work being done *to* happiness once happiness is politicized. If one needed any further warning, one need only look to the Venezuelan Ministry of Supreme Social Happiness, created in 2013. As the BBC reported at the time, the country had a 50 per cent inflation rate and suffered 'chronic shortages of basic goods'.[39] The Ministry was widely and routinely mocked throughout mainstream and social media in the West.

Such programmes beg an awkward question of institutions like Denmark's privately run Happiness Research Institute, as well as those fee-taking academic institutions that educate would-be happiness policymakers. What are the ethics of essentially operating a consultancy firm for making happiness strategies for anybody who can pay for the service? If Denmark has a name for doing well in happiness indices, then why not sell the Danish brand. Meik Wiking has experience with this, having published *The Little Book of Hygge: The Danish Way to Live Well* with Penguin in 2016. It remains at time of writing in the best-seller lists. Apparently his Institute is frequently visited by people from South Korea. In an extraordinary identification – almost Platonic – of individual striving for happiness and the embodiment of emotion in a nation state, Wiking says that South Korea is 'the poster child for the way a lot of countries feel, in that they've got far richer over the past decades without their quality of life or wellbeing necessarily increasing'. It struggles to convert 'wealth into wellbeing'. He points to the country's high suicide rate (27.3/100,000 in 2014) as indicative of a happiness problem. South Korea places 26th out of 128 in the Social Progress Index, though it is 119th in terms of its suicide rate. In striving for a better work–life balance, one of Wiking's recommendations is entrepreneurship, not as a cure for the misery of others, but as a cure for one's own unhappiness. 'Surveys show that entrepreneurs are generally happier than those who are salaried,' is one of the insights gained by the Institute, which provides a wonderfully loopy logic.[40] The happiness industry promotes socially progressive entrepreneurship to bring happiness to the lives of others, while noting that entrepreneurs are particularly happy and satisfied with their lives. Perhaps everyone should be an entrepreneur then? How does that work out for isolated members of society in the UAE, or in Korea? I have previously written of the curious tension in entrepreneurship between serving society (for a profit) and self-interested motivation, arguing that the great tide of new entrepreneurs of a social bent is an extension of the spirit of capitalism formulated by Max Weber, in which a 'man exists for the sake of his business instead of the reverse'.[41] They have a 'calling',

> driven by a burning drive to prove themselves (to themselves, as well as to their fellows), seeking an area in which to do so, preferably an area in which they can gain power, and preferably also one in which in some symbolic way they can vent their rage at the elites who have caused their troubles.[42]

Shortly after the Second World War Joseph Schumpeter pointed to this inevitable social instrumentality of entrepreneurial activity, noting that it 'impresses the stamp of its mentality upon the social organism'. This mentality bore 'the stamp of ideological preconception', but lacked the reflexivity to allow for a kind of critical entrepreneurship.[43] Back in 1949 Schumpeter was at the forefront of new research at the Harvard University Research Center in Entrepreneurial History, which explored the historicity of entrepreneurship and the stakes of its ideology or mentality (whether in the individual or writ large), but the impetus was lost and the new wave of *fin de siècle* entrepreneurs have entered the scene without the tools for critical reflection on what it means to 'do good' or 'make happy'.[44]

Return to Aristotle

This book began with an explanation of Aristotle's view of politics as the most excellent means towards 'happiness', which was unpacked and decoded to show that 'happiness' is hardly an adequate translation of that state of *eudaimonia* that comes with the highest good. We now come full circle, and again ask about the politics of happiness, but we find in our own age a distinct inversion of the Aristotelian scheme. For now we find that happiness has become a means to political power, which is its own justification. Insofar as happiness is shown to be an objectively measurable quality, it is then used to explain and to legitimize certain styles and expressions of political power, as if politics is designed to make citizens happy. Citizens, in turn, are debarred from political activity, for politicians will tell them that they are happy under their happiness regime. As with Aristotle's definition of *eudaimonia*, it is understood that people might be objectively identifiable as happy, even if they do not experience any happiness per se. But unlike Aristotle's *eudaimonia*, which was carefully defined according to the personal experience of an individual, today's happiness seems to be constructed independently of anyone's actual experience, whether we think of happiness as an emotion or a general disposition. When the 'happiest' nations on the planet also have the highest suicide rates on the planet, what substantial meaning can we ascribe to happiness any more?

Recently an attempt has been made by researchers based at the 'Emotion and Self-Regulation Laboratory' at the Hebrew University in Jerusalem to subvert the politicization of happiness regimes by re-invoking an Aristotelian thesis.[45] Rather than a simple pleasure/happiness correlation, the researchers looked for evidence that the capacity to feel contextually appropriate emotions led to greater happiness, even if the emotions in question were 'negative', such as anger or hate. The hypothesis is drawn from a cursory gloss of the *Nicomachean Ethics*, reducing the Aristotelian thesis to the following: 'Happiness, according to Aristotle, should involve feeling emotions that people deem to be appropriate given their needs and motives. Building on Aristotle's account, therefore, we define "feeling right" as feeling emotions that one considers to be desirable.'[46]

The results of the research undertaken are breathtaking confirmation of the hypothesis, that happiness consists in 'feeling right', not 'feeling pleasure'. The study is culturally reflexive, employing 2,324 university students from eight countries, and is meant to be representative of seven-eighths of 'world cultural regions'. It is, the researchers claim, the first empirical test of the Aristotelian thesis, and they conclude that while it holds true that the secret to happiness might involve 'feeling good' (that is, pleasure), it also involves 'feeling right', which might mean that happiness depends on anger or hatred, in a given situation. 'Happiness', they conclude, 'entails feeling emotions that are valued, as determined by the unique personal, social, and cultural context of each individual.'[47]

What if we unpick the hypothesis that this study tested? What if we show that the premise is flawed, that the reading of Aristotle is reductive and wrong, and that the conclusions are focused on individual emotional effort at the expense of the cultural context in which emotional striving and emotional *doing* takes place? What if we point out that this study of 'feeling right' is not cognizant of the practical component of feeling, and that the question of whether one can feel what one desires to feel is intertwined with social codes relating to the appropriateness of practices relating to different emotions? In other words, if a person wants to feel anger, is that person allowed also to express that anger in whatever way she feels necessary in order to 'feel right'? The same question applies to hatred. The implications for 'feeling right' are dangerous and alarming. What if the practices associated with 'feeling right' involve violence and oppression? What if hatred and anger are targeted at minorities? What if such feelings tap into political dynamics of oppression, exclusion and all levels of violence including ethnic cleansing? Are we to validate the 'happiness' so experienced in such moments because the perpetrators 'felt right' about it?

Such studies are naive in the extreme, despite the extraordinary level of press coverage they receive, and their employment of Aristotle as a hypothesis to test is almost laughably reductive. First, even if we concede that Aristotle was talking about 'happiness' when he was talking about *eudaimonia*, we have to remember that he was talking about a state that could only really be achieved through extensive experience, up to and including the whole course of life. Passing emotional states and their associated practices could be signs of virtuous existence, depending on how an emotion was handled, but such a passing state could not be equated with an individual's own feeling of happiness, satisfaction, *eudaimonia*, or whatever we should choose to call it. Second, a person's state of *eudaimonia* was supposed to be objectively measurable, which is to say that an individual's momentary or even longer-lasting feelings were immaterial in the final analysis of whether that person was good and therefore happy.

The key is that society decides on virtue, not the individual, for society supplies the parameters of virtuous practices and that which constitutes either deficiency of action or transgression through excess.

This element is wholly missing from such studies that focus entirely on emotional satisfaction. That they do so while invoking Aristotle is unfortunate. As we continue to probe at what makes us happy, and whether the question is even important any more (and if so, for whom?), we overlook the social and the moral at our peril. The happiness of a society of individuals is the neoliberal dream of, at best, the amoral, and at worst, the immoral. If we set out our stall to understand happiness as the emotional fulfilment of any emotion, including anger and hate, at the individual level, then we descend into a chaos fuelled by the happiness designs of the powerful and the violent. If we take at face value the bare fact that anger and hatred can be satisfying, that such emotions can make individuals feel right about themselves and the world, surely we cannot leave it at that. Society functions to delimit what is acceptable and to penalize those who operate outside its norms. This is not to sanctify any particular set of norms, or to preach any particular set of values, but simply to state that the values attached to feelings and their associated practices are policed by something bigger than the individual for the sake of something bigger than the individual.

In William Reddy's terms, this 'emotional regime' can be a happy place or it can be a place that causes a great deal of suffering.[48] In either case, however, happiness does not boil down to an individual's freedom to feel this way or that. Aristotle understood something like this. He understood that the practices of anger, for example, would determine whether or not *society* was satisfied with this particular expression of a passion. Finding the right form of habitual behaviour was key to the moral status of the individual and the moral state of the community as a whole. In a community where peaceful practices of justice are carried out by the state and by government, personal feelings of anger would have to be channelled through the appropriate institutions and process of law. Where individuals feel dissatisfied with such a check on their desire to unleash their rage, we would have to take the view, from the perspective of that society, that their dissatisfaction – their unhappiness at being unable to feel how they desired to feel – is necessary and even unimportant. Presumably the satisfaction derived from successfully pursuing one's righteous indignation through the courts would, in these circumstances, provide a superior form of satisfaction; a less immediate gratification of passionate flourishing, but a more satisfying outcome for having the ultimate sanction of society as a whole, as represented by its institutions. And in such a regime as this, the person who did give in to an immediate display of rage would, ultimately, not derive any satisfaction from it, even if it were momentarily to 'feel right'. Society would sanction the transgression, or display fear at the individual's apparent lack of control. The very functionality of society depends on such checks and sanctions.

All of this begs the question: how do we know, how can we know, that we are in a happy society, or that we as individuals are happy, or satisfied, with our lot? Since society's prescriptive norms for emotional practices tend to be inscribed without the members of society's conscious reflection, some might argue that it is impossible for the conformist to do what Aristotle ultimately desired: objectively measure our state of satisfaction. All we can do is measure our satisfaction according to the standards set for us.

This is perhaps a little bleak. Our alienation is not complete, for there is still that sense of individual dissatisfaction to fall back upon. When William Reddy conceptualized 'emotional suffering' he was principally concerned with the distance between an individual's feelings and the prescribed expressions of emotions in a given context. One can suffer through conformity and know full well that one is not happy, even if the state insists, as many states have done and still do, that one is. Moreover, if enough people find a connection in this source of individual unhappiness or suffering, then regime change can be brought about. Exposing the apparent naturalness of an emotional regime for the constructed political framework it actually is already goes some way to undermining it. When a sufficient number of people act in concert with the conscious aim of being freed from emotional constraint, then a regime falls and, perhaps, the emotional suffering of a polity suddenly gets cast in relief. A new emotional regime takes the place of the old. Those who thought they were happy under the previous scheme suddenly find the tables turned. The new happy means veiled suffering for them, unless they can successfully habituate themselves to the new order. And so on.

Moments of crisis and of upheaval, especially in times of political change among the shifting perception of belonging to a community, a society, a nation or a bigger polity, suddenly shine a light on social norms and on the apparently natural. Common assumptions and common sense suddenly look ungainly, out of place, falsehoods and nonsense. We live in such times. Are we happy? I suggest we do not refer to a happiness index to find out. But we might refer to one another.

CONCLUSION:
THE VALUE OF EXPERIENCE

I f this book has gone some way to elucidating the enormous scope
of the history of feelings, it has in equal measure made manifest
the inherent limitations of the history of *emotions*. That term –
'emotions' – which is as beguiling as it is maddening, itself defies a
clear definition, yet its use is nonetheless leading for that. It speaks
to a fixity of psychology, and of psychology itself as a transcendent
field of inquiry; or else is occupied by a kind of transcendental evolutionary biology, which tends to overlook changes to the human in
historical time as mere ripples in a much older and more profound
story. It works as a semantic shorthand for the kinds of things we
are looking for and trying to explain, but it misleads as often as it
helps. It captures certain kinds of phenomena, particularly relating
to *expression*, but it fails miserably to explain the experience of sensation, or the intermingling of cognition, reason and affection, and
it tends to pre-limit the scope of enquiry to those 'emotions' that
we already know. Those parts of affective life that are lost are likely
to remain that way, so long as our historical research is led by our
presentist predilections.

I have tried to avoid these pitfalls by talking in a general sense
about 'feelings', which remain semantically vague in contemporary
English, and about affective experiences in the languages of historical actors themselves. At the very least, when talking about feelings
the subject-matter is not automatically pre-limited to the terms of
what an fMRI scanner somewhere can see light up. But I am left
with a nagging doubt about how this contribution fits in the overall
scheme of historical knowledge and its relevance to contemporary
research on 'emotions'. It may be more useful to incorporate the

history of emotions, as a subset, into a broader category of scholarly research: experience. It seems to me that the question 'how did
it feel?' encompasses more than simply emotion, but also all kinds
of sensation, inflected by situated knowledge. The question points
to the category of experience in general. Its advantage is that the
specific object of enquiry is not laden with the risk of anachronism
in quite the same way as emotion. We do not need to find people
using past iterations of the word 'experience' in order to say that
experiences were being had, and nor does the deployment of the
word 'experience' in the present predetermine what is specifically
meant by the term. There is no comparative science – psychological or
neurobiological – of experience, as there is with emotion, to set us at
odds with disciplines beyond the boundaries of historiography. Yet,
in dealing with experience, we are perfectly equipped still to tackle
questions of emotion, and of whatever was there before emotion
meant anything. Since there are so many cross-disciplinary crossed
wires regarding emotion talk, it may actually help historians reach
out by avoiding reference to that which is always already pre-loaded
with fixed definitions and disciplinary methodologies.

By using the word 'experience' I think we also open up the
political possibilities of this kind of research to a much greater extent
than with the emotions conceived narrowly. Just taking the happiness
examples in Chapter Six, for example, there is a great deal of uncertainty about whether anybody in prescriptive happiness regimes really
feels happy, but there can be no question that everybody experiences
such regimes in one way or another. There is an affective register to
be explored, beneath the prescriptions and beyond the rhetoric of
emotional well-being. The implicit and symbolic violence of a government mandate to *make* happiness on a national scale, with a full
appropriation of what it means to be happy and what it takes to *do*
happy, should actually lead us to explore the impact of that violence,
not the extent of that happiness. To be sure, that research is difficult
and possibly dangerous to conduct, but it is no less pressing for these
considerations. In historical contexts there is less (or no) risk, which
makes the approach all the more attractive. What lies beneath the
surface of affective prescription? How did people feel about what
they were doing, or what was being done unto them? What did they
do about how they felt? What were the limits of what could be done,
and who set those limits? These questions have, to a great extent,

informed the episodes and examples explored in this book. They speak to something beyond the presence of a feeling itself, leading to an analysis of evaluation of feelings. Did feelings feel *right* or *wrong*, and who or what determined this? That question stalks us in the present as much as it ever harried people in the past.

Our feeling of what is right and what is wrong used to be called the 'moral sense' in English. Perhaps some people still frame it this way. Yet eighteenth- and nineteenth-century constructions of the moral sense, or of projections further back into history to examine the moral sense of the past, usually had in mind the unconsciousness of conscience. Somehow, whether by natural biological and/or evolutionary processes, or by divine intent, the moral sense was generally thought to be inborn. Where it was faulty, it was a fault of 'nature', broadly construed. Even those, such as Kant, who understood the importance of the senses in the experience of the world, nevertheless saw the senses as stable.[1] And even those nineteenth-century educational reformers who thought that the least worthy of humanity could be redeemed by being taken in hand, had to fight against a dominant tide of sentiment, especially from the world of biological science, eugenics and evolutionary theory, that moral taint – *unfitness* – was fixed. The history of emotions' major contribution, as I see it, is in shining a light on the institutions of power that make emotional prescriptions, that essentially frame and delimit 'moral economies'.[2] It is a light that picks out the cultural shaping of human feelings, even to the extent that what seems unconscious, or 'natural', has been significantly influenced by the cultural webs in which human biology is ensnared.[3] We are journeying towards a biocultural history of the moral sense, where we might better understand the power of an exhortation to see and to feel in this way or that about the world.[4] We can understand anew the internal struggle of people to try to feel right, and the changing stakes of failure in different kinds of context. When more substantially realized, we will have a history of experience that foregrounds the perceived, that is the *felt*, value of experience. And all of this, if we choose to do it, can be turned on ourselves and on the prescriptive cultural regimes in which we dwell. It would not be for the purpose of an endless and pointless moral relativism, but rather for the purpose of empowerment. Exposing the architecture of a dominant moral economy, revealing how the prescriptions are made and the power deployed, is the first step towards modifying or even dismantling it, towards making a framework in which those under the uncomfortable yoke of power can more easily feel right about their experiences. If I entertain a hope, therefore, it is that readers are given genuine pause for thought when they are next asked, 'how do you feel?'

REFERENCES

Introduction: Feeling for History

1 On the vagaries of empathy, see Susan Lanzoni, 'Introduction: Emotion and the Sciences: Varieties of Empathy in Science, Art, and History', *Science in Context*, XXV (2012), pp. 287–300; Lanzoni, 'A Short History of Empathy', *The Atlantic*, 15 October 2015. For some essential handwringing about the distinctiveness of something called empathy (*Einfühlung*), see Max Scheler, *Wesen und Formen der Sympathie*, 5th edn (Frankfurt, 1948). For a brief account of the 'slipperiness' of empathy, including a variety of neuroscientific angles, see Rob Boddice, *The History of Emotions* (Manchester, 2018), pp. 55–6, 124–8.

2 Richard Evans's *In Defence of History* (London, 1997) carved out the response to the nadir of postmodernity, namely Keith Jenkins, *Re-thinking History* (London, 1991). More intellectually rigorous and useful approaches, such as those of Hayden White, seemed the more menacing in the light of Jenkins's extremes. For the particular reference here, see Hayden White, 'The Historical Text as Literary Artifact', *Tropics of Discourse: Essays in Cultural Criticism* (Baltimore, MD, 1985), pp. 81–100.

3 Linda Connor, response to Paul Shankman, 'The Thick and the Thin: On the Interpretative Theoretical Program of Clifford Geertz', *Current Anthropology*, XXV (1984), pp. 261–80 (p. 271).

4 The notion of finding out how it felt to be there, then, is most clearly expressed in Lynn Hunt, 'The Experience of Revolution', *French Historical Studies*, XXXII (2009), pp. 671–8. Some historians of emotions have been reluctant to set this as their goal, seeing a fundamental barrier to experience in the historical record. I suppose this to be a lack of historical imagination in part, but a serious underrating of the capacity to *see* through reconstructed contexts, languages and gestures.

5 For other *longue durée* studies, see J. Liliequist, ed., *A History of Emotions, 1200–1800* (London, 2013); Barbara Rosewein, *Generations of Feeling: A History of Emotions, 600–1700* (Cambridge, 2016); Elena Carrera, ed., *Emotions and Health, 1200–1700* (Leiden, 2013). A more theoretically engaging account, which focuses largely on rhetoric, is Daniel M. Gross,

The Secret History of Emotion: From Aristotle's Rhetoric to Modern Brain Science (Chicago, IL, 2006).

6 Boddice, *History of Emotions*.

7 Readers should refer to my *History of Emotions* for a full account of this, but more programmatic accounts, including their intellectual rationale, can be found in Rob Boddice, 'The History of Emotions: Past, Present, Future', *Revista de Estudios Sociales*, LXII (2017), pp. 10–15; Rob Boddice (with Daniel Lord Smail), 'Neurohistory', in *Debating New Approaches in History*, ed. P. Burke and M. Tamm (London, 2018).

8 Boddice (with Smail), 'Neurohistory'.

9 Allusions to culture notwithstanding, this is the popular view espoused by Antonio Damasio, *Self Comes to Mind: Constructing the Conscious Brain* (New York, 2012); Damasio, *The Feeling of What Happens: Body and Emotion in the Making of Consciousness* (Orlando, FL, 1999). An essential critique was supplied by Gross, *Secret History of Emotion*.

10 A particularly fierce critique has been supplied by Roger Cooter, 'Neural Veils and the Will to Historical Critique: Why Historians of Science Need to Take the Neuro-turn Seriously', *Isis*, CV (2014), pp. 145–54. The threat of a new Dark Ages was uttered by Cooter in a paper presented at the Department of Social Studies of Medicine, McGill University, November 2017.

11 Jean-Paul Sartre, *Sketch for a Theory of the Emotions*, trans. Philip Mairet (London, 2002), pp. 11–14 (p. 10).

12 For example, Lisa Feldman-Barrett, 'Are Emotions Natural Kinds?', *Perspectives on Psychological Science*, 1 (2006), pp. 28–58.

13 See Daniel Lord Smail, *On Deep History and the Brain* (Berkeley, CA, 2008), pp. 147–8, 193–4.

14 For example, I.C.G. Waever et al., 'Epigenetic Programming by Maternal Behavior', *Nature Neuroscience*, VII (2004), pp. 847–54; R. K. Silbereisen and X. Chen, eds, *Social Change and Human Development: Concepts and Results* (London, 2010); E. Jablonka and M. J. Lamb, *Evolution in Four Dimensions: Genetic, Epigenetic, Behavioural, and Symbolic Variation in the History of Life* (Cambridge, MA, 2005).

15 For an example of the former, see Arne Öhman, 'The Biology of Fear: Evolutionary, Neural, and Psychological Perspectives', in *Fear Across the Disciplines*, ed. Benjamin Lazier and Jan Plamper (Pittsburgh, PA, 2012), pp. 35–50. The principal affect universalists are Paul Ekman and Silvan Tomkins: see, in particular, Silvan Tomkins, *Affect Imagery Consciousness*, 4 vols (New York, 1962–3, 1991–2); Paul Ekman and Wallace Friesen, *Pictures of Facial Affect* (Palo Alto, CA, 1976).

16 Defined in William Reddy, 'Against Constructionism: The Historical Ethnography of Emotions', *Current Anthropology*, XXXVIII (1997), pp. 327–51.

17 See in particular, Lisa Feldman-Barrett, 'Solving the Emotion Paradox: Categorization and the Experience of Emotion', *Personality and Social Psychology Review*, X (2006), pp. 20–46, and Feldman-Barrett, 'Are Emotions Natural Kinds?'

18 This neatly accords with what practice theorists have been saying for some time. See Monique Scheer, 'Are Emotions a Kind of Practice (and is that what makes them have a history)? A Bourdieuian Approach to Understanding Emotion', *History and Theory*, LI (2012), pp. 193–220.

19 There have been some beginnings: M. Pernau et al., *Civilizing Emotions: Concepts in Nineteenth-century Asia and Europe* (Oxford, 2015); Paolo Santangelo, *La rappresentazione della emozioni nella Cina tradizionale* (Modena, 2014); Barbara Schuler, ed., *Historicizing Emotions: Practices and Objects in India, China, and Japan* (Leiden, 2018).

20 See, for example, Alan G. Fix, *Migration and Colonization in Human Microevolution* (Cambridge, 1999); Alex Mesoudi, 'Pursuing Darwin's Curious Parallel: Prospects for a Science of Cultural Evolution', *Proceedings of the National Academy of Sciences of the United States of America*, CXIV (2017), pp. 7853–60.

21 This was the profound, though unsaid, implication of Charles Darwin's *On the Origin of Species* (London, 1859). For the implications at the level of scientific practice, see Rob Boddice, *The Science of Sympathy: Morality, Evolution and Victorian Civilization* (Urbana-Champaign, IL, 2016).

22 Here I mirror the intent of Michael Champion and Andrew Lynch, 'Understanding Emotions: "The Things They Left Behind"', in *Understanding Emotions in Early Europe*, ed. Champion and Lynch (Turnhout, 2015), pp. ix–xxxiv (p. xiv); and of Thomas Dixon, *From Passions to Emotions: The Creation of a Secular Psychological Category* (Cambridge, 2006).

23 If one overlooks her search for something transcendent and universal, this is the overriding impression given by the evidence of Anna Wierzbicka in *Emotions across Languages and Cultures: Diversity and Universals* (Cambridge, 1999).

24 See the discussion in Boddice, *History of Emotions*, pp. 73–6.

1 Archaic and Classical Passions

1 The master of the field is David Konstan, who has done more than anyone to foreground the importance of the history of emotions in antiquity. See David Konstan, *Pity Transformed* (London, 2001); Konstan, *Sexual Symmetry: Love in the Ancient Novel and Related Genres* (Princeton, NJ, 1994); Konstan, *The Emotions of the Ancient Greeks: Studies in Aristotle and Classical Literature* (Toronto, 2006); Konstan and N. Keith Rutter, eds, *Envy, Spite and Jealousy: The Rivalrous Emotions in Ancient Greece* (Edinburgh, 2003). Konstan inspired the Festschrift edited by Ruth R. Caston and Robert A. Kaster, *Hope, Joy, and Affection in the Classical World* (Oxford, 2016), and he also defines points of departure and debate, such as Ed Sanders, *Envy and Jealousy in Classical Athens: A Socio-psychological Approach* (Oxford, 2014). While Konstan is a firm advocate of the historicization of emotional experience, he has been criticized, notably by Sanders, for being too eager to make direct translations of Greek terms into English equivalents, as well as for drawing too strong a connection between the emotional experience of past and present, so as to derive a kind of immediate topical relevance

for the study of ancient emotions. Sanders himself seems to be inconsistent on this point (pp. 4–6).

2 While classics has produced more works on emotion than perhaps any other period, it is necessary to point out that much of this work has arisen independently of the development of the history of emotions per se, and often with quite different agendas. Where classicists expound on philosophy, literature, poetry and rhetoric with a mind to making sense of ancient texts, many have approached the subject of affective and emotional life from the point of view of contemporary psychology and cognitive science. This is a particular foible of philosophers, who tend to beat the particular with a universal stick. Some of this now looks rather out of place in the history-of-emotions landscape. See in particular Richard Sorabji, *Emotion and Peace of Mind: From Stoic Agitation to Christian Temptation* (Oxford, 2000) and Martha Nussbaum, *The Therapy of Desire: Theory and Practice in Hellenistic Ethics* (Princeton, NJ, 1994).

3 The action refers to events some four hundred years earlier, in the early twelfth century BCE, and there is much debate about the extent to which the Homeric epic preserves an earlier oral poetic tradition. In any case, the primary mode of receiving and rehearsing the *Iliad*, even in classical times, was through listening and through oral repetition.

4 From *cholos* we get the humoral substance of *choler* – bile – which has been preserved in modern languages in a variety of ways. In English, a choleric person is ill-tempered or angry, and the French *colère* is the common-usage word for 'anger'. Its rootedness in bodily disorder or disease is preserved in the word 'cholera' (see Chapter Two).

5 Leonard Muellner, *The Anger of Achilles: 'Mênis' in Greek Epic* (Ithaca, NY, 2004). My analysis broadly accords with his.

6 Homer, *The Iliad*, trans. Robert Fagles (London, 1990).

7 See, for example, William V. Harris, *Restraining Rage: The Ideology of Anger Control in Classical Antiquity* (Cambridge, MA, 2001), pp. 131–56.

8 See, for example, Lynn Kozak, *Experiencing Hektor: Character in the Iliad* (London, 2017).

9 Marilynn Desmond, 'Trojan Itineraries and the Matter of Troy', in *The Oxford History of Classical Reception in English Literature*, vol. 1, ed. Rita Copeland (Oxford, 2016), p. 262.

10 W. E. Gladstone, *Juventus Mundi: The Gods and Men of the Heroic Age* (London, 1869), pp. 508–9.

11 Saul Levin, 'Love and the Hero of the Iliad', *Transactions and Proceedings of the American Philological Association*, LXXX (1949), pp. 37–49 (p. 37). See also Katherine Callen King, *Achilles: Paradigms of the War Hero from Homer to the Middle Ages* (Berkeley, CA, 1987); Seth Benardett, *Achilles and Hector: The Homeric Hero* (South Bend, IN, 2005).

12 Muellner, *Anger of Achilles*, p. 119.

13 Homer, *Iliad*, 1.408–12.

14 Ibid., 21.521–5.

15 Ibid., 22.312–13.

16 Stephen Scully, 'Reading the Shield of Achilles: Terror, Anger, Delight', *Harvard Studies in Classical Philology*, CI (2003), pp. 29–47 (p. 40).

17 For a thorough account of the meaning and distinctly bodily qualities of *menos*, see Richard Sugg, *The Secret History of the Soul: Physiology, Magic and Spirit Forces from Homer to St Paul* (Newcastle, 2014), pp. 22–5.

18 Homer, *Iliad*, 22.346–7.

19 Homer, *The Iliad*, trans. A. T. Murray (Cambridge, MA, 1924).

20 David Konstan, 'Anger, Hatred, and Genocide in Ancient Greece', *Common Knowledge*, XIII (2007), pp. 170–87 (p. 177). Sara Ahmed, 'Collective Feelings: Or, The Impressions Left by Others', *Theory, Culture and Society*, XXI (2004), pp. 25–42 (p. 27).

21 Oliver Taplin, 'The Shield of Achilles within the "Iliad"', *Greece and Rome*, 2nd ser., XXVII (1980), pp. 1–21.

22 Homer, *Iliad*, trans. Stanley Lombardo (Indianapolis, IN, 1997), 19.401–6.

23 Ibid., 19.426–7.

24 Scully, 'Reading the Shield', pp. 40, 43, 45.

25 Homer, *Iliad*, trans. Lombardo, 19.33–4.

26 Rob Boddice, *The History of Emotions* (Manchester, 2018), pp. 11–14.

27 Mary Beard, *Confronting the Classics: Traditions, Adventures and Innovations* (London, 2013), pp. 32–3.

28 Aristotle, *Poetics*, trans. Malcolm Heath (London, 1996), 5.5.

29 See, among others, Hajo Holborn, 'Greek and Modern Concepts of History', *Journal of the History of Ideas*, X (1949), pp. 3–13; Kenneth J. Dover, 'Thucydides "As History" and "As Literature"', *History and Theory*, XXII (1983), pp. 54–63.

30 Thucydides, *The Peloponnesian War*, trans. Steven Lattimore (Indianapolis, IN, 1998).

31 Thucydides, *History of the Peloponnesian War*, trans. Rex Warner (London, 1974); Robert Lisle, 'Thucydides 1.22.4', *Classical Journal*, LXXII (1977), pp. 342–7.

32 Thucydides, *The Peloponnesian War*, trans. Martin Hammond (Oxford, 2009).

33 Thucydides, *Der Peloponnesische Krieg*, trans. Helmuth Vretska and Werner Rinner (Stuttgart, 2000).

34 Thucydides, *The Peloponnesian War*, trans. Thomas Hobbes [1629] (Chicago, IL, 1989); Thucydides, *History of the Peloponnesian War*, trans. Benjamin Jowett (Oxford, 1881).

35 Marc Cogan, *The Human Thing: The Speeches and Principles of Thucydides' History* (Chicago, IL, 1981). See also Elisabeth Young-Bruehl, 'What Thucydides Saw', *History and Theory*, XXV (1986), pp. 1–16, which subverts typical readings.

36 Thucydides, *Peloponnesian War*, 2.37. As per the study of Douglas Cairns, 'Metaphors of Hope in Archaic and Classical Greek Poetry', in *Hope, Joy, and Affection in the Classical World*, ed. Ruth R. Caston and Robert A. Kaster (Oxford, 2016), hope in ancient Greece was far from a universally positive emotion, and was often construed strongly in the negative.

37 For my reluctance to translate this simply to 'happiness', see the following section on Aristotle.

38 Thucydides, *Peloponnesian War*, 2.35–6.

39 Ibid., 2.47–54.

40 Ibid., 5.84–116.

41 For various takes on the meaning and employment of *eudaimonia*, much of which attempts to give it contemporary relevance and, indeed, apply it, see Martha Nussbaum, *Upheavals of Thought: The Intelligence of Emotions* (Cambridge, 2003), pp. 31–2; A. S. Waterman, 'The Relevance of Aristotle's Conception of Eudaimonia for the Psychological Study of Happiness', *Theoretical and Philosophical Psychology*, x (1990), pp. 39–44; R. M. Ryan, V. Huta and E. L. Deci, 'Living Well: A Self-determination Theory Perspective on Eudaimonia', in *The Exploration of Happiness: Present and Future Perspectives*, ed. Antonella Delle Fave (Dordrecht, 2013), pp. 117–39; A. S. Waterman, ed., *The Best within Us: Positive Psychology Perspectives on Eudaimonia* (Washington, DC, 2013). This is a mere selection. The popularity of *eudaimonia* in the burgeoning world of 'happiness studies' or 'positive psychology' (often called 'eudaimonic functioning' and contrasted to 'hedonic functioning') is mitigated by few cautionary notes, though the following has the advantage of pointing out that 'eudaimonia is not well-defined': Todd B. Kashdan, Robert Biswas-Diener and Laura A. King, 'Reconsidering Happiness: The Costs of Distinguishing between Hedonics and Eudaimonia', *Journal of Positive Psychology*, II (2008), pp. 219–33.

42 As early as 1926, Aristotle's translator Harris Rackham noted at the first instance of *eudaimonia* in *Nicomachean Ethics* (Cambridge, MA, 1926) that, while 'happiness' was the unavoidable translation, he did not 'interpret it as a state of feeling but as a kind of activity' (1095a). This was insightful: only now historians of emotions work with the notion that feeling states are also kinds of activity.

43 It is tempting here to flag the similarity to the psychological and physiological innovation of William James, who pointed out that 'we feel sorry because we cry, angry because we strike, afraid because we tremble', but the ends each thinker had in mind were wildly different. Aristotle's is a treatise on morals. James's is a work on emotions per se. Most importantly, for Aristotle (and the Greeks more generally) the passions came from without, from the world, and affected the body; James was working on the exact opposite premise, that emotional experience arose in response to internal and automatic visceral movement and activity. The final analysis puts them as kindred ideas, but with radically different appreciations of function. William James, *The Principles of Psychology*, vol. II (New York, 1890), pp. 449–50. For analysis, see Boddice, *History of Emotions*, pp. 23–5.

44 Aristotle, *The Nicomachean Ethics*, trans. J.A.K. Thomson (London, 2004), p. 32.

45 Ibid.

46 Ibid., p. 35.

47 Ibid., p. 38.

48 Ibid., p. 41.

2 Rhetorical and Bodily Feelings

1 For a general account, see Ruth Webb, 'Imagination and the Arousal of the Emotions in Greco-Roman Rhetoric', in *The Passions in Roman Thought and Literature*, ed. Susanna Morton Braund and Christopher Gill (Cambridge, 1997), pp. 112–27.

2 Robert A. Kaster, *Emotion, Restraint, and Community in Ancient Rome* (Oxford, 2005), p. 8.

3 For the concept of emotional improvisation, see Erin Sullivan, *Beyond Melancholy: Sadness and Selfhood in Renaissance England* (Oxford, 2016).

4 Thucydides, *History of the Peloponnesian War*, trans. C. F. Smith (Cambridge, MA, 1921), 1.22.

5 The historical merits of the speeches, both in terms of their content and their form, have been much debated. See, for sporadic example, Peter Kosso, 'Historical Evidence and Epistemic Justification: Thucydides as a Case Study', *History and Theory*, XXXII (1993), pp. 1–13 (pp. 10–11); J. Wilson, 'What Does Thucydides Claim for his Speeches?', *Phoenix*, XXXVI (1982), pp. 95–103; Maria Pavlou, 'Attributive Discourse in the Speeches in Thucydides', in *Thucydides between History and Literature*, ed. Antonis Tsakmakis and Melina Tamiolaki (Berlin, 2013), pp. 409–34; Marc Cogan, *The Human Thing: The Speeches and Principles of Thucydides' History* (Chicago, IL, 1981); M. Heath, 'Justice in Thucydides' Athenian Speeches', *Historia: Zeitschrift für Alte Geschichte*, XXXIX (1990), pp. 385–400.

6 For debates on these particular speeches, see A. Andrews, 'The Mytilene Debate: Thucydides 3.36–49', *Phoenix*, XVI (1962), pp. 64–85; Donald Kagan, 'The Speeches in Thucydides and the Mytilene Debate', *Yale Classical Studies*, XXIV (1975), pp. 71–94; P. A. Debnar, 'Diodotus' Paradox and the Mytiline Debate (Thucydides 3.37–49)', *Rheinisches Museum für Philologie*, CXLIII (2000), pp. 161–78; Clifford Orwin, 'The Just and the Advantageous in Thucydides: The Case of the Mytilenaian Debate', *American Political Science Review*, LXXVIII (1984), pp. 485–94. Plus see notes below.

7 Thucydides, *Peloponnesian War*, 3.36.

8 Ibid.

9 Ibid., 3.37–8.

10 Ibid., 3.40.

11 Edward M. Harris, 'How to Address the Athenian Assembly: Rhetoric and Political Tactics in the Debate about Mytilene (Thuc. 3.37–50)', *Classical Quarterly*, LXIII (2013), pp. 94–109; David Konstan, *Pity Transformed* (London, 2001), pp. 82–3; James A. Andres, 'Cleon's Hidden Appeals (Thucydides 3.37–40)', *Classical Quarterly*, L (2000), pp. 45–62 (p. 50).

12 Harris, 'How to Address', p. 100.

13 Ibid., pp. 108–9.

14 Thucydides, *Peloponnesian War*, 3.42–8.

15 Ibid., 3.42.

16 Translations that use 'passion' and 'mind' include those by J. M. Dent (1910), C. F. Smith (1921) and Benjamin Jowett (1881).

17 Thucydides, *Peloponnesian War*, 3.44.

18 Ibid., 3.50.

19 Landmark studies have shown the extraordinary possibilities of the deconstruction of past knowledge systems to reveal their internal political, technological and affective dynamics. See Lorraine Daston and Peter Galison, *Objectivity* (New York, 2007); Peter Burke, *What is the History of Knowledge?* (Cambridge, 2016).

20 Galen wrote on the temperaments (in Greek, κράσεων (*kraseon*) – mixtures, temperatures (climate), temperaments; in Latin the text is translated as *De temperamentis*). On Galen's understanding of the passions (overlooking the anachronistic title), see Christopher Gill, 'Did Galen Understand Platonic and Stoic Thinking on Emotions?', in *The Emotions in Hellenistic Philosophy*, ed. Juha Sihvola and Troels Engberg-Pedersen (Dordrecht, 1998), pp. 113–48; and Loveday C. A. Alexander, 'The Passions in Galen and the Novels of Chariton and Xenophon', in *Passions and Moral Progress in Greco-Roman Thought*, ed. John T. Fitzgerald (London, 2008), pp. 175–97. For the far-reaching implications of Galenic medicine on matters of the self and the passions, see Angus Gowland, 'Medicine, Psychology, and the Melancholic Subject in the Renaissance', in *Emotions and Health, 1200–1700*, ed. Elena Carrera (Leiden, 2013), pp. 186–219.

21 Claudia Mirrione, 'Theory and Terminology of Mixture in Galen: The Concepts of *krasis* and *mixis* in Galen's Thought', PhD thesis, Humboldt Universität zu Berlin, 2017, p. 265n.

22 *Hippocratic Writings*, trans. Francis Adams (Chicago, IL, 1952), pp. 9–19. The Greek text is presented by W.H.S. Jones, *Hippocrates: Collected Works* (Cambridge, MA, 1868).

23 Adams's translation (*Hippocratic Writings*, p. 15) offers 'the temper might be ruffled and they be roused to inconsiderate emotion and passion'. Under the basic rubric of history-of-emotions methodology, trying at all costs to avoid anachronism, the introduction of 'emotion' here cannot be justified so I have modified it.

24 The translation here is by Peter Brain, *Galen on Bloodletting: A Study of the Origins, Development and Validity of His Opinions, with a Translation of the Three Works* (Cambridge, 1986), p. 74.

25 *Claudii Galeni opera omni*, ed. Karl Gottlob Kühn, vol. XI (Leipzig, 1826), p. 267.

26 Brain, *Galen on Bloodletting*, p. 83. For the Greek and Latin, *Claudii Galeni*, vol. XI, p. 282.

27 Alexander Tuttle et al., 'Increasing Placebo Responses over Time in U.S. Clinical Trials of Neuropathic Pain', *Pain*, CLVI (2015), pp. 2616–26.

28 K. T. Hall, J. Loscalzo and T. J. Kaptchuk, 'Genetics and the Placebo Effect: The Placebome', *Trends in Molecular Medicine*, XXI (2015), pp. 285–94.

29 Patrick Wall, *Pain: The Science of Suffering* (New York, 2000), pp. 40, 42.

30 Pliny the Elder, *The Natural History*, trans. John Bostock and H. T. Riley (London, 1855), 32.42.

31 Ibid., 20.13.

32 Ibid., 20.51. The same plant in other cultures, especially in Asia Minor,
    was used to ward off the evil eye. Modern research has shown that the
    seeds at the very least do indeed have an analgesic or anaesthetic effect:
    Loubna Farouk et al., 'Evaluation of the Analgesic Effect of Alkaloid
    Extract of *Peganum harmala* L.: Possible Mechanisms Involved',
    Journal of Ethnopharmacology, cxv (2008), pp. 449–54.

33 Pliny, *Natural History*, 21.84.

34 Ibid., 20.70, 20.84.

35 Ibid., 22.33.

36 Javier Moscoso, 'Exquisite and Lingering Pains: Facing Cancer in
    Early Modern Europe', in *Pain and Emotion in Modern History*, ed. Rob
    Boddice (Basingstoke, 2014), pp. 16–35 (pp. 24, 31). See also Rob Boddice,
    Pain: A Very Short Introduction (Oxford, 2017) and Joanna Bourke,
    The Story of Pain: From Prayer to Painkillers (Oxford, 2014).

37 Plutarch, 'De esu carnium i', 'De esu carnium ii', in *Moralia*,
    ed. Gregorius N. Bernardakis (Leipzig, 1895). For English comparison
    (and the source of the unmodified translations here), see Plutarch,
    Plutarch's Morals, trans. revd William W. Goodwin (Boston, MA, 1874).

38 Konstan, *Pity Transformed*, pp. 53–4.

39 Boddice, *Pain: A Very Short Introduction*, pp. 5–10.

40 One ancient Greek word for something akin to 'disgust' affords
    one of those happy lexical moments when the Greek seems to capture
    better the experience of the word than does the modern English.
    The word is σικχός – *sikkhos* and refers also to the squeamish, which
    at least captures the state of nausea that the English contains. Then
    again, Greek affords us other options: ἀηδής (*aedes*) is literally a lack
    of sweetness of pleasantness, and is therefore 'distasteful' and might
    be nauseating. This seems to lack the necessary revulsion of 'disgust',
    though it is often translated as such; δυσχέρεια (*duskhereia*) is also
    frequently translated as 'disgust', though in a recent treatment Emily
    Allen-Hornblower has gone to great lengths to show not only what
    this word has in common with what we understand by 'disgust', but
    also where the word departs from such an understanding. This work,
    however, is characteristic of a general tendency to want to conjoin
    past and present. 'The ancients' conceptions of emotions are different
    from our own; there are methodological pitfalls to assuming a perfect
    equation between the two,' Allen-Hornblower correctly opines, but
    while she is not suggesting that the 'emotion(s) of δυσχέρεια . . . can
    be neatly mapped onto our own modern conception(s) of disgust', she
    nevertheless 'aim[s] to draw out some defining characteristics that they
    share'. I find this will to explore how past experience is the same as 'ours'
    far less interesting than an exploration of how it differs. Why does the
    contemporary category get privileged in the analysis? See Emily Allen-
    Hornblower, 'Moral Disgust in Sophocles' Philoctetes', in *The Ancient
    Emotion of Disgust*, ed. Donald Lateiner and Dimos Spatharas (Oxford,
    2016), pp. 69–86, n.11.

41 Richard Firth-Godbehere, 'The Two Dogmas of Disgust', *The History of
    Emotions Blog*, 31 August 2016, https://emotionsblog.history.qmul.ac.uk,
    accessed 3 November 2017.

42 Rob Boddice, *The History of Emotions* (Manchester, 2018), p. 158; Daniel Lord Smail, *On Deep History* (Berkeley, CA, 2008), p. 115.

43 Lateiner and Spatharas, eds, *Ancient Emotion of Disgust*. The editors basically concede historicity in their introduction to the volume, when they 'endorse the view that emotions are a cognitive phenomenon requiring evaluations, rather than just instinctive, "irrational" responses to external stimuli. Disgust is indeed a reflexive emotion centering on particularly embodied cognitions. By virtue of its visceral nature, disgust canonizes behavior and constructs social hierarchies by imposing prohibitions. By projecting aversive physical qualities upon morally or socially condemnable behavior, disgust serves as a mechanism to marginalize others' (pp. 1–2). By thus defining emotions and disgust, categorically, the study of things *like* disgust in the past becomes irrevocably hitched to the contemporary definition. It presupposes that, looking for disgust in the past, we already know what we are looking for, which is teleological and dangerously flirtatious with anachronism. For an account of why I think it is crucial that we stop attempting to define our terms at the outset, see Boddice, *History of Emotions*, pp. 41–9.

44 Lateiner and Spatharas, eds, *Ancient Emotion of Disgust*, p. 8.

45 Ibid., n. 19.

46 Boddice, *Pain: A Very Short Introduction*, p. 67.

47 The translation is by Tom Griffith (Cambridge, 2000), p. 136.

48 The question of desire is explicitly put by Rana Saadi Liebert, 'Pity and Disgust in Plato's *Republic*: The Case of Leontius', *Classical Philology*, X (2013), pp. 179–201, but the discussion is skewed by the insistence that the struggle here concerns disgust as a visceral reaction to the sight of dead bodies. The passage that immediately follows the anecdote of Leontius works against this interpretation, which is implicitly led by a willingness to *find* disgust where *we* might expect to find it. The whole point here is that these kinds of assumptions about the presence of 'disgust' at all have to be thrown out a priori.

49 Liebert summarizes the range of opinion on Leontius, 'Pity and Disgust', pp. 180–82, including bibliographic notes.

50 Carolyn Korsmeyer, *Savoring Disgust: The Foul and the Fair in Aesthetics* (Oxford, 2011), p. 42. Korsmeyer thereafter confuses the Platonic soul by saying that Leontius' 'desires are in conflict', when in fact his desire is in conflict with *reason*. She calls what Leontius is experiencing 'aesthetically alluring disgust', though she admits that 'it is not clear at this point just which terms are most apt', listing 'allure, attraction, pleasure, curiosity, magnetism'. The key for me is that while it makes sense to talk about the aesthetic *pull* of disgust in general, I cannot find a way to apply it to Leontius, for those expressions that we tend to want to apply to disgust are here part of his rational soul's attempt to beat off desire, and the desire is given by Plato (Socrates in the dialogue) as simply that: ἐπιθυμοῖ (*epithumoi*).

51 See Barbara Rosenwein, *Generations of Feeling: A History of Emotions, 600–1700* (Cambridge, 2016), pp. 24–34. This background is useful, but here and with Cicero (pp. 16–24) Rosenwein insists on conflating ancient categories of affective experience with 'emotions', which I find

to be a linguistic load that the originals cannot support. Cicero is a case in point. Rosenwein states that Cicero's word *perturbationes* was 'the Latin word he chose for the emotions' (p. 17). Rosenwein acknowledges that he was riffing on Greek *pathé*, but in his *Tusculan Disputations* Cicero could not have been more clear. When talking about *aegritudinem* – distress – as a master category, he was talking about disturbances of the soul (*animi perturbationen*), which, he said, the Greeks called πάθος (*pathos*). Lest there could be any confusion, he defined pathos as *morbum*: disease, signifying any troubled movement of the soul (*motus in animo turbidis*). In no way do these perturbed movements of the soul sound like 'emotions', for at the very least they *happen to* a person, rather than projecting *out of* a person. The reference to *pathos*, to that which is suffered as it were passively, ought to be a huge clue. Whatever we want to do with the affective life of the past, making it sound like or fit into our own emotional schema will hinder more often than it helps. See Cicero, *Tusculan Disputations*, trans. J. E. King (Cambridge, MA, 1927).

52 The translation that follows is my slight modification of that by Carolyn J.-B. Hammond: Augustine, *Confessions* (Cambridge, MA, 2014), 10.35, pp. 162–3. For a general account of Augustine on the passions, see James Wetzel, 'Augustine', in *The Oxford Handbook of Religion and Emotion*, ed. John Corrigan (Oxford, 2008), pp. 349–63, and Peter King, 'Emotions in Medieval Thought', in *The Oxford Handbook of Philosophy of Emotion*, ed. Peter Goldie (Oxford, 2010), pp. 167–87 (pp. 169–71).

53 Augustine, *Confessions*, 10.35, pp. 160–63.

54 Ibid., pp. 162–3.

55 Ibid., pp. 164–7.

56 Augustine, *City of God*, trans. Philip Levine (Cambridge, MA, 1966), 14.9, pp. 304–19.

57 Ibid., pp. 310–11.

58 Ibid., pp. 312–13. Canonical translations here employ 'mind' for *animo*, instead of 'soul', but the decision, given that Augustine has a perfectly good word for mind (*mens*) when he intends to use it, seems unjustified, especially in the context of the state of sin.

59 Ibid., pp. 312–13. Here he really does mean mind (*mentemque*), in contradistinction to the soul.

60 Ibid., pp. 313–14. That Augustine left room for more than one definition of apathy, and that this particular apathy was not achievable in the living, has been missed by a number of scholars. For an appraisal of the different kinds of apathy in Stoic, Cynical and Epicurean schools, see Sarah Catherine Byers, *Perception, Sensibility, and Moral Motivation in Augustine: A Stoic Platonic Synthesis* (Cambridge, 2013), pp. 68ff. and 68n.65.

61 Augustine, *City of God*, 14.9, pp. 304–5.

62 The connection is explicit in ibid., 14.3, pp. 270–71.

63 Ibid., 14.9, pp. 304–5. For extensive treatment of desire in Augustine, see Timo Nisula, *Augustine and the Functions of Concupiscence* (Leiden, 2012).

64 Augustine, *City of God*, 14.9, pp. 316–17.

65 For the twentieth-century theological account, see C. S. Lewis, *The Problem of Pain* [1940] (New York, 2001). The Christian idea(l) of pain

as just, or as virtue, or even as ecstasy, is long and storied. For general coverage, see Boddice, *Pain: A Very Short Introduction*, esp. Chapter Two; Bourke, *The Story of Pain*; Javier Moscoso, *Pain: A Cultural History* (Basingstoke, 2012). For temporally focused accounts, see Judith Perkins, *The Suffering Self: Pain and Narrative Representation in the Early Christian Era* (London, 1995); Esther Cohen, *The Modulated Scream: Pain in Late Medieval Culture* (Chicago, IL, 2010); Jan Frans van Dijkhuizen and Karl A. E. Enenkel, eds, *The Sense of Suffering: Constructions of Physical Pain in Early Modern Culture* (Leiden, 2009); John R. Yamamoto-Wilson, *Pain, Pleasure and Perversity: Discourses of Suffering in Seventeenth-century England* (Farnham, 2013).

66 Augustine's rhetorical work is part of the dynamic of the affective formation. For the importance of rhetoric in emotional formation, see Daniel M. Gross, *The Secret History of Emotion: From Aristotle's Rhetoric to Modern Brain Science* (Chicago, IL, 2006); for an overview of the revolution in psychological thinking wrought by social neuroscience, that is the connection between naming and feeling, see Lisa Feldman-Barrett, *How Emotions Are Made: The Secret Life of the Brain* (New York, 2017).

3 Motions and Machinations

1 For the astonishing range and history here, including the history of lost loves, see William Reddy, *The Making of Romantic Love: Longing and Sexuality in Europe, South Asia, and Japan, 900–1200 CE* (Chicago, IL, 2012); C. Stephen Jaeger, *Ennobling Love: In Search of a Lost Sensibility* (Philadelphia, PA, 1999).

2 For Augustine, see above. For Aquinas, see in particular Nicholas E. Lombardo, 'Emotions and Psychological Health in Aquinas', in *Emotions and Health, 1200–1700*, ed. Elena Carrera (Leiden, 2013), pp. 19–46; Barbara Rosenwein, *Generations of Feeling: A History of Emotions, 600–1700* (Cambridge, 2016), pp. 144–68; Constant J. Mews, 'Thomas Aquinas and Catherine of Siena: Emotion, Devotion and Mendicant Spiritualities in the Late Fourteenth Century', *Digital Philology*, 1 (2012), pp. 235–52.

3 Hildegard receives no mention in Rosenwein's *Generations of Feeling*. Hildegard's opera, *Ordo Virtutum*, is mentioned only briefly in J. Liliequist, ed., *A History of Emotions, 1200–1800* (London, 2013), pp. 51, 60, and the 'emotions' therein are explored in Julie Hotchin, '"Arousing sluggish souls": Hildegard of Bingen and the *Ordo Virtutum*', *Histories of Emotion*, 9 June 2015, https://historiesofemotion.com, accessed 12 December 2017. The question of emotions in figures that feature in Hildegard's world have been explored by Constant J. Mews, with some critical attention paid to Hildegard herself: 'Male–Female Spiritual Partnership in the Twelfth Century: The Witness of Abelard and Heloise, Volmar and Hildegard', in *Hildegards von Bingen Menschenbild und Kirchenverständnis heute*, ed. Rainer Berndt and Maura Zatonyi (Münster, 2015), pp. 167–86. For the broader context, see Constant J. Mews, 'Abelard, Heloise, and the Discussion of Love in the Twelfth-century Schools', in *Rethinking Peter Abelard: A Collection of*

Critical Essays, ed. B. S. Hellemans (Leiden, 2014), pp. 11–36; Constant
J. Mews, 'Bernard of Clairvaux, Peter Abelard and Heloise on the
Definition of Love', *Revista Portuguesa de Filosofia*, LX (2004),
pp. 633–60. Further context is provided in Barbara Newman, ed.,
Voice of the Living Light: Hildegard of Bingen and Her World (Berkeley,
CA, 1998). There is certainly a dissertation waiting to be written on
Hildegard's passions and affects.

4 Her visionary trilogy comprises *Scivias* (1142–51), *Liber Vitae Meritorum*
(1158–63) and *Liber Divinorum Operum* (1163/4–72). Her medical treatises
are *Physica* (1150–58) and *Causae et Curae* (before 1179). Her invented
language is documented in *Lingua Ignota* (before 1179). Her most
important musical piece is the opera/morality play *Ordo Virtutum* (*c.* 1151).

5 The numbering is consistent between the Latin transcriptions and the
English translations, making for ease of use. See L. Van Acker, ed.,
Hildegardis Bingensis Epistolarium, pars prima I–XC (Turnhout, 1991); L.
Van Acker, ed., *Hildegardis Bingensis Epistolarium, pars secunda*
XCI–CCLr (Turnhout, 1993); and L. Van Acker and M. Klaes-Hachmoller,
eds, *Hildegardis Bingensis Epistolarium, pars tertia* CCLI–CCCXC
(Turnhout, 2001). For the English translations, Joseph L. Baird and
Radd K. Ehrman, *The Letters of Hildegard of Bingen*, 3 vols (Oxford,
1994–2004).

6 For sketches of Hildegard's life, see Mark Atherton's introduction to
Hildegard von Bingen, *Selected Writings* (London, 2001), pp. ix–xliii.

7 Ibid., pp. xix–xx.

8 The important transformative effect on the brain of meditative reading
and writing practices has been explored in this context by Julia Bourke,
'An Experiment in "Neurohistory": Reading Emotions in Aelred's *De
Institutione Inclusarum* (*Rule for a Recluse*)', *Journal of Medieval Religious
Cultures*, XLII (2016), pp. 124–42.

9 All English translations are taken from Baird and Ehrman. Hildegard
to Bernard, Abbot of Clairvaux, *c.* 1146. Baird and Ehrman, *Letters*,
vol. I, p. 28, letter no. 1.

10 Hildegard to Bernard, *c.* 1146. Ibid., vol. I, p. 29, letter no. 1.

11 Baird and Ehrman, *Letters*, vol. I, p. 29n.4, allude to Hildegard's
explanation of her waking visions in one of the autobiographical
passages of her *Vita*.

12 Hildegard to the Monk Guibert, 1175. Ibid., vol. II, pp. 21–5, letter no. 103r.

13 The phrase 'context of possibilities' is from Fanny Hernández Brotons,
'The Experience of Cancer Illness: Spain and Beyond during the
Second Half of the Nineteenth Century', PhD thesis, Universidad
Carlos III de Madrid (2017), p. 20.

14 The concept of *viriditas* in Hildegard's work has been thoroughly
explored, but chiefly with regard to medieval medicine. See Victoria
Sweet, *Rooted in the Earth, Rooted in the Sky: Hildegard of Bingen and
Premodern Medicine* (London, 2010) and, more particularly, Victoria
Sweet, 'Hildegard of Bingen and the Greening of Medieval Medicine',
Bulletin of the History of Medicine, LXXIII (1999), pp. 381–403. See also
C. Meier, 'Die Bedeutung der Farben im Werk Hildegards von Bingen',
Frühmittelalterliche Studien, VI (1972), pp. 280–90.

15 Hildegard to Abbot Adam, before 1166. Baird and Ehrman, *Letters*, vol. 1, pp. 192–4, letter no. 85r/a.

16 The symbolism is explained as follows: the cloak represents 'pure innocence' with which she embraces all things. The shoes indicate that her paths 'lead through the best part of God's election'. The sun and moon in the right hand are indicative that God's right hand embraces all creation, dispensing divine love to the good everywhere. The ivory tablet – in its purity – is the Virgin Mary, and inside it is Christ, with sapphire representing his divinity.

17 Here I have modified the translation of Baird and Ehrman, who rather obscurely write 'divine love was the matrix from which He created all things'.

18 On Machiavelli and the 'emotions' in particular, see N. Hochner, 'Machiavelli: Love and the Economy of Emotions', *Italian Culture*, xxxii (2014), pp. 122–37; Jack Barbalet, 'Emotions in Politics: From the Ballot to Suicide Terrorism', in *Emotion, Politics and Society*, ed. Simon Thompson (Basingstoke, 2006), pp. 45–6; Haig Patapan, *Machiavelli in Love: The Modern Politics of Love and Fear* (Lanham, MD, 2006).

19 Niccolò Machiavelli, *Il Principe* [1513] (Florence, 1857), p. 53.

20 Niccolò Machiavelli, *The Prince*, trans. David Wootton (Indianapolis, IN, 1995), p. 79.

21 For Castiglione and the emotions (especially love), see James T. Stewart, 'Renaissance Psychology and the Ladder of Love in Castiglione and Spenser', *Journal of English and Germanic Philology*, LVI (1957), pp. 225–30; Wietse De Boer, 'Spirits of Love: Castiglione and Neo-Platonic in Discourses of Vision', in *Spirits Unseen: The Representation of Subtle Bodies in Early Modern European Culture*, ed. Christine Göttler and Wolfgang Neuber (Leiden, 2007), pp. 121–40.

22 Baldassare Castiglione, *Il cortegiano* (1528) (Vicenza, 1771), p. 20. All Latin references are from this edition.

23 Baldesar Castiglione, *The Book of the Courtier*, trans. Charles S. Singleton (New York, 2002), pp. 17–18.

24 Castiglione, *Il cortegiano*, pp. 29–30; Castiglione, *Book of the Courtier*, pp. 18–19.

25 Castiglione, *Il cortegiano*, p. 31.

26 René Descartes, 'Treatise on Man', in *The Philosophical Writings of Descartes*, vol. 1, trans. John Cottingham, Robert Stoothoff and Dugald Murdoch (Cambridge, 1985), p. 101.

27 René Descartes, *Discourse on Method*, trans. Laurence J. Lafleur (Upper Saddle River, NJ, 1956), p. 30.

28 Ibid., p. 36.

29 Ibid., p. 21.

30 Descartes, 'Treatise on Man', p. 169.

31 René Descartes, 'The Treatise on Man', in *The World and Other Writings*, ed. Stephen Gaukroger (Cambridge, 1998), p. 153.

32 Ibid., p. 155.

33 Descartes, *Discourse on Method*, p. 38.

34 Nicolaas A. Rupke, *Vivisection in Historical Perspective* (London, 1987), p. 26.

35 Ibid., p. 27.

36 Ibid.

37 For context see Joan DeJean, *Tender Geographies: Women and the Origins of the Novel in France* (New York, 1991), pp. 71–93.

38 The literature on hysteria is vast and still growing, in part at least because it is subject to continual historical reappraisal. See Rob Boddice, 'Hysteria or Tetanus? Ambivalent Embodiments and the Authenticity of Pain', in *Emotional Bodies: Studies on the Historical Performativity of Emotions*, ed. Dolorès Martin Moruno and Beatriz Pichel (Urbana-Champaign, IL, 2019); Elaine Showalter, *The Female Malady: Women, Madness and English Culture, 1830–1980* (London, 1985); Mark Micale, *Hysterical Men: The Hidden History of Male Nervous Illness* (Cambridge, MA, 2008); Mark Micale, *Approaching Hysteria: Disease and Its Interpretations* (Princeton, NJ, 1995); Sander L. Gilman et al., eds, *Hysteria Beyond Freud* (Berkeley and Los Angeles, CA, 1993).

39 Susan Winnett, *Terrible Sociability: The Text of Manners in Laclos, Goethe, and James* (Palo Alto, CA, 1993), p. 12.

40 For my use of 'moral economy', see Rob Boddice, *The History of Emotions* (Manchester, 2018), pp. 195–201.

41 Winnett, *Terrible Sociability*, p. 10.

42 Ibid.

43 The subject is given special treatment in Marin Cureau de la Chambre (1594–1669), *Nouvelle pensées sur les causes de la lumière, du desbordement du Nil et de l'amour d'inclination* (Paris, 1634), a compendious work that seems at once strange in its disparate topics, but at the same time on point in its location of the heart in a landscape of light and flood. See also Cureau de la Chambre's astonishingly cynical take on the poisonous character of love and the wounds to the soul done by beauty: Marin Cureau de la Chambre, *The Characters of the Passions* (London, 1649), pp. 20–35. For context, see Florence Dumora, 'Topologie des émotions. Les caractères des passions de Marin Cureau de la Chambre', *Littératures Classiques*, LXVIII (2009), pp. 161–75.

44 See Anne-Marie-Louise d'Orléans, Duchesse de Montpensier, *Against Marriage: The Correspondence of La Grande Mademoiselle*, ed. and trans. Joan DeJean (Chicago, IL, 2002); Carolyn C. Lougee, *Le Paradis des Femmes: Women, Salons, and Social Stratification in Seventeenth-century France* (Princeton, NJ, 1976); Suzanne Desan and Jeffrey Merrick, eds, *Family, Gender, and Law in Early Modern France* (University Park, PA, 2009).

45 Immanuel Kant, *Kritik der Urteilskraft* (1790) (Leipzig, 1922), p. 120. English translations tend to make for confused reading here. *Zärtliche Rührungen* are sometimes translated as 'tender emotions', though it is clear that by *Rührungen* Kant is referring to something inward – a feeling of being moved or stirred – not to an outward projection of this. Hence it becomes a problem only when it rises to the level of *Affekt*, which tends to be translated as 'affect', but here means something more like 'emotion', since it is has a presence in and impact on the world. See the passage in question in Immanuel Kant, *Critique of Judgement*, trans. Werner S. Pluhar (Indianapolis, IN, 1987), p. 133.

46 Alexander Bain, *The Emotions and the Will*, 2nd edn (London, 1865), pp. 70–93 (p. 72).

47 Herbert Spencer, *The Principles of Psychology*, vol. II, 2nd edn (London, 1870), pp. 622–4.

4 The Age of Unreason

1 See the review of recent work on the embodiment of reason, or of the relation of reason and senses, in Simon Swift, 'Mary Wollstonecraft and the "Reserve of Reason"', *Studies in Romanticism*, XLV (2006), pp. 3–24.

2 See the historical case study in William Reddy, *The Navigation of Feeling: A Framework for the History of Emotions* (Cambridge, 2001). See also Colin Jones's take on the high stakes of smiling over the course of the French Revolution: *The Smile Revolution in Eighteenth-century Paris* (Oxford, 2014).

3 See, for example, Lisa L. Moore, Joanna Brooks and Caroline Wigginton, eds, *Transatlantic Feminisms in the Age of Revolutions* (Oxford, 2012); Marla R. Miller, *The Needle's Eye: Women and Work in the Age of Revolution* (Amherst, MA, 2006); Harriet B. Applewhite and Darline G. Levy, eds, *Women and Politics in the Age of the Democratic Revolution* (Ann Arbor, MI, 1993).

4 John Wild, ed., *Spinoza: Selections* (New York, 1930), p. 210. This edition helpfully contains the whole of the *Ethics* as well as additional works and correspondence. Where I compare this translation directly with Spinoza's Latin, the source for the Latin is Benedicti de Spinoza, *Ethica*, hypertext edition created by Rudolf W. Meijer. http://users.telenet.be, accessed 5 July 2018.

5 Wild, *Spinoza*, p. 218.

6 Ibid., p. 181.

7 Ibid., pp. 262–3.

8 For a broad treatment of Spinoza and the 'emotions', see Susan James, *Passion and Action: The Emotions in Seventeenth-century Philosophy* (Oxford, 1997). See also Karolina Hübner, 'The Trouble with Feelings, or Spinoza on the Identity of Power and Essence', *Journal of the History of Philosophy*, LV (2017), pp. 35–53.

9 Proponents of the 'affective turn' in sociology and cognate fields *might* trace such a genealogy, but it is difficult to connect them to proponents of the 'affective turn' – a different one – in the humanities. See, for example, Patricia Ticineto Clough and Jean Halley, eds, *The Affective Turn: Theorizing the Social* (Durham, NC, 2007). A more explicit connection exists between Spinoza and the philosopher Gilles Deleuze and his followers, as well as in the work of 'deep ecologists'. See Eccy de Jonge, 'An Alternative to Anthropocentrism: Deep Ecology and the Metaphysical Turn', in *Anthropocentrism: Humans, Animals, Environments*, ed. Rob Boddice (Leiden, 2011), pp. 307–19. Others make a greater leap: Antonio Damasio, *Looking for Spinoza: Joy, Sorrow, and the Feeling Brain* (Orlando, FL, 2003).

10 Rob Boddice, *The History of Emotions* (Manchester, 2018), p. 49.

11 Wild, *Spinoza*, p. 281.

12 Ibid.

13 Ibid., p. 266.

14 Ibid., pp. 266–81 (pp. 266–7, 270–71).

15 Ibid., p. 217.

16 Ibid., p. 380.

17 Nicole Eustace, *Passion is the Gale: Emotion, Power, and the Coming of the American Revolution* (Chapel Hill, NC, 2008).

18 For the concept of the 'emotional frontier', see K. Vallgårda, K. Alexander and S. Olsen, 'Emotions and the Global Politics of Childhood', in *Childhood, Youth and Emotions in Modern History: National, Colonial and Global Perspectives*, ed. Stephanie Olsen (Basingstoke, 2015).

19 Harvey J. Kaye, *Thomas Paine and the Promise of America: A History and Biography* (New York, 2005), p. 43; Michael Foot and Isaac Kramnick, eds, *The Thomas Paine Reader* (London, 1987), p. 10.

20 Thomas Paine, *Common Sense* (Philadelphia, PA, 1776), p. 3.

21 Ibid., p. 4.

22 Ibid., p. 11.

23 Thomas Paine, *The Age of Reason* (New York, 1827), p. 5.

24 Ibid., p. 6.

25 Paine, *Common Sense*, p. 39.

26 Caroline Robbins, 'The Lifelong Education of Thomas Paine (1737–1809): Some Reflections upon His Acquaintance among Books', *Proceedings of the American Philosophical Society*, CXXVII (1983), pp. 135–42 (p. 140). Paine even cited Spinoza in *The Age of Reason*. See Jack Fruchtman Jr, *The Political Philosophy of Thomas Paine* (Baltimore, MD, 2009), pp. 34–5.

27 Paine, *Common Sense*, p. 17.

28 Ibid., pp. 17–18.

29 Ibid., p. 31.

30 Ibid., p. 41.

31 Ibid., p. 42.

32 Ibid.

33 Ibid., p. 43.

34 Ibid., p. 58.

35 Ibid., p. 55.

36 Ibid., p. 17.

37 Jean-Jacques Rousseau, *Émile, ou de l'éducation* (Amsterdam, 1762). Wollstonecraft famously attacked Rousseau's ideas in her *Vindication of the Rights of Woman* (1792).

38 Mary Wollstonecraft, *A Vindication of the Rights of Woman* [1792] (London, 1891), p. x.

39 Ibid., pp. 31–2. The problem with the 'nature' or human status of women has been dealt with at length by Joanna Bourke, *What It Means To Be Human: Reflections from 1791 to the Present* (London, 2011). It was not a question limited to the eighteenth century, but continued to dog the politics of education and enfranchisement well into the twentieth century. See, for example, Rob Boddice, 'The Manly Mind? Re-visiting the Victorian "Sex in Brain" Debate', *Gender and History*, XXIII (2011), pp. 321–40.

40 Ralph M. Wardle, *Collected Letters of Mary Wollstonecraft* (Ithaca, NY, 1979); Mary Wollstonecraft, *Letters Written during a Short Residence in Sweden, Norway and Denmark* (Fontwell, Sussex, 1970). The principal source for her private life, aside from letters, is the memoir penned by her husband: William Godwin, *Memoirs of the Author of A Vindication of the Rights of Woman* (London, 1798). There are many biographies of admirable quality, for example, Lyndall Gordon, *Mary Wollstonecraft: A New Genus* (London, 2005); Janet Todd, *Mary Wollstonecraft: A Revolutionary Life* (New York, 2000); Eleanor Flexner, *Mary Wollstonecraft: A Biography* (New York, 1972). For general context specific to the question of gender and sentimentality, see Claudia L. Johnson, *Equivocal Beings: Politics, Gender, and Sentimentality in the 1790s: Wollstonecraft, Radcliffe, Burney, Austen* (Chicago, IL, 1995).

41 Mary Wollstonecraft to Gilbert Imlay, 4 October 1795. Wardle, *Collected Letters*, pp. 315–16.

42 Wollstonecraft to Imlay, *c.* 10 October 1795. Wardle, *Collected Letters*, pp. 316–17.

43 Samuel Johnson, *A Dictionary of the English Language*, 10th edn (London, 1792).

44 Wollstonecraft to Imlay, *c.* November 1795. Wardle, *Collected Letters*, pp. 317–18.

45 Syndy McMillen Conger, *Mary Wollstonecraft and the Language of Sensibility* (Rutherford, NJ, 1994), p. 34.

46 For the context, see Gareth Williams, *Angel of Death: The Story of Smallpox* (Basingstoke, 2010); for the life of Jenner, see Rob Boddice, *Edward Jenner* (Stroud, Gloucestershire, 2015); Richard B. Fisher, *Edward Jenner: A Biography* (London, 1991). What follows is drawn from Jenner's correspondence, held at the Royal College of Physicians, the Royal College of Surgeons and the Wellcome Library, all in London, as well as from the published letters in Genevieve Miller, *Letters of Edward Jenner* (Baltimore, MD, 1983). The original biography of Jenner, by his friend John Baron, remains an essential if partial source: *The Life of Edward Jenner*, 2 vols (London, 1838).

47 I have told it elsewhere. See Rob Boddice, 'Bestiality in a Time of Smallpox: Dr Jenner and the "Modern Chimera"', in *Exploring Animal Encounters: Philosophical, Cultural, and Historical Perspectives*, ed. Dominik Ohrem and Matthew Calarco (Cham, 2018); Boddice, *Edward Jenner*, pp. 41–83.

48 Royal College of Physicians (London), Edward Jenner Diary, 15 March 1796. RCP MS372.

49 Edward Jenner to Thomas Pruen, 21 November 1808. Wellcome Library, London, MS 5240/11.

50 Jenner to Pruen [1809]. Wellcome Library, London, MS 5240/25.

51 Jenner to Pruen [1809]. Wellcome Library, London, MS 5240/28.

52 Depression as a clinical and diagnosable phenomenon has an interesting history of its own, and we must remain vigilant in resisting the temptations of 'retrospective diagnosis'. Conceptions of what illnesses are (or are not) directly impact practices of being ill and being treated, running to the heart of the experience of illness itself. See, for example,

Åsa Jansson, 'Mood Disorders and the Brain: Depression, Melancholia, and the Historiography of Psychiatry', *Medical History*, LV (2011), pp. 393–9. See also Edward Shorter, *How Everyone Became Depressed: The Rise and Fall of the Nervous Breakdown* (Oxford, 2013) for a useful reminder of the mutability of diagnostic categories, though it is worth stating too that there is no underlying 'science' of depression that works for all time. Scientific knowledge about what depression is and how to treat it is no less contextually situated and culturally produced than anything else. For a brilliant study of the kinds of feelings that were possible in a context before depression existed, see Erin Sullivan, *Beyond Melancholy: Sadness and Selfhood in Rennaissance England* (Oxford, 2016).

53 Jenner to Thomas Charles Morgan, 11 July 1809. Miller, *Letters*, no. 46.

54 Jenner to Morgan, 9 October 1809. Miller, *Letters*, no. 49.

55 Baron, *Life of Edward Jenner*, vol. II, pp. 141–2.

56 Jenner to Pruen, 14 February 1810. Wellcome Library, London, MS 5240/31.

57 Jenner to Pruen, 23 October 1815. Wellcome Library, London, MS 5240/59.

58 Jenner to Pruen, 2 January 1816. Wellcome Library, London, MS 5240/60.

59 Ibid.

60 Jenner to Dr Thomas Harrison Burder, 5 February 1816. Miller, *Letters*, no. 76.

61 Jenner to Pruen, 27 June 1816. Wellcome Library, London, MS 5240/61; Jenner to Pruen, 9 December 1816. Wellcome Library, London, MS 5240/63; Jenner to Edward Davies, 2 March 1821. Wellcome Library, London, MS 5237/1.

5 Senselessness and Insensibility

1 The classic study is G. J. Barker-Benfield, *The Culture of Sensibility: Sex and Society in Eighteenth-century Britain* (Chicago, IL, 1992).

2 Mr John Dashwood is said to be 'rather cold hearted' and his wife 'a strong caricature of himself' (pp. 4–5); Lady Middleton is defined by a 'repulsive . . . cold insipidity' (p. 27); and Marianne's first assessment of Colonel Brandon is that he 'must have long outlived every sensation' (p. 29) of love, suggesting that age itself dried or cooled the heart. The suggestion that he might be a match for her is, in her opinion, an 'unfeeling' one (p. 28). There are many other examples of such crude juxtapositions of highly refined feelings and blunt callousness, such that this is the dynamic that drives the plot. Jane Austen, *Sense and Sensibility* [1811] (Oxford, 2004). Some have argued that, among elite men in Britain in particular, the tide against sensibility turned around the beginning of the nineteenth century, lest it betray an effeminacy that could be too readily associated with the French. Hence the emergence of the ruddy, candid and bluff Englishman, of few words and, apparently, fewer emotions. See Michèle Cohen, 'Manliness, Effeminacy and the French: Gender and the Construction of National Character in Eighteenth-century England', in *English Masculinities, 1660–1800*, ed. Michèle Cohen and Tim Hitchcock (Harlow, 1999).

For a comparative view of the historicity of the famed 'stiff upper lip', see Thomas Dixon, *Weeping Britannia: Portrait of a Nation in Tears* (Oxford, 2015).

3 Peter Heath and J. B. Schneewind, eds, *Immanuel Kant: Lectures on Ethics* (Cambridge, 1997), pp. 212–13.

4 To wit, the overarching argument of Rob Boddice, *A History of Attitudes and Behaviours toward Animals in Eighteenth- and Nineteenth-century Britain: Anthropocentrism and the Emergence of Animals* (Lewiston, NY, 2008).

5 Allan Young, 'Empathic Cruelty and the Origins of the Social Brain', in *Critical Neuroscience: A Handbook of the Social and Cultural Contexts of Neuroscience*, ed. Suparna Choudhury and Jan Slaby (Oxford, 2012).

6 See note 4 of this chapter.

7 Bernard Mandeville, *The Fable of the Bees*, 3rd edn (London, 1724), pp. 189–90.

8 Jeremy Bentham, *An Introduction to the Principles of Morals and Legislation* (London, 1789), pp. 309–10n.

9 Rob Boddice, 'The Moral Status of Animals and the Historical Human Cachet', JAC: *A Journal of Rhetoric, Culture and Politics*, XXX (2010), pp. 457–89.

10 Penal Code – Cruelty to Animals, Bentham MSS, University College London (UCL), LXXII, 214 (*c.* 1780). Transcribed and reprinted in Lea Campos Boralevi, *Bentham and the Oppressed* (Berlin, 1984), pp. 228–9. See also Bentham's letter in favour of vivisection in the *Morning Chronicle*, 13 March 1825.

11 Penal Code, Bentham, MSS, UCL.

12 Charles Darwin, *The Descent of Man*, 2nd edn (London, 1874), p. 90.

13 See Rob Boddice, *The Science of Sympathy: Morality, Evolution and Victorian Civilization* (Urbana–Champaign, IL, 2016), plus the concluding section of this chapter for the context of anaesthesia.

14 Letter to *The Times*, 19 April 1881.

15 As physiologists in particular began to see the emotions as rooted in bodily, visceral activity, rather than as an immaterial product of the mind, so research into them demanded strict control, lest the emotions of the scientists themselves affect the emotional responses of their experimental subjects (often dogs). Hence the development of a physiological research agenda in the pursuit of emotions led to the development of strategies of emotional elimination from the laboratory. This might be seen as a strand of that scientific endeavour to see, as it were, objectively, which of course is no less an affective viewpoint than any other, but objectivity comes with the difficult analytical challenge of being an affect that explicitly claims not to be. For the rise of the physiology of emotions and the emotionlessness of scientists in this context, see Otniel Dror, 'The Scientific Image of Emotion: Experience and Technologies of Inscription', *Configurations*, VII (1999), pp. 355–401; Otniel Dror, 'The Affect of Experiment: The Turn to Emotions in Anglo-American Physiology, 1900–1940', *Isis*, XC (1999), pp. 205–37; Otniel Dror, 'Techniques of the Brain and the Paradox of Emotions,

1880–1930', *Science in Context*, XIV (2001), pp. 643–60; for general background about the rise of objectivity in scientific research, and of objectivity as an affect, see the monumental work by Lorraine Daston and Peter Galison, *Objectivity* (New York, 2007).

16 Andrew Ure, 'An Account of Some Experiments Made on the Body of a Criminal Immediately after Execution, with Physiological and Practical Observations', *Quarterly Journal of Science and the Arts*, VI (1819), pp. 290–91.

17 For the connection, see Ben Dawson, 'Modernity as Anthropolarity: The Human Economy of *Frankenstein*', in *Anthropocentrism: Humans, Animals, Environments*, ed. Rob Boddice (Leiden, 2011), pp. 155–81 (p. 173).

18 David Ferrier, 'The Croonian Lecture: Experiments on the Brain of Monkeys', *Philosophical Transactions of the Royal Society of London*, CLXV (1875), pp. 433–88.

19 United Kingdom Parliament, Report of the Royal Commission on the Practice of Subjecting Live Animals to Experiments for Scientific Purposes, C. 1397, testimony of John Colam, p. 83.

20 Lizzy Lind-af-Hageby and Leisa Katherina Schartau, *The Shambles of Science* (London, 1903), pp. 19–26 (p. 20). 'Shambles' here plays on a sense of *travesty* as well as on an archaic reference to the butcher's slab. The classic study of the case is Coral Lansbury, *The Old Brown Dog: Women, Workers, and Vivisection in Edwardian England* (Madison, WI, 1985).

21 Lind-af-Hageby and Schartau, *Shambles of Science*, p. 21.

22 *The Times*, 4 August 1875.

23 Charles Darwin, *The Expression of Emotions in Man and Animals* (London, 1872). For a worthy summary of the relationship with Crichton-Browne, which unfortunately incorrectly characterizes Darwin's argument as having to do with natural selection, see Stassa Edwards, 'The Naturalist and the Neurologist: On Charles Darwin and James Crichton-Browne', *The Public Domain Review*, 28 May 2014, https://publicdomainreview.org, accessed 14 November 2017.

24 The correspondence on this subject took place between May 1869 and January 1873, straddling the publication of the *Expression*, although the letters cluster chiefly in 1871. See Darwin Correspondence Project, www.darwinproject.ac.uk, accessed 15 November 2017.

25 For a general appraisal, see Phillip Prodger, *Darwin's Camera: Art and Photography in the Theory of Evolution* (Oxford, 2009).

26 Ekman famously adjoined his name to Darwin's by critically editing a new edition of Darwin's *Expression* (Oxford, 1998), augmenting it with an introduction that cemented a kind of intellectual genealogy, further reinforced by the superimposition of Ekman's pictures of facial affect on the cover. For worthy criticism of the photographic method, see Ruth Leys, 'How Did Fear Become a Scientific Object and What Kind of Object Is It?', in *Fear Across the Disciplines*, ed. Jan Plamper and Benjamin Lazier (Pittsburgh, PA, 2012), pp. 51–77.

27 For a broader discussion of this theme, which includes the two paintings here discussed, see Christopher Lawrence and Michael Brown, 'Quintessentially Modern Heroes: Surgeons, Explorers, and Empire, c. 1840–1914', *Journal of Social History*, 50 (2016), pp. 148–78.

28 Michael Brown, 'Surgery and Emotion: The Era before Anaesthesia',
    in *The Palgrave Handbook of the History of Surgery*, ed. Thomas Schlich
    (Basingstoke, 2017), pp. 327–48; Michael Brown, 'Redeeming Mr
    Sawbone: Compassion and Care in the Cultures of Nineteenth-century
    Surgery', *Journal of Compassionate Health Care*, IV/13 (2017).

29 G. Böhme, *Atmosphäre: Essays zur neuen Ästhetik* (Frankfurt am Main,
    2000); A. Reckwitz, 'Affective Spaces: A Praxeological Outlook',
    Rethinking History, XVI (2012), pp. 241–58. See also B. Anderson,
    'Affective Atmospheres', *Emotion, Space and Society*, II (2009), pp. 77–81.
    For a narrative account of a cognate shift in emotional atmosphere
    (in the physiological laboratory), see Boddice, *Science of Sympathy*,
    pp. 75–86.

30 David Hume, *Treatise of Human Nature* [1738] (Oxford, 1888), p. 576.

31 Frances Burney to Esther Burney, 22 March 1812. Frances Burney,
    Journals and Letters, ed. Peter Sabor and Lars E. Troide (London, 2001),
    p. 442.

32 Adam Smith, *The Theory of Moral Sentiments* [1759] (London, 2009), p. 45.

33 As positively summarized by Stephanie J. Snow, *Blessed Days of
    Anaesthesia: How Anaesthetics Changed the World* (Oxford, 2008).

34 Rob Boddice, 'Hurt Feelings', in *Pain and Emotion in Modern
    History*, ed. Rob Boddice (Basingstoke, 2014), pp. 1–10; Rob Boddice,
    Pain: A Very Short Introduction (Oxford, 2017). This is confirmed
    by contemporary neuroscientific research that has attempted on
    the one hand to merge notions of physical and emotional pain
    as phenomenologically and neurologically consonant, and on the
    other to re-conceptualize injury stimuli that are not experienced
    meaningfully as pain as something else. See in particular Nikola
    Grahek, *Feeling Pain and Being in Pain*, 2nd edn (Cambridge,
    MA, 2007); Naomi I. Eisenberger, 'Does Rejection Hurt? An fMRI
    Study of Social Exclusion', *Science*, CCCII (2003), pp. 290–92; and more
    broadly, Geoff MacDonald and Lauri A. Jensen-Campbell, eds, *Social
    Pain: Neuropsychological and Health Implications of Loss and Exclusion*
    (Washington, DC, 2011).

35 Matt Cartmill called it 'the Bambi syndrome' in *A View to a Death in the
    Morning* (Cambridge, MA, 1993), pp. 161ff.

36 Herbert Spencer, *The Principles of Psychology*, vol. II, 2nd edn (London,
    1870), pp. 622–4. This analysis was not in the first edition of 1855.
    Spencer was clearly responding to his times, particularly aiming to
    explain and account for altruism – a neologism – both where it was
    misdirected and how it might be better applied. For broader context,
    see Thomas Dixon, *The Invention of Altruism: Making Moral Meanings
    in Victorian Britain* (Oxford, 2008). Spencer is the subject of Chapter
    Five of that study.

37 As Michael Fried points out, 'we know almost everything that could be
    known about the scene Eakins chose to depict', including the specifics
    of the operation, which had been refined by Gross. My observations on
    the painting are a contribution to what has previously been unknown
    (or unexplored) about the affective context of the scene, which
    inevitably takes us beyond the scene itself. See Michael Fried, *Realism,*

Writing, Disfiguration: On Thomas Eakins and Stephen Crane (Chicago, IL, 1987), p. 6. For the sources of what we know about the painting, see Gordon Hendricks, 'Thomas Eakins's *Gross Clinic*', *Art Bulletin*, LI (1969), pp. 57–64; Lloyd Goodrich, *Thomas Eakins: His Life and Work*, vol. I (New York, 1933), pp. 49–54; Elizabeth Johns, *Thomas Eakins: The Heroism of Modern Life* (Princeton, NJ, 1983).

38 Goodrich, *Thomas Eakins*, vol. I, p. 125.

39 Some debate has emerged about the sex of the patient. I masculinize here because the condition more often strikes boys than girls, but in essence I would claim that the sex of the patient is immaterial. The painting depicts an inscrutable body because the anaesthetic has *objectified* it. It is no longer a human being but surgical *stuff*, and will be so until the anaesthetic effect wears off. The only gender dynamic that matters in this image is that between surgeon and cringing mother. See Jennifer Doyle, 'Sex, Scandal, and Thomas Eakins's *The Gross Clinic*', *Representations*, LXVIII (1999), pp. 1–33 (pp. 5, 21). Doyle does not consider the medical context, which might have led her to confirm a suspicion that the patient is a male child.

40 This interpretation seems to me altogether more likely and more justifiable by the public discourse surrounding surgical innovation and anaesthesia than the Oedipal fantasies of Fried, recapitulated to some extent and modified by Doyle. While Fried is right that the mother figure's gesture 'amplifies the demand that we look', under the duress of being appalled by the sight, there is no substantial justification for the suggestion that this somehow 'suggests an encounter with castration', or that the wound on the leg is a 'vaginal gash'. Doyle, 'Sex, Scandal', pp. 5, 22–3.

41 Goodrich, *Thomas Eakins*, vol. I, p. 50.

42 Quoted in ibid., pp. 51–2.

42 S.G.W. Benjamin, *Art in America: A Critical and Historical Sketch* (New York, 1880), p. 208.

44 Quoted in Goodrich, *Thomas Eakins*, vol. I, p. 51.

45 Quoted in Hendricks, 'Thomas Eakins's *Gross Clinic*', p. 63.

46 The broader context of this new affective moral economy is the subject of my book *Science of Sympathy*, the cover of which is adorned by *The Gross Clinic*. I did not talk about the painting in that book, but for me the narrative of the painting perfectly encapsulates its whole argument.

47 Goodrich, *Thomas Eakins*, vol. I, p. 126.

48 William Osler, 'Aequanimitas', *Aequanimitas, with other Addresses to Medical Students and Practitioners of Medicine*, 2nd edn (Philadelphia, PA, 1925), pp. 3–11 (pp. 3–6).

6 The Ministry of Happiness

1 Eva Illouz, *Cold Intimacies: The Making of Emotional Capitalism* (Oxford, 2006), p. 4.

2 See, for example, A. Killen, *Berlin Electropolis: Shock, Nerves, and German Modernity* (Berkeley, CA, 2006); Joanna Bourke, *Dismembering the Male: Men's Bodies, Britain, and the Great War* (London, 1996); David

Cantor and Edmund Ramsden, eds, *Stress, Shock, and Adaptation in the Twentieth Century* (Rochester, NY, 2014); Ian Dowbiggin, *The Quest for Mental Health: A Tale of Science, Medicine, Scandal, Sorrow, and Mass Society* (Cambridge, 2011).

3 Allan V. Horwitz and Gerald N. Grob, 'The Troubled History of Psychiatry's Quest for Specificity', *Journal of Health Politics, Policy and Law*, XLI (2016), pp. 521–39.

4 This is the paradox of emotional practice explored by Stephanie Olsen, *Juvenile Nation: Youth, Emotions and the Making of the Modern British Citizen, 1880–1914* (London, 2014). For a similar story of love as the defining motivation for battle, see V. Kivimäki and T. Tepora, 'War of Hearts: Love and Collective Attachment as Integrating Factors in Finland during World War II', *Journal of Social History*, XLIII (2009), pp. 285–305.

5 See, for example, Nicoletta F. Gullace, 'White Feathers and Wounded Men: Female Patriotism and the Memory of the Great War', *Journal of British Studies*, XXXVI (1997), pp. 178–206.

6 The phrase is *dulce et decorum est pro patria mori*. Wilfred Owen, 'Dulce et Decorum Est' (*c.* 1918).

7 Bourke, *Dismembering the Male*.

8 John Helliwell, Richard Layard and Jeffrey Sachs, eds, *World Happiness Report 2017* (New York, 2017), p. 3.

9 'About the OECD', www.oecd.org, accessed 20 December 2017.

10 Helliwell, Layard and Sachs, *World Happiness Report 2017*, p. 3.

11 'Journal of Happiness Studies', *Springer Link*, https://link.springer.com, accessed 21 December 2017.

12 '2017 Social Progress Index', www.socialprogressindex.com, accessed 27 October 2017.

13 Tamar Hellman, 'Happiness and the Social Progress Index', *Social Progress Imperative*, www.socialprogressimperative.org, 30 October 2017.

14 Roger T. Webb et al., 'National Cohort Study of Suicidality and Violent Criminality among Danish Immigrants', PLOS ONE, X (2015).

15 'Life Satisfaction', OECD *Better Life Index*, www.oecdbetterlifeindex.org, accessed 21 December 2017.

16 'Denmark', OECD *Better Life Index*, www.oecdbetterlifeindex.org, accessed 30 October 2017.

17 Pablo Diego Rosell, 'Gallup's Well-being Index: Measuring the Attributes of A Life Well Lived', www.amateo.info, accessed 30 October 2017.

18 *New Economics Foundation*, http://neweconomics.org, accessed 30 October 2017.

19 *Happy Planet Index*, http://happyplanetindex.org, accessed 30 October 2017.

20 L. Bruni and P. L. Porta, eds, *Handbook on the Economics of Happiness* (Cheltenham, 2008).

21 Eva Illouz, 'The Culture of Management: Self-interest, Empathy and Emotional Control', in *An Introduction to Social Entrepreneurship: Voices, Preconditions, Contexts*, ed. Rafael Ziegler (Cheltenham, 2009), pp. 107–32 (p. 108). See also Illouz, *Cold Intimacies*.

22 For an entry into this subject, see D. Bok, *The Politics of Happiness: What Government Can Learn from the New Research on Well-being* (Princeton, NJ, 2011); V. De Prycker, 'Happiness on the Political Agenda: PROS and CONS', *Journal of Happiness Studies*, 11 (2010), pp. 585–603.

23 Some examples, showing the breadth of the subject across disciplinary lines, include Maira Kalman, *And the Pursuit of Happiness* (New York, 2010); Philip Booth, ed., *And the Pursuit of Happiness: Wellbeing and the Role of Government* (London, 2012); Setha M. Low, *Behind the Gates: Life, Security, and the Pursuit of Happiness in Fortress America* (New York, 2003); President's Council on Bioethics, *Beyond Therapy: Biotechnology and the Pursuit of Happiness* (Washington, DC, c. 2004); Arthur Brooks, *The Conservative Heart: How to Build a Fairer, Happier, and More Prosperous America* (New York, 2015); Roger Rosenblatt, *Consuming Desires: Consumption, Culture, and the Pursuit of Happiness* (Washington, DC, 1999); Shimon Edelman, *The Happiness of Pursuit: What Neuroscience Can Teach Us about the Good Life* (New York, 2012).

24 Jeremy Bentham, 'Anarchical Fallacies – Being an Examination of the Declaration of Rights Issued during the French Revolution', in *Works*, ed. John Bowring (Edinburgh, 1838–43), vol. VIII, p. 501.

25 Samuel Johnson, 'Happiness', in *A Dictionary of the English Language: A Digital Edition of the 1755 Classic by Samuel Johnson*, ed. Brandi Besalke, http://johnsonsdictionaryonline.com, accessed 1 November 2017.

26 For a review of 'positive psychology' or 'happiness studies' in the twentieth century, see Daniel Horowitz, *Happier? The History of a Cultural Movement that Aspired to Transform America* (Oxford, 2017).

27 David Cameron, 'PM Speech on Wellbeing', 25 November 2010, www.gov.uk, accessed 21 December 2107.

28 Brian Wheeler, 'Whatever Happened to the Happiness Agenda?', BBC News, 16 January 2014, www.bbc.co.uk, accessed 30 October 2017.

29 Ann M. Simmons, 'UAE's Minister of Happiness Insists Her Job is No Laughing Matter', *Los Angeles Times*, 6 March 2017, www.latimes.com, accessed 31 October 2017.

30 Tim Hulse, 'The Pursuit of Happiness', *British Airways Business Life*, September 2017, pp. 58–62 (p. 59).

31 'Happiness Meter to Gauge Dubai Residents' Mood Coming Soon', *Gulf News*, 16 November 2017, http://gulfnews.com, accessed 16 November 2017. See the official explanation at Wisam Amid, '2.1: Happiness Meter History', *Happiness Agenda*, http://en.happinessagenda.ae, accessed 15 November 2017.

32 'Major Initiatives', *Greater Good Science Center*, https://ggsc.berkeley.edu, accessed 31 October 2017; *Oxford Mindfulness Centre*, http://oxfordmindfulness.org, accessed 31 October 2017.

33 Illouz, *Cold Intimacies*, p. 12.

34 On the transformation of citizens into clients in the happiness regimes of neoliberal societies, see Edgar Cabanas, 'Rekindling Individualism, Consuming Emotions: Constructing "Psytizens" in the Age of Happiness', *Culture and Psychology*, XXII (2016), pp. 467–80. For a longer historical view, see Sabine Donauer, *Faktor Freude: Wie die Wirtschaft Arbeitsgefühle erzeugt* (Hamburg, 2015).

35 Arlie Russel Hochschild, *The Managed Heart: The Commercialization of Human Feeling* (Berkeley and Los Angeles, CA, 1983).

36 'Yemen: Urgent Investigation Needed into UAE Torture Network and Possible U.S. Role', Amnesty International, 22 June 2017, www.amnesty. org, accessed 31 October 2017.

37 Bureau of Democracy, Human Rights and Labor, 'United Arab Emirates', *Country Reports on Human Rights Practices for 2016*, www.state.gov, accessed 31 October, 2017.

38 See Juliane Brauer, 'Disciplining Young People's Emotions in the Soviet Occupation Zone and the Early German Democratic Republic', in *Childhood, Youth and Emotions in Modern History: National, Colonial and Global Perspectives*, ed. Stephanie Olsen (Basingstoke, 2015), pp. 178–97; Juliane Brauer, '"... das Lied zum Ausdruck der Empfindungen werden kann": Singen und Gefühlserziehung in der frühen DDR', *Emotionen in der Bildungsgeschichte, Jahrbuch für Historische Bildungsforschung*, XVIII (2012), pp. 126–45.

39 Emily Thomas, 'Venezuela to Create "Ministry of Happiness"', BBC News, 26 October 2013, www.bbc.co.uk, accessed 31 October 2017.

40 Hulse, 'Pursuit of Happiness', p. 62.

41 This particular gloss on Weber belongs to Ronan MacDonald, 'Schumpeter and Max Weber: Central Visions and Social Theories', in *Entrepreneurship and Economic Development*, ed. P. Kilby (New York, 1971), pp. 71–94 (pp. 78–9).

42 Everett Hagen, 'How Economic Growth Begins: A Theory of Social Change', in *Entrepreneurship and Economic Development*, ed. Kilby, pp. 123–37 (p. 136).

43 Joseph Schumpeter, 'Economic Theory and Entrepreneurial History', in *Change and the Entrepreneur: Postulates and Patterns for Entrepreneurial History* (Cambridge, MA, 1949), pp. 63–84 (pp. 72, 81–2).

44 Rob Boddice, 'Forgotten Antecedents: Entrepreneurship, Ideology and History', in *An Introduction to Social Entrepreneurship*, ed. Ziegler, pp. 133–52.

45 Maya Tamir et al., 'The Secret to Happiness: Feeling Good or Feeling Right?', *Journal of Experimental Psychology*, CXLVI (2017), pp. 1448–59. This study is far from alone in trying to reanimate Aristotle for our age. See, for example, Joar Vittersø, *Handbook of Eudaimonic Well-being* (Cham, 2016), which includes chapters on 'eudaimonic psychology' and on *eudaimonia* as 'a way of living', plus much more. The term is endlessly applicable, though I suspect completely unknown beyond academic bowers. See, for examples of disciplinary breadth, Michael Ross Potter, 'Reconciling Ethical Asymmetry in Agency Oversight: Striving for Eudaimonia among Legislative Staff in West Virginia', *Global Virtue Ethics Review*, VII (2016), pp. 137–65; J. B. Fowers et al., 'Enhancing Relationship Quality Measurement: The Development of the Relationship Flourishing Scale', *Journal of Family Psychology*, XXX (2016), pp. 997–1007 (where 'flourishing' is their translation of *eudaimonia*); Andrew West, 'The Ethics of Professional Accountants: An Aristotelian Perspective', *Accounting, Auditing and Accountability Journal*, XXX (2017), pp. 328–51; Matthew A. Fuss, 'Eudaimonia: Using Aristotle

to Inform Organizational Communication in order to Reimagine Human Resource Management', PhD thesis, McAnulty College and Graduate School of Liberal Arts, 2016. One could produce a seemingly endless list, the contents of which would be subject to the same kind of criticism that I level at Tamir et al.

46 Tamir et al., 'Secret to Happiness', p. 1.

47 Ibid., p. 10.

48 William Reddy, *The Navigation of Feeling: A Framework for the History of Emotions* (Cambridge, 2001), pp. 122–9. See my summary in Rob Boddice, *The History of Emotions* (Manchester, 2018), pp. 70–77.

Conclusion: The Value of Experience

1 See Immanuel Kant, *Critique of Pure Reason*, trans. Werner S. Pluhar (Indianapolis, IN, 1996).

2 I here use the definition of Lorraine Daston in 'The Moral Economy of Science', *Osiris*, 2nd ser., X (1995), pp. 2–24. See Rob Boddice, *The History of Emotions* (Manchester, 2018), pp. 194–201.

3 This is a riff on Clifford Geertz, who riffed on Max Weber, in 'Thick Description: Toward an Interpretive Theory of Culture', *The Interpretation of Cultures* (New York, 1973).

4 Boddice, *History of Emotions*, pp. 201–4; Rob Boddice (with Daniel Lord Smail), 'Neurohistory', in *Debating New Approaches in History*, ed. P. Burke and M. Tamm (London, 2018).

SELECT BIBLIOGRAPHY

For a general bibliography of the history of emotions, with related literature in the history of the senses, I refer the reader to *The History of Emotions* (Manchester, 2018). That extensive list provides the intellectual, theoretical and methodological ingredients that have both inspired this book and enabled it to be written. In lieu of repeating that list, which would not offer any specific guidance to a reader of this book, I have compiled a small selection of texts that I think are the most important introductory works for the field, to orientate the reader who wants more. In addition, I have here compiled a bibliography of key works pertaining specifically to the different periods covered in this book, and organized as such. By no means does this list include all the works referred to herein, for that would be unwieldy and unhelpful, but rather serves as a guide to the essential literature on the history of emotions, senses and experience – of *feeling* in general – across the broad swathe of historical time. I have tried to limit the literature here to those works that provide general coverage, with some exceptions (especially in the classical world). Where works on individual emotions are included, readers should expect to find in them important insights on general theoretical and methodological questions. The structure of this list reflects a general tendency of historians of emotions to reproduce and recapitulate rather traditional models of periodization (the exception is Barbara Rosenwein, and I have elided the medieval and early modern so as to accommodate the broad temporal approach of her work). While I present the work in this way, I do not necessarily recommend that work in this area continues to be so organized. This book aims to blur or break some of those traditional boundaries in its content, but nevertheless inevitably draws on other scholarly research that does the opposite. One of the abiding messages of a book like this one is that, for almost every period, the history of the affective life of the past is wide open for further study and expansion. If what I have here compiled seems already rather abundant, I can nevertheless attest to, and encourage, the enormous possibilities for its augmentation.

Key Theoretical, Methodological and Introductory Works in the History of Emotions and the History of the Senses

Boddice, R., *The History of Emotions* (Manchester, 2018)

Daston, L., 'The Moral Economy of Science', *Osiris*, 2nd ser., x (1995), pp. 2–24

Davidson, J., and S. Broomhall, eds, *A Cultural History of the Emotions*, 6 vols (London, 2018)

Dixon, T., '"Emotion": The History of a Keyword in Crisis', *Emotion Review*, iv (2012), pp. 338–44

Feldman-Barrett, L., *How Emotions Are Made: The Secret Life of the Brain* (New York, 2017)

Gross, D. M., *The Secret History of Emotion: From Aristotle's Rhetoric to Modern Brain Science* (Chicago, il, 2006)

Howes, D., and C. Classen, *Ways of Sensing: Understanding the Senses in Society* (New York, 2013)

Jütte, R., *A History of the Senses: From Antiquity to Cyberspace* (Cambridge, 2005)

McGrath, L. S., 'Historiography, Affect, and the Neurosciences', *History of Psychology*, xx (2017), pp. 129–47

Plamper, J., *The History of Emotions: An Introduction* (Oxford, 2015)

Prinz, J., *The Emotional Construction of Morals* (Oxford, 2007)

Reddy, W., *The Navigation of Feeling: A Framework for the History of Emotions* (Cambridge, 2001)

Rosenwein, B., 'Worrying about Emotions in History', *American Historical Review*, cvii (2002), pp. 821–45

Scheer, M., 'Are Emotions a Kind of Practice (and is that what makes them have a history)? A Bourdieuian Approach to Understanding Emotion', *History and Theory*, li (2012), pp. 193–220

Smail, D. L., *On Deep History and the Brain* (Berkeley and Los Angeles, ca, 2008)

Smith, M. M., *Sensing the Past: Seeing, Hearing, Smelling, Tasting, and Touching in History* (Berkeley and Los Angeles, ca, 2008)

Stearns, P. N., and C. Z. Stearns, 'Emotionology: Clarifying the History of Emotions and Emotional Standards', *American Historical Review*, xc (1985), pp. 813–36

Stearns, P. N., and S. Matt, eds, *Doing Emotions History* (Urbana-Champaign, il, 2014)

Wassmann, C., 'Forgotten Origins, Occluded Meanings: Translation of Emotion Terms', *Emotion Review*, ix (2017), pp. 163–71

Key Works on Ancient Greece and Rome

Caston, R. R., and R. A. Kaster, eds, *Hope, Joy, and Affection in the Classical World* (Oxford, 2016)

Chaniotis, A., ed., *Unveiling Emotion: Sources and Methods for the Studies of Emotions in the Greek World* (Stuttgart, 2012)

—, and P. Ducrey, eds, *Unveiling Emotions*, vol. ii: *Emotions in Greece and Rome: Texts, Images, Material Culture* (Stuttgart, 2014)

Fitzgerald, J. T., ed., *Passions and Moral Progress in Greco-Roman Thought* (London, 2008)

Konstan, D., *The Emotions of the Ancient Greeks: Studies in Aristotle and Classical Literature* (Toronto, 2006)

—, and K. Rutter, eds, *Envy, Spite and Jealousy: The Rivalrous Emotions in Ancient Greece* (Edinburgh, 2003)

Lateiner, D., and D. Spatharas, eds, *The Ancient Emotion of Disgust* (Oxford, 2016)

Morton Braund, S., and C. Gill, eds, *The Passions in Roman Thought and Literature* (Cambridge, 1997)

Sihvola, J., and T. Engberg-Pedersen, *The Emotions in Hellenistic Philosophy* (Dordrecht, 1998)

Key Works on the Medieval and Early Modern Periods

Boquet, D., *L'ordre de l'affect au moyen âge: autour de l'anthropologie affective d'Aelred de Rievaulx* (Caen, 2005)

—, and P. Nagy, *Sensible Moyen Âge: une histoire des émotions dans l'Occident médiéval* (Paris, 2015)

Broomhall, S., ed., *Early Modern Emotions: An Introduction* (New York, 2016)

Champion, M., and A. Lynch, eds, *Understanding Emotion in Early Europe* (Turnhout, 2015)

Eustace, N., *Passion is the Gale: Emotion, Power, and the Coming of the American Revolution* (Chapel Hill, NC, 2008)

Jaeger, C. S., *Ennobling Love: In Search of a Lost Sensibility* (Philadelphia, PA, 1999)

Lilicquist, J., ed., *A History of Emotions, 1200–1800* (London, 2013)

Rosenwein, B., *Emotional Communities in the Early Middle Ages* (Ithaca, NY, 2006)

—, *Generations of Feeling: A History of Emotions, 600–1700* (Cambridge, 2016)

Sullivan, E., *Beyond Melancholy: Sadness and Selfhood in Renaissance England* (Oxford, 2016)

Waldow, A., ed., *Sensibility in the Early Modern Era: From Living Machines to Affective Morality* (London, 2016)

Key Works on the Modern Period

Biess, F., and D. M. Gross, eds, *Science and Emotions after 1945: A Transatlantic Perspective* (Chicago, IL, 2014)

Boddice, R., *The Science of Sympathy: Morality, Evolution and Victorian Civilization* (Urbana-Champaign, IL, 2016)

Bourke, J., 'Fear and Anxiety: Writing about Emotion in Modern History', *History Workshop Journal*, LV (2003), pp. 111–33

—, *Fear: A Cultural History* (London, 2005)

Daston, L., and P. Galison, *Objectivity* (New York, 2007)

Dixon, T., *From Passions to Emotions: The Creation of a Secular Psychological Category* (Cambridge, 2006)

Frevert, U., et al., *Emotional Lexicons: Continuity and Change in the Vocabulary of Feeling, 1700–2000* (Oxford, 2014)

Key Works on Contemporary Emotions

Ahmed, S., *The Cultural Politics of Emotion* (Edinburgh, 2004)
—, *The Promise of Happiness* (Durham, NC, and London, 2010)
Berlant, L., *Cruel Optimism* (Durham, NC, and London, 2011)
Hochschild, A. R., *The Managed Heart: Commercialization of Human Feeling*
    (Berkeley and Los Angeles, CA, 1983)
Horowitz, D., *Happier? The History of a Cultural Movement* (Oxford, 2018)
Illouz, E., *Cold Intimacies: The Making of Emotional Capitalism*
    (Cambridge, 2007)

ACKNOWLEDGEMENTS

I took on this project as a conscious attempt to put into practice my account of the theory and methods of the history of emotions that I formulated in a 2018 book published by Manchester University Press. In the course of researching and writing that book, I collected a lot of material that pertained directly to the subject but did not fit with a strictly historiographical approach. Much of it is deployed here, in what is necessarily a selective, but hopefully essential narrative.

As always, I have incurred a number of debts in the course of writing this book. My expertise was developed at the Languages of Emotion Excellence Cluster at Freie Universität Berlin and at the Center for the History of Emotions at the Max Planck Institute for Human Development, also in Berlin. My active years in these places, from 2011 to 2016, could hardly fail to have been formative, and my gratitude to the personnel of these institutions is continued in an ongoing and fruitful exchange. This has been complemented by further engagement with other centres and networks for the history of emotions, particularly at Queen Mary University of London, and across Australia and Finland. Ancients in the field of the history of emotions are few and far between, but I have derived assistance and encouragement from Stephanie Olsen, Joanna Bourke, Susan Matt, Peter Stearns, Thomas Dixon, William Reddy, Daniel Lord Smail, Ville Kivimäki, Matthew Milner (saving me from Latin calamity), Michele Cohen (who first sent me to the land of *Tendre*), Juliane Brauer and Karen Vallgårda in particular. My exploration of ancient Greece began in 2006 at the European College of Liberal Arts (now Bard College), Berlin, where the Dean told me, sensing my perturbation at teaching so far from my comfort zone, that I should consider myself to be taking payment to educate myself. It was a sound notion. The opportunity to revisit Homer, Plato and Thucydides on numerous occasions, as well as Descartes and Spinoza, was facilitated by Michael Weinman at Bard. Thanks to him, and to Geoff Lehman and Tracy Colony for allowing me to impose on their seminars and be challenged by their students.

I must thank Martin Lücke for being a most congenial and liberal department head at Freie Universität Berlin, where this book was conceived and researched, under the auspices of a Deutsche Forschungsgemeinschaft grant. This book is the legacy project of that generous funding and has been completed at the Department of Social Studies of Medicine at McGill University, Montreal, with funding from the European Union's Horizon 2020 research and innovation programme under the Marie Sklodowska-Curie grant agreement No. 742470.

Tony Morris made this book happen. I'm so grateful for such a can-do cornerman.

On a personal note, my thanks go to supportive family and friends who grant me the time and space necessary to think and to write, but especially to the aforementioned Stephanie Olsen, whose expertise is combined with sympathy and forbearance. And finally to Sébastien, for being a fountain of joy in my own history of feelings.

PHOTO ACKNOWLEDGEMENTS

Thanks to the below sources of illustrative material and/or permission to reproduce it.

Benedictine Abbey of S. Hildegard, Elbingen, Germany: p. 81; British Museum, London: p. 27 (foot); from René Descartes, *L'homme . . . et un traité de la formation du foetus* (Paris, 1664): p. 96; from René Descartes, *Tractatus de homine, et de formatione foetus . . .* (Amsterdam, 1667), pp. 91, 94; photo © iwm (Imperial War Museum, London): p. 167; Museo Archeologico Nazionale, Naples: p. 27 (top); photos Metropolitan Museum of Art (Open Access): pp. 68, 134, 138, 139; Philadelphia Museum of Art, Pennsylvania: pp. 153, 154 (on loan from the University of Pennsylvania, Philadelphia); from Mr de Scudéry [*sic*], *Clélie, histoire romaine*, vol. I (Paris, 1654): p. 99; photo The Print Collector / Alamy Stock Photo: p. 96; photos courtesy u.s. National Library of Medicine, Bethesda, Maryland: pp. 91, 94; Tate, London: p. 117; Wellcome Library, London (photo Wellcome Images): p. 61; photo Yale Center For British Art, New Haven, Connecticut: p. 137.

Wellcome Images have licensed the works on pp. 61, 150 and 151 under a Creative Commons Attribution 4.0 International license: readers are free to share – to copy and redistribute these works – or to adapt – to remix, transform and build upon these works – for any purpose, even commercially, under the following conditions: they must attribute the works in the manner specified by the author or licensor (but not in any way that suggests that they endorse you or your use of the works) and if they alter, transform, or build upon the works, they may distribute the resulting works only under the same or similar licenses to those listed above). They may not apply legal terms or technological measures that legally restrict others from doing anything the license permits.

INDEX

Page numbers in *italics* refer to illustrations